THE NEMESIS OF REFORM

The Republican Party During the New Deal

•

THE NEMESIS OF RE FORM

The Republican Party During the New Deal

●

CLYDE P. WEED

COLUMBIA UNIVERSITY PRESS

New York

Columbia University Press
New York   Chichester, West Sussex
Copyright © 1994 Columbia University Press
All rights reserved

Library of Congress Cataloging-in-Publication Data

Weed, Clyde P.
    The nemesis of reform: the Republican Party during the New Deal/
Clyde P. Weed.
        p.   cm.
    Includes bibliographical references (p.   ) and index.
    ISBN 0–231–08486–2 (acid-free paper)
    1. Republican Party (U.S. : 1854-)   2. United States—Politics
and government—1929-1933.   3. United States—Politics and government—1933-1945   4. Presidents—United States-Election—
    1936.   5. New Deal, 1983-1939.   I. Title.
    JK2356.W44   1994
    324.2734'09'043—dc20   94–6094
                                                            CIP

For my mother and

the memory of my father

Contents

•

PART ONE   The Republican Era

PART TWO   Descent to Minority Status

List of Tables and Figures

•

Figures

Preface

•

So often the study of the relationship between political parties and governmental institutions becomes the history of policy innovation or social and political change. So it has gone with the 1930s where, despite an outpouring of literature on the period, the sources of non–New Deal culture remain strangely unexplored.

As an undergraduate I thought it curious that a successful mass organization such as the GOP could lose its way so quickly in the 1930s, and I can recall wondering about the sources of its confusion at the time. In graduate school I became interested in the problems of political opposition and minority parites in general, and this gradually led me back to considering the fate of the Republicans in the 1930s. I have found their judgments and electoral strategies to be more important to what happened in the 1930s than had previously been suggested, while also noting a similarity to the debates that went on within the Democratic party in the 1980s.

I have not belabored these similarities at length here, but the attentive reader may at several points recall the adage Truman Capote chose as a title: "Other voices, other rooms."

The reexamination of fundamental values cannot help but be a painful process, as the Republicans of the period rapidly discovered. However I hope to show how important this process in the chaotic days of 1935–1936 was with regard to what has happened since.

The process of constructing a work of this kind has left me with many intellectual debts that I simply can never repay. The trail begins in my graduate years at Columbia University where the almost legendary lectures of Professor Charles V. Hamilton first reawakened my interest in the crisis politics of the 1930s. He also served as a bulwark of encouragement at the end of the writing process, when, of course, I most needed support. Only he can be aware of how much I have owed him over the years.

Professor Eric R. A. N. Smith, formerly on the faculty of Columbia University and now at the University of California at Santa Barbara, read this work with unending patience at critical stages. He was essential not only in the formulation of ideas but also in establishing conditions where more readers will understand what I am trying to say than would otherwise have been the case.

I also owe great thanks to Professor Alan F. Westin, whose skeptical questions were matched only by his support when convinced. Professor Robert Shapiro has continually given of his time, despite the demands of his own research and teaching; without him the publication process would have been far more hazardous to navigate.

I am also immensely grateful to Professors Bruce Schulman of UCLA and Richard Pious of Barnard College for their enormously sensitive reviews while then serving as anonymous referees for Columbia University Press. Both have contributed far more to the work than I had a right to expect. Kate Wittenberg of Columbia University Press contributed support and subtle editorial judgments at every stage of the process; my colleagues at Southern Connecticut University also have been a source of general encouragement and have furnished useful observations during the latter stages of the project.

Finally, my wife, Betsy, has slaved endlessly over the task of typing the manuscript—and all the cutting and pasting entailed—with a grace and humor I have not always deserved. It is to her I must dedicate this book, as she has been ever willing to accept most of what I am and indefatigable in her willingness to abide the rest.

Redding, Connecticut and
Cooperstown, New York

THE NEMESIS OF REFORM

The Republican Party During the New Deal

•

Introduction:

Previous Concepts

of Political Realignment

•

This work attempts to reconsider the dynamics of political realignment in the light of perspectives developed by both political scientists and historians. It is not meant to be a history of the Republican party during the 1920s and 1930s but rather intends to integrate the observations and analyses of the historical community into a broader theory of political change in party systems.

The emphasis of the study is on the process of innovation in party systems and the modification of electoral strategies. By focusing on party strategies, interest groups, and the process by which elites innovate new party positions, an attempt is made to move beyond the study of voting behavior in mass realignments. Thus the Republican congressional party of the period is considered as only one element of this overall process. The study emphasizes the neglected but important role that minority parties have played in the realignment process.

Political realignment in its most basic sense could be defined simply as a durable change in previous patterns of voting behavior. Viewed from the standpoint of national politics, the existing rationale for the division of voters between parties gives way to a new one. It has long been recognized that some elections in American history, so-called critical realigning elections, have been far more important than most in their long range consequences for the American political system.[1] Such elections "settle" clusters of substantive issues in a more clear cut fashion than do ordinary elections. Historically, each realigning election began a new political cycle during which, with one exception, one of the major parties clearly dominated presidential voting, while also bringing about substantial change in previous party alignments on both the congressional and local levels.[2]

Most analysis of historical realignments has focused on the identification of realigning periods and the delineation of patterns of fundamental discontinuity in voter allegiance. According to realignment theory, long periods of electoral stability are disrupted by realigning periods which inaugurate basic change in mass electoral responses. After a period of intense political conflict, a new period of relative stability follows, in which the balance of power between the parties has been fundamentally altered and voter coalitions rearranged.

Some elaborations on realignment theory have attempted classification of all elections into various typologies; other analyses include "critical periods" covering several elections rather than concentrating on a single realigning election.[3] Further elaborations have attempted to integrate later statewide results into the patterns established by critical realignment on the presidential level.[4]

E. E. Schattschneider defined a political party as "first of all, an organized attempt to get power. Power is here defined as control of the government."[5] This succinct analysis delineates a fundamental precondition for the survival of any major party: The existence of a major party depends on its present possession of political power or its prospects of a bid for power that can be made with reasonable expectation of success.

Political realignment, through its alteration of previously established patterns of political behavior, wreaks havoc on a party relegated to minority status. A stunning defeat at the polls—by deranging the party's structure, prevailing interests, and level of direct influence on events—makes innovation a very attractive strategy. A political party unable to achieve reconciliation with the changing needs and values of a consistent majority of citizens risks extinction. Thus, political realignment can be said to force some form of innovation on minority parties in the same fashion that consistently declining sales force adaptation on the part of marketing units.

The electoral results of the 1930s drove home the importance of adaptation to Republican strategists of the period. The election of Franklin Roosevelt to the presidency in 1932 ended twelve years of Republican government.[6] Having already lost control of the House of Representatives in 1930 and losing the Senate in the Roosevelt landslide, the GOP suddenly assumed the unaccustomed role of a minority party. While the party's fall from power in 1932 primarily reflected the historic opposition of the electorate to an administration that had presided over an economic depression, at the same time a a long-range revolution in the character and scope of American politics was already under way. A massive number of urban voters, concentrated principally in the industrial centers of the Northeast and the Midwest, surged into the American electorate through the Democratic party, consolidating what Samuel Lubell has termed "the revolt of the city."[7]

No less formidable a challenge to the Republicans was the new course of public policy fashioned by the Roosevelt administration. To combat the depression and respond to the demands of its rural and urban constituents, the New Deal embarked upon an eclectic program designed to induce both recovery and social reform. Much New Deal legislation implicitly repudiated the primary reliance on individual, private, and community efforts that had formed the cornerstone of the voluntaristic Republican ideology of the 1920s. The initial New Deal efforts of 1933 and 1934 were supported by a broad "all-class coalition" in American society.[8] New Deal legislation repeatedly involved some degree of positive interference in the economy, which received retrospective endorsement by the electorate.

In contrast, the Republican party, which was long conditioned to playing an influential, if not dominant, role in American politics, suddenly found itself cast in the role of a frustrated and divided minority party with a drastically reduced congressional and local base, attempting an adjustment to a dynamic new set of political realities.[9]

Innovation in Party Systems During Political Realignment

The dominant paradigm in theories of party competition is the Downsian model. In his influential work, *An Economic Theory of Democracy,* Anthony Downs formulated explanations for party behavior that can be utilized to predict party responses to the conditions of partisan realignment.[10] He sees political parties as groups of rational individuals seeking to advance private ends by influencing the policymaking process. In order to maximize electoral gains, a party, in his view, would alter its appeals in response to changes in policy preferences by the electorate. Downs thus assumes that parties are rational actors, designing electoral strategies to maximize electoral gains.

Descriptions of the history of actual party behavior during the early stages of realignment contradict the Downsian view. Realignment observers such as Walter Dean Burnham and James Sundquist have noted *increased* ideological polarization between major parties during periods of partisan realignment.[11] They observe that during such periods the movement of the minority party to a position of polar opposition to the innovations of the majority party has been an essential step in the successful consummation of political realignment.

For Downs such movement would seem irrational. The strict logic of party competition should lead parties to give up more and more of their own preferences in order to maximize their electoral strength. In short, rapid convergence should occur. Within a rationalist economic perspective, the question remains: Why does polarization between the parties increase in the early years of these periods?

The behavior of the Republican party in the 1930s sheds light on this problem. When confronted with a nationwide surge to the Left during the period from 1930 through 1936, the Republicans, by "Downsian lights," should have moved to the political left, or at least much closer to the center, in order to maximize vote-gathering capacity. Instead, by 1935 the dominant eastern elements of the party had moved from an unwillingness to criticize many New Deal measures to the view that the party's most advantageous electoral course was not convergence, but ideological criticism of the New Deal. The effect of this was to minimize electoral appeal and doom the Republicans to a minority status that even now has not been wholly overcome.

Realignment theory seems to have fallen on hard times in the 1990s. While most scholars agree that something important has happened to the current party balance on a presidential level, the scant evidence of mass attitude change has left researchers uncertain as to how to classify the electoral patterns that have developed on a presidential level since the waning of the New Deal electoral coalition in 1968.[12] Polsby and Wildavsky as well as James Q. Wilson have considered the possibility that realignments among political elites can occur independent of changes in mass voting behavior. This study will posit the existence of such an elite realignment during the 1930s and argue for the need to alter the focus of studies of the New Deal period that have traditionally centered on changes in mass electoral responses.[13]

Toward a Theory of Minority Party Innovation During Political Realignment

Two primary conclusions arise from my investigation. First, I argue that a complete explanation of minority party behavior must move beyond models based solely on electoral response, and should consider the operation of interest groups within the party coalition as these groups respond to an altered public policy environment. Realignment has always involved the notion of dramatic changes in both electoral response and the national governing process. While parties must act to maximize electoral support, they have to do so in a fashion that does not lose the support of key interest groups. Yet the effects of political realignment on policy elites within party coalitions have received very little attention. As I shall show, the Republican party by 1935 reflected a coalition of groups that had come to feel extraordinarily threatened by the policy changes induced by the political realignment then under way, and this severely limited the party's ability to undertake electoral adjustments.

Second, this study considers whether political parties recently placed in a minority status may—as a result of past electoral success—suffer "perceptual problems" that retard immediate evaluation of, and adjustment to, the rapidly altered conditions of political realignment.

This study will introduce a "perceptual model" to the study of party behavior before the legitimization of modern polling. My view is that the fate of the GOP was sealed not so much by an unwillingness to act in a Downsian fashion as by the inability of Republican leaders to comprehend what was actually occurring during the period.

By concerning itself with the identification of aggregate electoral patterns that emerge retrospectively from periods of accelerated partisan change, realignment theory can, in its efforts to delineate broader electoral cycles, obscure unique features of individual electoral contests. As a result the importance of contemporary evaluations of political conditions, or the existence of "perceptual problems," can be entirely overlooked (or reduced to minimal importance) when one retrospectively examines party behavior.

Yet the existence of such factors forms an integral part of an explanation of the movement of the Republican party to a position of ideological polarization during the 1935–1936 period. Heretofore no examination of minority party dynamics has attempted to explain the movement of minority parties to positions of polar opposition during periods of partisan realignment. Since political parties face the same distribution of voters, it has never been apparent why their appeals can diverge so during such periods. An understanding of the role of perceptual problems during the period constitutes an important extension of our understanding of historical electoral dynamics.

I also hope that this book will fill an important gap in the literature of the New Deal and the decline of the reform impulse during the post–1936 period. Although various scholars have considered the political and institutional forces hostile to the New Deal, the internal dynamics behind Republican electoral strategies have been subjected to only the briefest kind of historical treatment at the expense of a broader understanding of the period.[14] This has occurred despite the fact that the GOP formed the bulk of the conservative coalition that came to oppose the continuation of the domestic New Deal after 1936. While state structures and state capacities are now recognized as important independent variables in the development of New Deal policy, I shall show that political elites also had an underappreciated, important independent effect. Finally, in light of contemporary discussions of the decline of the New Deal electoral coalition and the revival of a kind of mass-based conservatism in the 1980s, a consideration of the sources of non–New Deal political culture has taken on renewed importance.

Two limitations to the study should be mentioned at the outset. First, this is a study of the minority party's reaction to the New Deal on a national level: the complex mosaic of state and local politics is simply too involved to consider in a study of this kind. While it is conceivable that on the state and local level the minority party could follow a different course than that taken on the national level, little evidence suggests this was the case. The GOP was almost swept out of state legislatures in the western United States, remaining competitive in only a few northeastern states including their New England bulwarks of the 1920s and later.[15] The behavior of individual congressmen was also tied more closely to local political organizations in the 1930s than currently, and, as a result, local evaluations of political conditions were important to the party's congressional wing. Clearly the pressure for policy innovation was replicated on a local level through 1936 for most elected Republican officials.

Second, this is a study of the GOP's reaction to the *domestic* New Deal up to the advent of the congressional conservative coalition in 1938. It is not a consideration of Republican reactions to foreign policy questions. The period between the London Economic Conference in 1933 and Hitler's occupation of the Sudentenland in September of 1938 was a time when domestic political questions were of primary importance in American politics. The circumstances surrounding the isolationist/ interventionist debate have already been widely considered and, moreover, involved congressional alignments of a very different nature than those that affected consideration of the domestic New Deal through 1938.

The book, although divided into three parts, has four sections, plus a coda. Chapters 1 and 2 describe the "voluntaristic" Republican coalition of the 1920s and its rapid breakdown in the 1930s. The pattern established by New Deal efforts at national planning had dramatic effects on the GOP and its constituencies.

Chapters 3, 4, and 5 chronicle the efforts of the Republicans to effect the party's restoration between 1933 and 1936. Perceptual problems on the part of most party leaders became central to the political realignment of the period.

Chapter 6 discusses the Landon presidential campaign in 1936 with an emphasis on the reconstruction of knowledge then available to party strategists. Confusion over the direction of events was far deeper and more persistent than the often-discussed *Literary Digest* fiasco would suggest.

Chapters 7, 8, and 9 examine the Republican congressional party during the domestic New Deal. Both the regular Republican congressional party and the party's national committee are considered here. Given the importance of the Republicans to the emergence of the modern conservative congressional coalition in 1938, their failure to form consistently effective coalitions with disafffected elements of the Democratic party from 1933 through 1936 demands scrutiny. Previously only the GOP's progressive insurgents have received sustained attention, despite the fact that the party's regulars were the heart of the conservative coalition that began to operate effectively by the Seventy-fifth Congress. This is also a study, then, of a congressional delegation—accustomed to persistent political influence—suddenly cast into a political wilderness.

Furthermore, while it is almost a truism that national committees wield little power in a nonresponsible party system, within opposition parties they can exercise subtle but nevertheless important influence at different points. In such areas as publicity, research, or the evaluation of political conditions in constituencies national committees, particularly within minority parties, can become a genuine center of influence, The Republican party's internal struggles during this period shed light on the relative strength of different factions within the party as they sought to adjust to rapidly changing political circumstances.

The conclusion returns to the subject of minority party behavior during periods of accelerated partisan change, considered in light of the material presented throughout the work.

PART ONE

The Republican Era

•

CHAPTER ONE

The Anatomy of the Republican Party in the 1920s: The Restoration of "Sound Republicanism"

•

Political parties often serve as conduits for social change. Nevertheless, it is also important to note that they can reflect the legacies of preexisting factional conflict. Despite its electoral success in the 1920s, the Republican party continued to reflect the previous decade's schisms between the party's progressive and conservative wings.

The election of Warren Harding to the presidency in 1920 brought about a decisive restoration of Republican dominance. Simultaneously, through a combination of design and good fortune, the conservative old guard of the Republican party, after almost a decade of diminished influence, reassumed its role as the dominant faction in Republican party councils. America's entry into World War I had abruptly fragmented the broad cross-party base of progressive reform that had been characteristic of both political parties during the elections of 1912 and 1916.[1] By 1920 adverse reaction to American participation in the League of Nations had drawn most insurgent western Republicans back into the party's fold, finally providing an opportunity to heal the split between conservative eastern Republicans and the western members of the party.[2]

The newfound unity that characterized party efforts in 1920 seemed to demonstrate the political acumen of the party's conservative old guard. In 1912 William Howard Taft, Boies Penrose, Elihu Root, and the other leaders of the Republican old guard had reasoned that it was better to keep control of the party's machinery even if it meant losing an election rather than winning the election through resort to Rooseveltian radicalism.[3] This rigid, uncompromising attitude in the face of an insurgency within the party in 1912 had eventually been proven correct. A general reaction against Wilsonian progressivism had set in, and the party reassumed power under systematic conservative control. By 1920 it was apparent that the old guard would no longer be forced to choose between political expediency and the politics of principle: an unyielding attitude had sacrificed neither.[4]

Despite this newfound party unity, the GOP's triumph of 1920 owed much to conditions beyond the party's control. Nativism, tinged with various forms of anti-radicalism, had seeped deeper into the popular imagination as the war effort progressed, exacerbating conflicts that seemingly had been dormant in American society during the progressive period.[5]

The onset of economic recession in early 1920 deepened popular disaffection with the undertaking of heroic efforts, thus wreaking havoc on the Wilsonian electoral coalition of 1912–1916. In terms of real wages, postwar inflation had ravaged labor's wartime gains, while midwestern farmers had become increasingly disillusioned with the administration's wartime price ceilings on farm products.[6] Irish-, German-, and Italian-Americans felt that the concept of self-determination for European states had been compromised by the decisions taken at Versailles, while the majority of all Americans had simply grown weary of the exertions and dislocations required by the conduct of the war effort.[7]

The accumulation of popular disaffection pointed to Republican electoral success in 1920, but the magnitude of the victory stunned most observers. Harding received 16.1 million votes (60.3 percent), compared to 9.1 million (34.1 percent) for James Cox. The GOP now controlled the House of Representatives by the margin of 303 to 131, the largest in the party's history. In the Senate the Republicans increased their margin to 24 with the capture of 10 previously Democratic seats.[8]

The magnitude of the Harding victory seemed to indicate the maturation of a new political force. Yet the political successes of 1920 had come about not so much from a sudden upsurge of conservatism, or "fidelity to the Constitution," as from the underlying dissatisfaction with the dislocations of the war effort, which had allied western progressives and eastern immigrants with conservatives.[9] While the ideological battle appeared to have been won by the American Right in 1920, the experiences of the ensuing decade would demonstrate that key elements of the Republican electoral coalition cared little for the application of "classical economics" and later on—under the impact of economic crisis—even less for the Republican party.

Factions in the Republican Party

The old guard of the Republican party viewed the election of 1920 as the successful culmination of a political crusade. As noted, the party's renaissance had been accomplished through the enunciation of conservative appeals while party machinery remained in the hands of old guard spokesmen. The core of Republican old guard strength remained, in 1920 as in the previous decade, in the eastern United States, where its appeal was dominant in Connecticut, Delaware, Maine, Massachusetts, New Hampshire, New Jersey, New York, and Pennsylvania.

Although the political creed of the old guard of the Republican party was elastic enough to allow for some variation in attitudes, regular party leaders reflected a remarkably persistent conservative ideological outlook by 1920. They also represented the dominant conservative eastern contingent of the Republican party that had reassumed control of party councils.

Western Rural Insurgency and the GOP

Western Republicans remained a minority within party ranks, but continued to articulate the discontents of that region throughout the 1920s. The decade was one of chronic agricultural depression, and the party's western wing remained preoccupied with the "farm problem." Western Republicans continued to favor tariff protection for agricultural products, efforts to promote cooperative marketing, and endeavors to raise farm prices directly through the McNary-Haugen price stabilization system.[10] Thus the core of western insurgent Republican support was found primarily in states west of the Mississippi Valley—such as Iowa, Kansas, Nebraska, and the Dakotas—and in such states as Ohio, Michigan, and Illinois.

The Republican insurgents of the 1920s would remain primarily concerned with the problem of depressed farm prices during a period of general prosperity—as opposed to the broader national questions that had occupied the rural insurgents of the Populist period. This suggests there was a local, provincial quality to the Republican insurgency of the 1920s, representing, as it did, a disaffected minority. After 1920 the insurgents in the GOP were too few to effectively challenge the conservative leadership on most national issues. The most they could do was threaten the eastern old guard with electoral defeat if it failed to respond to agricultural demands—an argument that seemed somewhat hollow in light of the 1920 results.

Throughout the decade, the heart of the Republican insurgents' problem was the heavy single-party background that prevailed in their home states. Representing districts and states long committed to the Republican party, insurgents were both unable and unwilling to risk formal alliances with the Democrats or to formally support third-party efforts.[11] Even at the height of the Progressive era (1908–1916), when the prestige of the old guard was at an all-time low, the Progressive insurgents in the GOP judged that their constituents would not support a complete break with the Republican party.[12] As it turned out, they were correct: the resurgent old guard Republicanism of 1920 proved to be a more enduring force than Progressivism.

Yet Republican insurgency remained an active, contentious force within party ranks after 1920. Despite their relegation to minority status by the onrush of urbanization, insurgents continued to draw upon the language of the older, broader radical agrarian tradition, couching their demands in the anti-monopoly rhetoric that had served as a powerful rallying point for agrarian interests during the Populist period.[13]

In spite of these lingering conflicts, the Republican party remained a fertile seedbed for the development of the new managerial designs and forms that characterized the organizational revolution of the early twentieth century. Robert K. Murray recognized that such organizational innovation continued to prosper under the benign neglect of the Harding administration. However, as Murray also noted, these positive innovations have been obscured by the subsequent preoccupation of historians with the seamier events of the Harding years.[14] Thus, during the period so often characterized as one of "normalcy," there was nonetheless a continuing rise in the development of new organizational and technological expertise in response to the challenges and dilemmas of the time.

The Republican Party and the Associative State

In order to understand the response of the Republican electoral coalition to the political crises of the 1930s, it is necessary to delve beneath the familiar nostrums of "normalcy" so often associated with the Republican ascendancy of the 1920s. Viewed in retrospect, the support that some elements of the traditional GOP gave to early New Deal policies was a logical outgrowth of attitudes and policy-making structures developed during both the World War I emergency and the "associational" activities of the 1920s.[15]

The industrial mobilization policies of the First World War had proved to be remarkably palatable to major American corporations. While the period saw the final abandonment of laissez-faire precepts and the formal elevation of the federal government to the role of director of war-related industry, the diverse and specialized expertise central to the operation of modern industrial processes gave business leaders a systemic advantage in dealing with the often hastily constructed government agencies.[16] Thus an ad hoc system of national planning, largely characterized by industrial self-government, moved to the forefront of emergency planning. By July 1917 the War Industries Board had been organized to oversee the largely private administration of business procedures during wartime. Networks of private boards, staffed by individuals often drawn from the particular industries concerned, oversaw a voluntary cartelization of the American economy on an industry-by-industry basis.[17]

The successful prosecution of the war left an indelible imprint on the minds of industrial managers.[18] The war experience seemed to indicate what could be achieved through industrial self-government when the economy was largely freed from antitrust restraints and was directed toward mutually agreeable ends by the coordinated efforts of a benign government. While most American business viewed the prospect of postwar political control with little enthusiasm, the potential value of trade associations, the usefulness of the government to firms competing with foreign enterprises, and the possibility of federal intervention— without the suggestion of any permanent interference in the process of industrial decision-making—would remain vivid images for industrial planners of the period.

It is hardly surprising, then, that the wartime program of industrial self-government evolved into the "associational" activities of the 1920s.[19]

Associationalism involved the deliberate encouragement of voluntary institutions—particularly trade associations, professional societies, company unions, and farm cooperatives—to foster cooperation within a particular trade or industry. Of course the idea of business cooperation was not novel in the America of the 1920s: trade associations antedated the Civil War, but their development prior to the First World War had been hindered by the Sherman Antitrust Act.[20] Legitimization had come from the successful management of the war effort; trade associations had been found useful to wartime industrial coordination, and the methods of cooperation had not been forgotten.[21]

At the hub of these coordinative efforts was Harding's secretary of commerce, Herbert Hoover. While Hoover's particular view of governmental activism was not shared by such conservative party regulars as Andrew Mellon and Calvin Coolidge, it nevertheless formed one of the cornerstones of Republican domestic policy in the 1920s.[22]

The Hoover literature of the 1970s and 1980s is rich with descriptions of the efforts of Hoover and others to develop a nonstatist machinery that would nonetheless allow for more than automatic self-adjustment of the nation's economy. Of particular concern to both Hoover and the business community were efforts to control the economic fluctuations that resulted in declines in aggregate demand and increases in unemployment.[23] In November 1920 a Hoover-sponsored report by the Federated American Engineering Societies examined "waste in industry." Central to the study was the belief of Hoover and others that unemployment and labor problems were linked to a narrower problem, namely, inefficient organization of production.[24] Contrary to prevailing management sentiment, the study argued that labor unrest was not the cause of inefficiency and waste, and that the key to stability and increased productivity was sound business planning in response to short- and long-term market fluctuations.[25] Metcalf notes that the report, published in June 1921, "summed up the views of Hoover . . . at the time he became Secretary of Commerce," which involved "the application of knowledge, analysis and planning to the management of business enterprises."[26]

Critical to this effort was an increased interest in the collection of systematized economic statistics. As secretary of commerce, Hoover quickly moved to improve the data collection of the Bureau of the Census, and established a monthly survey of current business. He was sympathetic to the desire of businessmen for statistical information which could be shared among individual firms to contribute to economic stability, and sought to increase the department's role as "a real business information service to the country" and "an economic interpreter to the American public generally."[27] However, for Hoover the key to economic planning lay not with the collection of the statistics per se, but in their use as tools for the development of voluntary cooperation between differing elements of specific industries. For example, Hoover sought to bring stability to the bituminous coal industry through a series of voluntary, cooperative, and private efforts to control entry into, and predatory pricing among, the industry's marginal producers.[28]

Under Hoover's careful supervision, as secretary of commerce and later as president, trade associations patterned after the U.S. Chamber of Commerce proliferated during the 1920s. Entire industries were brought into close and regular contact with Congressional committees, cabinet departments and executive agencies. Thus the modern pattern of continual interaction between specific agencies of government and particular industrial groupings can be traced to the 1920s period. To dedicated associationalists, this activity enabled industry to address such concerns as predatory pricing, information exchange, and product standardization without sacrificing the safeguards of and tendency toward the introduction of innovations, which were seen as inherent to the price mechanism and legitimate competition. Associationalists believed that these new institutions, unlike the early trusts of the American experience, or the politicized cartels of the European one, would promote both efficiency and public service, utilizing the services of an increasingly enlightened corporate leadership committed to both profit and stewardship in public life.[29]

Despite the proliferation of the "new" Hoover scholarship on associational efforts, nagging questions remain as to the overall impact of these efforts on the Republican coalition. To what degree was associationalist behavior typical of the older basic industry elements of the Republican coalition? Hoover may never have worked out in his own mind the tension between the ideal of enhanced associational coordination and the efforts at cartelization that later emerged within much of the Republican coalition—instead his condemnation of the proposals for industrial recovery developed by 1932 suggest the limits of his own private vision vis-á-vis the thinking of industrial elites. In short, it seems important when analyzing the "state-building" of the period to distinguish between associational efforts and cartelization, recognizing that events after the 1920s called into question the long-term validity of the associationalist vision.

Nevertheless, government-business cooperation was evident by the mid-1920s in such areas as housing, unemployment, child labor, emergency relief, and retirement programs.[30] During the 1920s, business leadership reached a zenith in public esteem that led to its portrayal as a kind of ultimate American profession; business leaders were thought to be producing a technological revolution that utilized new patterns of both industrialization and science.

Despite that fact that Hoover was viewed with suspicion by the party's conservative old guard, he emerged as the leading candidate for the presidential nomination in 1928 after President Coolidge declined to seek renomination. Hoover's successes at the Department of Commerce, his reputation for technical professionalism, and his long history of involvement in humanitarian efforts were enchanced by his remarkable ability to secure favorable publicity on a nonpartisan basis.[31]

Herbert Hoover thus appeared to be an ideal custodian of Republican prosperity. His very lack of early partisan commitment could be utilized to portray him as a kind of omniscient administrator who combined both scientific and technical knowledge.[32] One Republican leaflet termed Hoover "ten candidates in one" and went on to depict him as an expert in areas such as aviation, engineering, conservation, and international affairs.[33]

When Hoover assumed the presidency in 1929 he surveyed with considerable satisfaction the condition of associational development which he had helped to guide at the Department of Commerce throughout the 1920s. The number of national voluntary associations had multiplied from approximately seven hundred in 1919 to over two thousand by 1929.[34] In Hoover's view, associationalism had preserved the essentials of American individualism by avoiding centralized decision-making and relying upon appeals to community and individual responsibility to lessen the gap between the public and the private interest.

However, the onset of the depression would demonstrate the clear limits of Hoover's voluntary associationalism during a period of privation and scarcity. As industrial profits continued to decline, moreover, the Hoover precedent of encouraging effective coordination among industrial groups through governmental sponsorship would enable such interests to formulate demands for forms of governmental assistance that Hoover and most elements of the Republican party had never envisioned. Unwittingly, Republican associationalism had introduced business group to a form of cooperative planning that would, under the impact of crisis, carry many of them away from the Republican electoral coalition.

The Limits of Volunteerism: Herbert Hoover and the Great Depression

The American economy suffered a severe and enduring contraction during the period that began in October of 1929, with the stock market crash triggering America's worst depression. In fact, by mid–1930 it was clear that the initial panic in the stock market had developed into a major economic downturn, the severity and persistence of which had been anticipated by few observers. During the Hoover period, unemployment would reach 25 percent of the civilian work force, while both prices and industrial output declined more than one-third from 1929 levels.[35] The depression was unprecedented and worldwide, as the international system of trade, capital flow and finance fell into disarray.

Until the end of 1930 one could say that Hoover maintained a position of leadership among those seeking direct solutions to the depression. Some members of Hoover's cabinet, including Secretary of the Treasury Andrew Mellon, counseled noninterference—a view that combined an adherence to classical economic theory with a distrust of centralized governmental control and direction.[36]

However, this view was strongly rejected by Hoover and a majority of his cabinet. Hoover's broadened outlook of cooperative individualism, together with the development of new forms of the government-business organizations of the 1920s, suggested to him that the downward spiral could be arrested, even reversed.[37] These efforts to short-circuit the "liquidationist" phase of the depression thus became central to the Hoover administration's activities.[38]

Working within this associationalist framework, the president began receiving an increasing number of national leaders making pilgrimages to the White House. One predictable result of these conferences was a series of optimistic statements and forecasts that began to issue with regularity from the White House. Of greater importance, however, was the pledge of industrial leaders to commence efforts to maintain existing wage scales, stabilize employment, and increase private construction and relief activities.[39]

Hoover initially undertook these efforts to imbue the industrial community with clear feelings of optimism. As a leading member of the engineering profession, he was in an excellent position to influence that important industrial reform group.[40] In addition, his experience as a fundraising philanthropist during the war years suggested that he had an intimate understanding of and experience with the uses of publicity and fund-raising techniques employed to arouse public response to major crises. Finally, Hoover's experiences at the Department of Commerce had involved continual contact with the nation's industrial and banking leaders, and he judged his tenure there to have been a conspicuous success.[41]

After 1930, of course, Hoover's leadership position was increasingly challenged. Herbert Stein has noted, however, that Hoover's continued emphasis on state and local governmental activity—undertaken with private sector support—is more comprehensible in light of the relatively small size of the federal government at that time. Stein observed:

> In 1929, total federal expenditures were about 2.5 percent of the gross national product, federal purchases of goods and services about 1.3 percent and federal construction less than 0.2 percent. . . . A very large percentage change in the revenue or expenditure side of such small budgets would have been required to make a significant dent in the national economy.[42]

Under such circumstances, it was perhaps natural, initially, to define presidential leadership in terms of its relationship to state, local, and voluntary efforts at relief.

Still, it is difficult to resist the conclusion that Hoover would have remained implacably hostile to federal solutions, even if more readily available mechanisms had existed. What rapidly separated Hoover from his increasingly numerous critics after 1930 was not so much his conviction of the need for programs to combat the depression as his lifelong belief that they could be funded privately—or at least by combined public and private resources.[43] He objected less to the concept of planning as than to the federal government's determination of the projects to be planned and funded. Hoover saw the social problems of the 1930s quite clearly, but, after 1930, he seemed often to oppose direct efforts to address them.

President Hoover came to embody, in an extreme fashion, most of the paradoxes America carried into the 1930s. As Barry Karl has noted, Hoover wanted trade associations, but he was unwilling to utilize government to give them legal authority.[44] He wanted effective farm organizations to develop both pricing and production arrangements, but he was unwilling to use government authority to bring them about, even in the wake of decades of the failure of voluntarism. He wanted local communities to be diligent in their efforts to provide for their needy citizens, but this was to be accomplished without federal assistance, lest it affect the American tradition of individual and local self-help. While the word *volunteerism* has been used to describe Hoover's approach to combating the depression, the term diminishes the overall concept involved and overlooks the firm grounding such an attitude had within the American reform tradition.[45] In Karl's words, "He [Hoover] saw the needs, but the solutions terrified him, for they implied that the revolutionary changes taking place elsewhere in the world could now be threatening to happen here."[46]

Continually preoccupied with international economics, Hoover put forth analyses of the depression that seemed increasingly abstract to individuals confronting the diminishing public resources available through local organizations. Whereas Hoover's management of the crisis had probably reflected prevailing attitudes in both parties in 1930, by 1932 perception of the crisis had begun to change. Still, confidence in Hoover and his solutions diminished only gradually and never entirely disappeared, as is shown by the Republican party's ability to poll 15 million votes (39.6 percent) in 1932, despite having presided over an unprecedented economic disaster.

Whatever else Herbert Hoover's ardent admirers might claim for him in the years after 1932, they could not credibly argue that he was an effective political manager of the economic crisis as it came to affect the Republican party. As he gradually came to view the very exercise of electoral politics as something that prolonged a sense of general crisis, Hoover became increasingly withdrawn from party affairs, thus hastening the rapid demise of the Republican electoral coalition.

The Initial Breakdown of the GOP Coalition Under the Impact of Economic Crisis

Such a profound economic crisis eventually cut across class lines, with devastating impact on the Republican electoral coalition. Predictably, Hoover's differences with the insurgent Republicans of the West quickly became irreconcilable. His experience at the Department of Commerce should have suggested to Hoover that farmers, unlike other laborers, had come to exercise a potent influence on congressional politics. While this influence extended back to the Populist period, it had blossomed in the 1920s through direct entry into the realm of pressure group politics and, under the impact of depression, constituted too formidable a force to be ignored.[47] Hoover's continual effort to attribute increasing demands for agricultural relief to a radical fringe seeking special interest legislation had little actual effect on public attitudes toward agricultural assistance.[48] Further, it provided a justification for most progressive Republicans to desert the party's leadership, so that by 1931, the breakdown of unity within Republican ranks was so serious that even a major economic upturn before the 1932 election would not have unified the party. The actions of such insurgent leaders as Borah, La Follette, Norbeck, and Johnson reflected a broader pattern of votes by western Republicans against the Hoover administration's positions.[49]

On the surface it appeared that the Republican party was confronted with a schism that simply redrew the lines of an ongoing conflict between the progressive and old guard elements of the party. While there is some merit to this analysis, the breakdown of the Republican coalition was based on far more than the disaffection of progressive Republicans.[50]

By the end of 1930 the internal cohesion of the American business community had begun to break down. While the American economy of the early 1930s was an intricate industrial system, reflecting an enormous variety of interests, it is possible to delineate a range of attitudes and responses among business interests that were identified with the Republican party, and to trace their evolution through the period. It is argued here that the economic crisis of the 1930s fostered a broad range of proposed solutions to economic distress among conservative business groups, and that the ensuing diversity of those groups' political behavior partially accounts for the enfeebled Republican efforts in the campaign of 1932, as well as for the effective breakdown of Republican opposition to the New Deal during its early period.

By 1931 it was apparent that voluntary efforts to maintain wage, employment, and price levels had been unsuccessful, and that the Depression could no longer be viewed as normal, either in duration or effect. Rising evidence of market failure and the continued existence of anti-statist impulses produced a series of calls for planned production under the auspices of trade associations—such associations to be granted immunity from the antitrust laws. This would permit industry's use of production quotas, pricing formulas and agreements, and entry controls.

While interest in the revision of antitrust provisions had been confined previously to the "profitless prosperity" industries of the 1920s, the continued impact of the Depression had made such sentiments a majority position among industrialists by 1931.[51] What was needed, so the argument ran, was the legalization of those trade association activities that would lead to increased industrial cooperation. The primary implementation of this cooperation would be the establishment of a series of planning boards, made up of representatives from industry, which would pass upon prices, wages, and levels of corporate production. Control would be democratic, rationalized and self-imposed by all the major industry groups—a vision that recalled the unity and success of the World War I planning experience.[52]

A leading voice in this discussion within the largely Republican groups was General Electric's president, Gerald Swope, whose popular "Swope Plan" advocated cartelization of the national economy under the auspices of federal control.[53] Central to Swope's plans, however, was the creation of greatly enhanced unemployment compensation plan, pension systems, and disability programs. In a precursor of divisions that would reemerge during the NRA period, neither the U.S. Chamber of Commerce nor the National Association of Manufacturers (NAM) would endorse any plan for industrial reform measures that went beyond cartelization of industry under suspended antitrust provisions.[54]

When the industrial champions of the "welfare capitalism" of the 1920s lost confidence in their own solutions and began to urge that they be given new power to plan and rationalize their own operations with government assistance, they ran directly into Herbert Hoover. Hoover continued to champion his lifelong belief in voluntary associationalism. The president maintained that the Swope Plan was "the most gigantic proposal of monopoly ever made in history" and refused to have anything to do with it, or the other proposals for cartelization then being suggested by both the U.S. Chamber of Commerce and the NAM.[55]

These divergent attitudes were indications of the widening schisms within conservative factions that would hinder the Republican party's desperate campaign efforts in 1932, and its later attempts to oppose the "all class" proposals of the early New Deal. The still formidable tradition of classical economics and the enduring pull of partisan loyalty were arrayed against the notions of a cooperative, rational effort to manage economic affairs in a fashion that recalled the unity of the World War I experience. The lack of precision surrounding those notions allowed interest groups that were traditionally hostile to government direction to view such efforts as little more than exercises in self-direction.

While Hoover continued to command a clear majority of support within the business community—in part due to his position on the tariff—the ever-growing clamor for active intervention in economic life threatened permanent disruption of the Republican electoral coalition as the 1932 campaign approached. Paradoxically, Hoover's efforts in the 1920s to stimulate industrial cooperation through the development of trade associations had now placed him in the position of opposing the recommendations of many of the very groups he had nurtured.

Never entirely comfortable with nor particularly interested in Republican party affairs, Hoover withdrew from such matters after the 1930 elections presented him with a Congress under partial Democratic control.[56] The election results seemed to indicate that the chief executive and his party needed to demonstrate more effective leadership in combating the economic depression; otherwise, the GOP declines of that year would be compounded in 1932. By 1932, however, it was apparent that even a unified Republican effort would have confronted insurmountable electoral difficulties; the fragmented effort the GOP was to mount was the harbinger of a rout.

CHAPTER TWO

The Fragmentation of the

Republican Coalition

•

Despite a proliferation of historically based works, the evolution of Republican electoral strategy in the 1930s has been widely misunderstood and underchronicled. For example, most scholarly analysis of the 1932 election has focused on the initial emergence of the New Deal Democratic coalition; the abrupt fragmentation of the Republican coalition has received far less attention.[1] Yet the unraveling of the Republican party's electoral coalition presented party strategists with a series of strategic problems, some of which, such as the farm problem, were far more visible at the time than others.

The disenchantment of GOP western elements was widespread and apparent. The possibility of a revolt by the western wing against a second Hoover candidacy made progressive Republicans the subject of much political speculation throughout 1932. The idea of a third-party effort was briefly considered by the party's westerners but then rejected. The results of the Progressive bolt of 1912 and the La Follette effort of 1924 seemed to demonstrate the limitations of such actions.[2] Consideration was then given to a direct challenge to Hoover's renomination, despite the odds against any kind of success.[3] By the end of 1931, however, it was clear to the progressive wing that the prospect of denying Hoover the renomination was hopeless.[4]

With Hoover the incumbent nominee, individual western progressives faced the personal decision of whether to now support him. Many issued ambivalent statements regarding their preference in the presidential election and avoided direct association with the party's national ticket; only Charles McNary and Arthur Capper would actively endorse and make speeches for Hoover; other progressives, such as Robert La Follette, Hiram Johnson, George Norris, and Lynn Frazier, openly supported Roosevelt.[5]

To many observers the condition of the GOP recalled the disarray of Republican efforts in 1912, when Theodore Roosevelt's "Bull Moose" effort had split the party. There would not be a separate insurgent effort led by a former Republican president, but the depth of insurgent disaffection was apparent. Not surprisingly, Roosevelt undertook a series of measures designed to gain the support, or benevolent neutrality, of progressive Republican senators. During campaign tours of the West, he appealed to individual progressive senators to join the Democratic effort and offered conspicuous praise of Republican progressives when campaigning in their states.[6] In September, Roosevelt also announced the formation of a "National Progressive League," with George Norris as its chairman, that was designed to attract Republican and independent support for his candidacy.[7]

The effect of these appeals was to neutralize any serious Republican efforts to reconstruct the alliance of eastern and western wings that had been the cornerstone of the party's strategy in the 1920s. At the same time, progressive Republicans, by rejecting the party's national ticket and confining their efforts to state and local contests in 1932, established a pattern of behavior that would have profound repercussions after the Republican congressional contingent was relegated to minority status. William E. Borah foresaw this when he wrote Walter Lippmann:

> I found myself out of harmony with both the candidates in this campaign, particularly upon economic and monetary questions. It did not seem to me there was any program whatever before the people purporting toward relief,—[sic]and this vote was a protest vote. However, I sincerely hope that the new president will be equal to the task. I shall have no embarrassment whatever in support of [sic] a program simply because it is a Democratic program.[8]

Other problems within the party's electoral coalition were more difficult to evaluate with precision. Harry Harriman, president of the U.S.
Chamber of Commerce, told Hoover during the course of the 1932
campaign that business support would not be forthcoming if Hoover
failed to endorse the proposals for cartelization of the national economy
that had been proposed by the Chamber.[9] While this was clearly an
exaggeration, Republican campaign efforts were hindered by the large
drop in campaign funds that the party experienced between 1928 and
1932. Although one would intuitively expect a drop in campaign contributions in a depression year, the financial condition of the party historically associated with American business and a high tariff is striking.
Louise Overacker, writing in October 1933, noted that the $2.54 million
raised by the Republicans in 1932 was less than 40 percent of the $6.6
million contributed to the party's campaign efforts in 1928.[10] Although
the GOP retained an absolute edge (overall contributions of $2.649
million compared to the Democrats' $2.378 million) donations to the
Democrats exceeded those of every other campaign for which records
existed, even in the midst of severe economic distress.[11] In addition, the
Democratic party attracted substantial support from large financial interests that in 1928 had retained their historical association with the Republican party. The following table reproduces Overacker's analysis of the
pattern of large campaign contributions in 1932.

Large contributions were the rule in 1932 and, as shown below,
substantial amounts of them went to the Democrats. For example, "bankers and brokers" made virtually equal contributions to the two parties,
while those in such categories as "railways, airways and public utilities"
and "professional people" gave the Democratic party more financial support than that accorded the GOP. While, at first glance, it appears that
manufacturing interests continued to provide the GOP with disproportionate support, less than half the manufacturing interests on the 1928
GOP list gave anything at all to the party in 1932.[12] The data thus
depict not only relatively even financial support for the parties, but also
a decision on the part of many long-time Republican supporters to "sit
out" the 1932 election.

It will be recalled that by 1932 both the Chamber of Commerce and
the NAM had come to disagree with Hoover over proposals for cartelization of the national economy. The proposed New Deal recovery program,
on the other hand, could be seen as a positive attempt to restore industrial

TABLE 2.1

Distribution by Economic Interests of Contributions of $1,000
or More to the National Committee, 1932

Economic Interests	DEMOCRATS		REPUBLICANS	
	Amount	Percent	Amount	Percent
Bankers and brokers	$301,100	24.2	$335,605	20.5
Manufacturers	130,950	10.5	431,647	26.3
Mining and oil	54,000	4.4	158,500	9.7
Railroads, airways & public utilities	76,500	6.1	67,500	4.1
Professional people	152,043	12.2	121,800	7.4
Publishers, advertising	88,500	7.1	22,000	1.4
Retail stores	30,200	2.4	36,000	2.2
Unclassified	125,300	10.2	142,840	8.7
Unidentified	284,403	22.9	323,050	19.7
TOTAL	$1,242,996	100.0	$1,638,942	100.0

SOURCE: Louise Overacker, "Campaign Funds in a Depression Year," *APSR* 27 (October 1933): 776.

prosperity by government intervention, and this was what large elements of the business community had sought, but never received, under Hoover. Thus, one could certainly conclude that disaffection within the business community resulted in both in the absolute drop in Republican campaign contributions and in the allocation of contributions between the parties by certain economic interests, as set forth in Table 2.1.

An "Across-the-Board" Surge to the Democratic Party

It is important to recognize that the disaffection of certain business groupings was part of a broader "across-the-board" movement of high-income groups away from the Republican coalition as a result of the persistence of the Depression. That the 1932 vote was a protest vote that cut across all the income groupings of the population has been demonstrated by an examination of the *Literary Digest* poll of 1932. The magazine conducted presidential polls in 1924, 1928, 1932, and 1936 and, of course, its 1936 poll results have become a textbook example of how sampling bias can skew the results obtained in the poll. By using a sample drawn from telephone books and automobile registration lists, the *Digest* poll was wittingly sampling a group attentive middle-class voters, rather than a true cross section of the nation's voters.[13] However, its clear sampling bias favoring middle-class voters can serve as an index of the attitudes toward the Hoover administration held by a constituency that was strongly Republican.[14] In contrast to the 1936 poll, the *Digest*'s 1932 sample had provided an accurate reflection of political sentiment in the nation at large. The 1932 poll predicted that Roosevelt would receive 59.8 percent of the popular vote, whereas the actual election figures gave him 57.42 percent.[15] The *Digest* projections were also accurate on the state level; their forecast of an Electoral College result of 474 to 57 was strikingly close to the actual result of 472 to 59.[16] The 1932 *Digest* inaccurately predicted the results in only two states, Delaware and Pennsylvania, both of which the magazine gave to Roosevelt.[17] The accuracy of the 1932 *Literary Digest* poll suggests that attitudes toward the Hoover administration in 1932 did not break down primarily on a class basis. The 1932 Democratic majority was relatively uniform throughout the population and, thereby, affected elements of the Republican electoral coalition in a fashion that would become more evident in 1933–1934.

Republican campaign efforts were further vexed by the conservative nature of many Democratic campaign appeals. While it is apparent, in retrospect, that major elements of the New Deal program were foreshadowed in the campaign, such concerns as labor relations, housing programs, deficit spending, and increased income taxes were only lightly touched upon by Roosevelt in 1932.[18] In addition, Roosevelt called for a 25 percent reduction in government expenses, a budget that was to be balanced annually, and a consolidation of federal bureaus. He asked for an end to deficit spending and insisted upon the maintenance of a sound currency.[19] Marriner Eccles, an early New Deal administrator, later observed, "Given later developments, the campaign speeches often read like a giant misprint, in which Roosevelt and Hoover spoke each other's lines."[20]

The Collapse of Republican Campaign Strategy

The ongoing dissolution of the Republican coalition enabled Democratic strategists to consider the capture of several eastern states which, until 1932, had been considered strongly Republican.[21] This forced Republican strategists to concentrate their diminishing electoral resources in the final weeks of the campaign on efforts to retain their northeastern base and resulted in the final concession of the midwestern farm belt to the Democratic party.

Even the clearly partisan statements coming from Republican head-quarters in the Waldorf-Astoria began to take on a hollow ring; as late as October 29 the Republican National Committee would claim only eleven "sure" states for Hoover, representing a total of 151 electoral votes, 115 short of the total of 266 then required for election.[22] It was apparent, even to the national committee, that the electoral coalition of the 1920s had been deprived of its western base and had been fragmented, at least temporarily. Facing the most serious defeat visited upon the party since 1912, and becoming increasingly aware of the likelihood of this, the regular Republican organization grew disillusioned and resigned as the election drew near.

By early November the composite view of a survey of informed political observers and the public opinion polls then in operation was that Franklin Roosevelt would score a decisive victory.[23] The *New York Times* forecast a massive Democratic victory with Roosevelt amassing between 400 and 450 electoral votes; it also predicted Democratic control of the Senate as well as further Democratic gains in the House of Representatives.[24] These preelection predictions and polls were to prove strikingly accurate.

On November 8 Roosevelt received 22,821,857 popular votes compared to Hoover's 15,761,841, while slightly over a million votes were divided among several minor party candidates.[25] As is usually the case, the outcome was even more one-sided in the Electoral College, with the Democrats carrying forty-two states with 472 electoral votes, and the Republicans carrying six states with a total of 59 electoral votes. Although Hoover fared slightly better than William Howard Taft had in his three-way race in 1912, the only states outside of New England that Hoover carried were Pennsylvania and Delaware. The Republican dreams of a competitive two-party system in the South were abruptly shattered when the region again produced its customary lopsided Democratic majorities. Nowhere were the results more disappointing than in the West, where insurgent Republicans had demonstrated so little interest in Hoover's efforts. While the West clearly did not determine the electoral outcome, the capture of all its electoral votes by Franklin Roosevelt completely broke down the northeastern-western alliance that had enabled Republicans to dominate presidential elections since 1896. Eugene Edgar Robinson wrote:

> The west, however, went Democratic at the level of the county vote as it had never done before. Of 664 counties in the west in 1932, Roosevelt had carried all but 18. Hoover did not carry a single county in Texas, Arizona, Nevada or Washington. He carried only one county each in Montana, Idaho, Wyoming, Oregon and his own state of California.[26]

Thus, while it is apparent that economic conditions in 1932 would have resulted in the repudiation of the Republican party under any circumstances, the election also offered ample evidence of the legacy of the factional infighting that had been apparent in Republican ranks since 1912. Without benefit of a formal third-party effort, Republican western insurgents had helped to produce results similar to those achieved in 1912, and the split again contributed to the decisive election of the Democratic candidate. The emerging divisions within the GOP formed an important element of contemporary perceptions of the 1932 results. Walter Lippmann wrote Theodore Roosevelt, Jr.:

> The last ten days of Hoover's campaign were pretty desperate and lost him thousands of votes among conservative Republicans who would not stand for his tariff speeches and his appeals to fear. At the end about thirty percent, as I figure it, of the Republican party, swung over to Franklin, causing a split almost as great as that in 1912.[27]

Far more than the presidential coalition had been shattered. The turnover in Congress was considerably more dramatic and conclusive than what had been predicted only days before. The Republicans lost 103 seats in the House of Representatives, where the balance now stood at 313 Democrats to 117 Republicans. Most of these seats were lost in the Midwest, in such states as Illinois, Indiana, Iowa, Kansas, Michigan, Minnesota, Missouri, and Ohio. The Republicans suffered further losses in California and Washington. While only one-third of the Senate had faced the electorate, Republican control was nevertheless decisively repudiated as the party lost 12 seats, 10 of them in midwestern and western states. The 36 remaining Republican senators now confronted 59 who were Democrats (with 1 independent). Even amidst severe economic depression, the election results must have been shocking to individual Republicans who had grown accustomed to persistent electoral success.

PART TWO

Descent to Minority Status

•

CHAPTER THREE

Efforts at Republican Party
Restoration and the 1934
Congressional Campaign: The
Counterrevolution That Was Not

•

Models of rationalized electoral competition would predict a move leftward by the Republican party in the aftermath of the electoral devastation visited upon it in 1930 and 1932. Despite some resistance among the party's diehard congressional conservative elements, and by the Republican National Committee, the party's overall behavior provides initial confirmation of the predictions of such models, undertaken amidst the party's clear demoralization.

Reflecting the disorganization and factionalism that now characterized Republican efforts, few methodical preparations preceded the congressional elections of 1934. Moreover many Republican representatives were displaying increased interest in campaign efforts that were independent of the national committee. In 1933 House Minority Leader Bertrand Snell announced the formation of a new Republican Congressional Campaign Committee that was not affiliated with the national committee organization.[1] In January 1934 Senate Minority Leader Charles McNary announced the formation of a new Republican Senatorial Campaign Committee. In a conciliatory gesture to the party's western wing, McNary appointed six western Senators to the nine-member committee. A further overture toward the party's insurgents in the West was reflected in McNary's statement that the new committee would support all party candidates regardless of ideology. "There will be no discrimination with respect to the definition of the word 'Republican,' " he remarked.[2]

The formation of these independent campaign committees was the result of a series of concerns. Both GOP conservatives and insurgents felt that the national organization was in a shambles; consequently, they were unwilling to see campaign funds channeled through it.[3] It is also apparent that many Republican office-holders wanted little to do with the national committee's intemperate attacks on the politically popular New Deal. John O'Laughlin wrote to Herbert Hoover:

> The onlooker has little difficulty in perceiving the lack of cohesion which prevails among the representatives of the party in the head-quarters of the National Committee and in Congress. . . . Efforts on the part of a few have failed largely because of absence of determined leadership and because courage is missing and self-interest dominant. The fear of Roosevelt's popularity is acting as a brake upon these officeholders whose single thought is the sentiment of their constituents. . . . Human interest is in the ascendancy and whatever is conceived to be best for the individual, that will the individual do.[4]

The divided Republican responses so evident throughout the 1932 campaign reemerged as the party formulated its electoral appeals for 1934. Some conservative spokesmen began escalating criticism of the New Deal in early 1934. Speaking at a Lincoln Day Dinner in New York City, Congressman James Beck of Pennsylvania attacked the New Deal for its "encroachments on the Constitution and on the rights of the individual" and labeled it a dangerously eclectic scheme of government whose "boundaries are not prescribed and whose objectives are not clear."[5] Minority Leader Snell declared in a radio address that "the period of emergency was over" and called for the restoration of normalized political debate.[6] Early in the year both Theodore Roosevelt, Jr., and Ogden Mills attacked New Deal "regimentation" in major speeches to Republican groups. It was apparent that the old guard viewed the upcoming congressional elections as an opportunity to finally engage the New Deal.

Even in the East, however, the developing conservative campaign began to encounter opposition. In Pennsylvania Governor Gifford Pinchot, a former Bull Mooser, attempted without success to unseat conservative Senator David Reed in the senatorial primary, forcing old guard Republicans to wage a vigorous primary campaign on Reed's behalf. Walter Lippmann summarized contemporary perceptions of the condition of the GOP:

> There are as yet no signs that the Republican party has found an issue on which it can unite. In fact there are many signs which indicate that the schism which rent it in 1912, was healed in 1920, and broke out again in 1932, is deeper than ever. In Pennsylvania, which was one of the six states carried by the Republicans against Roosevelt, a Republican, Governor Pinchot, running as a supporter of Roosevelt, polled about 45 percent of the votes in the Republican primary. In New York, the Republican State Chairman is openly opposed to attacking the national administration. The Western Republicans are, of course, as insurgent as ever, and what seems to have happened is that their insurgency has pervaded the east. Franklin Roosevelt seems to have produced about that same sort of division in the Republican party as did Theodore Roosevelt.[7]

As Lippmann recognized, New York provided another example of the significant divisions that had come to exist even within conservative eastern-state organizations. W. Kingsland Macy, the New York Republican State Chairman, broke with party regulars over the issue of the proper approach toward the New Deal. While old guard spokesmen in that state, such as Ogden Mills, Charles Hilles, and Theodore Roosevelt, Jr., maintained that Republican state-level campaigns should reflect a forthright stance against the New Deal, Macy wanted those campaign appeals confined to state and local issues. Instead of criticizing the New Deal, he argued, the party should stand on a progressive platform that embodied the principles of Theodore Roosevelt and Charles Evans Hughes. He remarked, "It is no longer good political strategy to abuse and denounce everyone and everything without regard to the facts or the temper of the times."[8] Macy further antagonized conservatives by issuing statements highly critical of House Minority Leader Snell and other local conservative leaders.[9] Attempting to circumvent Macy, the conservative element of the New York party then formed its own campaign and finance committees to promote the election of conservative regular candidates for Congress and for state offices. In a final, acrimonious confrontation at the state convention in September, the old guard adopted a platform critical of the New Deal, and ousted Macy from the state chairmanship.[10] Still, the entire episode served to underscore the divisions apparent even in regular state organizations.

In June 1934 the "reorganized" national committee entered the congressional campaign, giving needed direction and unity to the party's conservative elements. The committee's "Declaration of Principles" assailed New Deal "dictatorship" and officially placed the national party machinery in strong opposition to the administration's recovery program. National Chairman Henry Fletcher announced unilaterally that all party agencies, including the congressional and senatorial campaign committees, were to undertake joint efforts in the congressional elections.[11] It was thereby apparent that party conservatives remained firmly in control of the GOP apparatus at the national level.

During early 1934 it was clear that the national committee's conservative leadership desired a congressional campaign that focused on the alleged excesses of the New Deal. This reflected the old guard view that much support for the New Deal was predicated on the "emergency" conditions that had existed during 1933–1934. By this analysis, the general success of conservative appeals to the electorate remained self-evident despite the party's recent reversals, and efforts to "stagger to the left" could only result in the abrogation of both political principle and success at the polling booths. Even a partial restoration of prosperity and business confidence would diminish support for the Roosevelt administration; accordingly, substantial modification of electoral appeals was both unnecessary and unwise. The adoption of a policy of "holding fast" in the face of insurgency had been successful as recently as the election of 1920, and the old guard felt that such tactics would ultimately foster similar results. While entertaining no hope of "rolling back" the entire New Deal following the 1934 congressional elections, the old guard felt that the abatement of emergency conditions would result in Republican congressional gains.[12]

However, the party leadership's determination to make the campaign a direct assault on the New Deal succeeded only in producing additional party schisms. Many party regulars viewed such a course as politically inexpedient. Most insurgent Republicans were, of course, in open sympathy with many elements of the Roosevelt program. Finally, the national committee again faded into the background as the campaign progressed, and Republican appeals were largely shaped by individual candidates in consultation with state and local leaders. The result was a catholicity of electoral appeals that ranged across the political spectrum.

Some old guard candidates, recognizing that in all probability they faced defeat, waged battles for "conservative principles." Old guard Senators David Reed of Pennsylvania and Simeon Fess of Ohio embodied this intransigent attitude, with Reed denouncing the innovations of the Democratic administration in unequivocal terms.[13] Simeon Fess confided to Herbert Hoover:

> I speak the simple judgment of my heart when I say I would rather be defeated in antagonizing this program of economic absurdities than to have been elected either by advocating them or sneaking in as noncommittal.[14]

In New Jersey conservative Republican Hamilton Kean also waged an openly anti–New Deal campaign. However, with that state's Republican party unable to raise even minimal campaign funds, he entered the campaign with few illusions.[15] West Virginia's conservative senator, Henry Hatfield, openly acknowledged that the odds of his returning to the Senate were long.[16] Missouri's old guard spokesman, Roscoe Patterson, waged a bitter fight against New Deal policies, but before election day, the Missouri Republican organization all but conceded the senatorial contest to Patterson's opponent, Harry S. Truman.[17] Despite these examples, however, most conservative Republicans remained reluctant to directly challenge Roosevelt's political popularity during the 1934 campaign. Prior to his own electoral defeat that year, Senator Felix Hébert of Rhode Island wrote to Herbert Hoover:

> Politically, we here in this part of the country feel it is not wise to attack the Chief Executive of the nation. . . . In fact, some of our own people in our own organization have much respect for him and for what he is endeavoring to do and they want to give him some further time to work out his policies.[18]

Many conservative Republicans remained silent as to the New Deal or announced that they supported the administration when it pursued "sound" policies.[19] Consequently, unity broke down even among regular party elements. For example, the *New York Times* noted a lack of enthusiasm at the New York Republican State Convention for a keynote address that strongly criticized administration policies.[20] In Maryland the Republican State Convention endorsed a platform that asserted that its candidates for statewide office would cooperate with New Deal recovery policies even more closely than did the conservative Democratic governor, Albert Ritchie.[21] And in Pennsylvania, a state then regarded as heavily Republican, local officials endorsed Democratic congressional candidates in five districts.[22] In Massachusetts the party organization could find no well-known candidate to undertake a race against the Democratic incumbent, Senator David Walsh, and was forced to settle on a political unknown, Robert M. Washburn.[23]

Moreover, it was becoming increasingly apparent that the Republican party was now almost incapable of mounting a coordinated national effort. Even western party regulars, such as Senate Minority Leader Charles McNary, had been critical of the choice of Henry Fletcher as national chairman. This initial distrust gradually evolved into open hostility, as the national chairman publicly began to encourage wholesale opposition to the policies of the Democratic administration. It was clear that Fletcher had little understanding of, or sympathy for, the party's progressive elements. For their part, progressive Republicans simply ignored the national organization. There was a single, apparently fruitless, meeting between Fletcher and Senator Borah in June; in July, Borah went home to conduct his own campaign, independent of national committee assistance. Senate Minority Leader McNary took no active part in the campaign at all. In October he wrote to Senator James Couzens of Michigan: "I have made no speeches and shall remain dormant for the rest of the campaign."[24] In the West, then, both progressives, and party regulars lacked cohesiveness and unity.

Early in 1934 Senator Arthur Vandenberg of Michigan lashed out at New Deal policies in a fashion characteristic of his old guard colleagues. However, finding himself in a tightly contested race against a candidate who stressed support of the administration, Vandenberg began to tell constituents that certain aspects of the recovery program were "beneficial and fine."[25] In Wisconsin Republican efforts disintegrated completely. Senator Robert La Follette, Jr., and his brother Philip made the decision early in 1934 to leave the Republican party completely and form the

Progressive Party of Wisconsin. The Republican candidate for the Senate, John Chapple, then campaigned on a platform more "radical" than that of Senator La Follette.[26] Disgruntled Wisconsin conservative Republicans referred to Chapple as the "Upton Sinclair of Wisconsin," while Chapple renounced all connections with the national Republican organization and refused offers of financial assistance from the party.[27]

Midwestern Republicans were, of course, continually aware of the importance of the farm vote. It became difficult to criticize Democratic recovery policies without being drawn into a discussion of one's attitude toward New Deal agricultural measures. Most midwestern candidates rejected the idea of directly criticizing the policy, and some openly endorsed it. When National Chairman Henry Fletcher denounced the AAA in an Illinois speech, several downstate Republicans were quick to protest. Fletcher then became so angry that he threatened to refuse to speak at the Illinois Republican State Convention. Frank Knox, a future Republican vice presidential nominee, confided to his wife that it had required major efforts to calm the national chairman in an effort to preserve ostensible party harmony.[28]

Kansas leaders also clearly had little sympathy for the old guard strategy. Governor Alfred Landon and the party's more liberal faction resisted the efforts of the national leadership—as well as those of the conservative elements of the Kansas party—to promote attacks on the entire New Deal. William Allen White wrote Frank Knox, "We just can't follow Ogden Mills and Jim Wadsworth and Snell and that eastern crowd." In view of President Roosevelt's great personal popularity, direct political attacks would be unwise, White concluded.[29] Accordingly, references to the New Deal in the Kansas Republican platform were only mildly critical.[30] Kansas Senator Arthur Capper, who retained strong ties to the regular party organization, openly rejected the Fletcher position of all-out condemnation of the administration's program. And as the campaign wore on even the most conservative western Republicans tended to ease their attacks on the New Deal. For example, Republican congressional candidates in Illinois issued a joint statement saying that the purposes of the AAA were laudable and that Republican candidates had no quarrel with its goals and objectives. They were, according to the statement, opposed to its repeal or modification by interests unsympathetic to agriculture.[31] As a result, Senator Lester Dickinson's attacks on the AAA while on a speaking tour reportedly caused anxiety among local

Indiana candidates.[32] Old guard Senator Arthur Robinson of Indiana avoided all mention of the president, confining his criticisms to bureaucracy and spending.

Some Republican candidates cut themselves off entirely from the national organization, even refusing to permit the national committee to send its campaign literature or workers to their districts without permission.[33] A number of prominent national speakers who had been active in previous campaigns, such as Ogden Mills and Theodore Roosevelt, Jr., found their role in western campaigns minimized.[34] Congressman Chester Bolton, head of the Republican Congressional Campaign Committee, remarked that no one in the entire Ohio congressional delegation was willing to engage in direct criticism of administration policies.[35]

Party schisms were evident throughout the Far West as well. The most serious incident occurred in New Mexico, where Senator Bronson Cutting, a consistent supporter of many New Deal programs, managed to secure renomination only after a bitter fight with party conservatives. But the state's old guard refused to back the senator and threw their support, instead, to the Democratic senatorial candidate, Dennis Chavez. Thus New Mexico's conservative Republicans found themselves in the curious position of being allied with the national Democratic administration in a major state campaign against the candidate of the Republican party.

In September Republican efforts were abruptly further vexed by the election results in the heavily Republican state of Maine: the Democrats reelected their candidate for governor and captured two of Maine's three congressional seats.[36] Republican strategists had hoped that a few Republican victories in the Maine election would lend some momentum to their efforts in the last six weeks of the campaign. The party's candidates in Maine had been highly critical of the New Deal, and such conservative spokesmen as Frank Knox, Theodore Roosevelt, Jr., and Senator Lester Dickinson had campaigned extensively throughout the state.[37] Yet most of the party's candidates were defeated.

The results shocked party conservatives: only two years before Hoover had carried the state by thirty-seven thousand votes. Increasingly fearful of running counter to the appeal of the Democratic program, after September party conservatives ventured fewer criticisms of the administration's recovery programs.[38] In large measure simple political expediency came to dictate patterns of behavior. Despite the continued efforts of a few old-guard candidates and the national committee to directly attack the innovations of the Seventy-third Congress, Republican attempts to carry out a united crusade against the New Deal had broken down completely.

The Condition of the Republican Electoral Coalition in 1934

It is important to recognize that the popular base of Republican support in 1934 was even narrower than that of the coalition that had supported Hoover's desperate efforts in 1932. This was widely recognized by party strategists throughout the congressional campaign. The initial appeal of the all-class coalition of the early New Deal had disaffected many traditionally Republican constituencies. Senator Daniel Hastings, serving on the Republican Senatorial Campaign Committee, wrote to Herbert Hoover:

> I am so disgusted. I am tempted to resign the Senate and stop worrying about my inability to do any good. Do you know it is impossible for me to raise money to help Republican Senators who have a good chance to be reelected? I do not understand what these people of means can be thinking.[39]

House Minority Leader Snell wrote to the former president:

> It has been one of the hardest years to raise funds that I have ever known. We are severely handicapped for that reason. . . . The businessmen talk about the protection they need, etc. They just do not want to put up their own money to get it.[40]

Republican National Chairman Henry Fletcher wrote:

> I am going along under a great handicap from lack of funds and a discouraging lack of interest or courage on the part of those who are in a position to help and who are vitally interested in the preservation of our economic system.[41]

This was more than ritualistic complaining. The Fletcher papers show clearly that the abrupt decline in party funding in 1932—first identified by Overacker—grew far more acute during the 1933–1934 period. The Republican "Statement of Net Income" for 1933–1934 indicates that the party ran a deficit of $191,000 in 1933 and received only $7,721 in contributions during the final quarter of that year.[42] Even more important, the party was unable to finance adequately its efforts during the congressional elections of 1934, ending the campaign with a total of $352 in liquid assets.[43] Long accustomed to well-financed campaign efforts, the Republican party suddenly found itself without the means to open a campaign office in the western states, while its midwestern headquarters in Chicago initially could not afford desks.[44]

Even under such dire circumstances, however, the Republican minority entertained hope of substantial congressional gains.[45] Every off-year election in the twentieth century had seen the party in control of the executive branch lose congressional seats (a phenomenon already recognized by political observers in 1934), and virtually all contemporary political analysts—including such unsympathetic observers as the editorial staff of *The Nation*—predicted some Republican gains.[46] In the wake of the devastation inflicted on the Republican's representation in Congress in 1930, and again in 1932, it seemed inconceivable that some reversal of Democratic trends would not take place. On the eve of the election the *New York Times* reported that Democratic strategists felt that their own losses would be fewer than forty House seats.[47] Republican strategists were, thus, completely unprepared for the unprecedented off-year results that followed.

To the Republican's dismay, the Democrats, in defiance of both off-year tradition and contemporary expectations, again gained seats in Congress. The GOP's already diminished senatorial contingent fell from thirty-five to twenty-five. The eastern old guard senatorial group sustained the deepest damage, with by far the most disheartening loss the defeat of the effective parliamentarian and spokesman, David Reed of Pennsylvania. Four other eastern conservatives met a similar fate, as Henry Hatfield of West Virginia, Hamilton Kean of New Jersey, Felix Hébert of Rhode Island, and Frederick Walcott of Connecticut were all removed from the party's councils. In Maryland a Democrat won the seat of Phillips Goldsborough, who had chosen not to stand for reelection. Abruptly, then, the old guard had lost six of its spokesmen in the

Northeast and only ten eastern conservatives remained in the Republican senatorial contingent.

Regular Republicanism also suffered severe setbacks in the West. Conservatives Simeon Fess of Ohio, Arthur Robinson of Indiana, and Roscoe Patterson of Missouri failed in their efforts to gain reelection to the Senate, reducing the party's regular western contingent to only five members. Although four of the western insurgent Republican senators had stood for reelection, all returned, leaving the strength of the insurgent bloc unchanged at ten members. Robert La Follette, Jr., however, had now taken on the Progressive party designation.

House Republicans saw their numbers drop from 117 to 104. The party had gained 19 seats, while losing 32, thus accounting for the net loss of 13. The heaviest GOP losses were in the previously Republican state of Pennsylvania, where 12 seats were lost and in Wisconsin, where 5 seats were captured by the Progressive Party. Eastern House Republican representation declined from 66 to 52. Such important leaders as Robert Luce of Massachusetts, Charles Bakewell of Connecticut, and Carroll Beedy of Maine suffered defeat. Perhaps as important, a number of prominent eastern members of Congress, such as James Beck and Edward Stokes of Pennsylvania, had declined to run for reelection, choosing to return to private pursuits. Thus, the eastern conservative bloc suffered both numerical attrition and the loss of effective leadership.

The number of western House Republicans actually increased by one, from 49 to 50. This reflected the fact that the few new seats the party had won were primarily in the Midwest, with congressional seats gained in rural Michigan, three in Illinois and three in Minnesota.[48] While the Republican western congressional delegation had changed little in absolute numbers, its progressive element nevertheless incurred significant losses and defections. Within the Wisconsin Republican congressional delegation, 5 former progressive Republicans had defected to the Progressive Party. Other prominent congressional progressives, such as North Dakota's James Sinclair and Michigan's Frank James, had been defeated by Democratic candidates. Thus, the defeat of some progressive western Republicans left the party's western wing with a House delegation that contained enhanced conservative strength, a factor that would later take on increased importance.

The New Deal, in Arthur Krock's words, had won "the most overwhelming victory in the history of American politics."[49] The *Literary*

Digest termed the midterm contest "black Tuesday" for the Republican old guard, while lauding the president's appeal as "astonishing . . . historic . . . and unique."[50] Although the Republicans had been well aware of the extraordinary dimensions of Roosevelt's personal popularity and the ineffectuality of their own divided campaign efforts, no preelection forecast had provided an indication of yet another electoral rejection of this dimension. Whatever resignation or stoicism had accompanied the defeats of 1930 and 1932 now gave way to bitterness and mutual recrimination. Defeated old guard leader Senator David Reed wrote to Herbert Hoover:

> My defeat has actually brought me a sense of great relief, although it is disheartening to realize that the people of any great American state are susceptible to the kind of campaign that was put on by our adversaries. I have not said so publicly because it would sound like the wail of a disappointed man, but the truth is that millions of dollars of federal money were poured into the state for so-called "relief" during the four or five days immediately before the election. . . . It was more like an auction than an election and I do not regard it as a repudiation of Republican principles or as an endorsement of anything but ready cash.[51]

Old guard Senator Simeon Fess also confided to Hoover:

> It is a season for contemplating the gratitude of republics. . . . The depression of 1929 for which party leadership had little if any responsibility is an illustration of how public men suffer from unjust judgments. . . . If the injury could be limited to the leaders and not extend to the country we could pass it on as a characteristic of republics but when it opens the way for a spurious leadership to be given a blank check to use the treasury for the purpose of promoting economic nonsense by buying public support . . . it strikes at the very heart of the system of popular governments.[52]

Senator Arthur Vandenberg of Michigan repeated a similar charge to the former president: "This expenditure prospectus is almost beyond belief.

Unintentionally or *otherwise,* it involves amazing political repercussions. It is calculated virtually to Tammanyize the whole United States."[53] Hoover himself expressed similar sentiments in a letter to Senator Henry Hatfield of West Virginia after Hatfield's defeat:

> I was greatly shocked to see the result in West Virginia. . . . It is fairly impossible for a candidate in these times to say, in effect, too much money is being spent in this state when his opponent gives assurances that he believes in spending more and is the only man who can secure it.[54]

These remarks are reflective of much old guard sentiment regarding the effect of relief expenditures on the 1934 electoral results.

It is difficult to evaluate with any precision the Republican charges made during this period.[55] What is central to our purposes here, however, is the effect that these sentiments had on Republican electoral evaluations at the time. Confronting what they considered to be "politicized" administration of relief funds between 1933 and 1934, it was a rare defeated Republican office-holder who did not privately blame the results on the "relief vote." What is missing from conservative Republican analysis is any suggestion that the political changes brought about by positive intervention in the economy through relief could be real and durable—that is, that they could remain sources of partisan division after the conditions of economic emergency had receded. To many old guardsmen, therefore, the idea of permanent alteration of voting patterns in light of the 1934 results remained clouded by the subject of relief administration.

Such sentiments were not shared by the party's insurgent wing. To them, the campaign had amounted to nothing less than a final repudiation of the party's conservative leadership, the rejection of which was a prerequisite for the party's survival. The defeat of many old guardsmen seemed to raise again the question of party reorganization, as well as the larger problem of alteration of electoral appeals. Such sentiments offered confirmation of the Downsian prediction of a move to the political center by large elements of the Republican party. Within days of the congressional elections, Senator William Borah of Idaho stated, "Unless the Republican party is delivered from its reactionary leadership and reorganized in accordance with its one time liberal principles, it will die like the Whig party of sheer political cowardice."[56] In a mild pique, he added, "We can talk and talk but the Republican party is going to the left just as surely as I am alive."[57] In the midst of continued privation and suffering throughout the nation, the Republican senator depicted his old guard colleagues as offering legalistic objections to the administration of the New Deal. In reality, he argued, the GOP had been unable to formulate a practical response to the New Deal: "They have offered the Constitution—but the people can't eat the Constitution." The absence of a practical program, Borah felt, had left Republican voters with "no place to go but to the Democrats."[58]

Senator George Norris wrote that in the absence of an inflationary program, conservative Republicans actually had little to propose.[59] William Allen White indicated similar sentiments when he wrote, "It isn't good politics to weep and wail over our decaying liberties unless we point the way to some kind of program which will solve the problem without the decay of liberty."[60]

Originally, then, the primary drive for party redefinition came from the party's western elements, in a renewal of the longstanding struggle between the party's conservative eastern wing and its insurgent western wing. William Borah became the primary catalyst of the movement, with other western Republicans quickly following his lead. The extent of the divisions in the party were made clear by Senators Borah and Gerald Nye in their speeches in New York City in late 1934. They called for the ousting of "diehards" from control of the party machinery and a positive program that would emphasize "protection of the rights, liberties and economic privileges of the average man and woman from the dangers of 'monopoly and concentration of wealth.' "[61] Senator Nye predicted the final dissolution of Republicanism in the West if the party did not adjust its appeals to accommodate the interests of agrarians, laborers, and consumers.[62]

It is apparent that such criticism, as was typified by the Borah and Nye speeches, had some effect. A number of young Republican groups, for example, echoed Borah's criticisms and joined in the demand for party reform. Leaders of Young Republican organizations in such eastern states as New York, Pennsylvania, and New Jersey wrote to Borah expressing strong praise for his efforts. In addition, some eastern leaders supported these efforts. Theodore Roosevelt, Jr., stated before the National Republican Club of New York that

> there is a direct relationship between the drop in the Republican share of the vote and the type of political thought credited to the defeated candidates and the organization they represented. The more the individual campaign was considered as representing ultra-conservatism and reaction to the old machine, the worse the defeat at the polls.[63]

However, it quickly became apparent that such sentiments for reform still reflected a minority viewpoint among eastern Republicans. Kingsland Macy, the ousted New York State Republican Chairman, was one of the few eastern leaders to support the demands of the party's western progressives.

Further, it is fair to say that Senator Borah was ill equipped to lead a systematic effort at party reorganization. A strongly independent man, he found it difficult to persuade even fellow western progressives to support his efforts. Senator James Couzens of Michigan, who had strong ties to the progressive group, accused Borah of offering little constructive criticism and suggested that he seek the national chairmanship in order to "draft" a party platform of his own.[64] Other progressive leaders, such as Senators Norris, La Follette, and Johnson, also showed little interest in the controversy and continued to function in a sympathetic working relationship with the New Deal reform program.[65]

Old Guard Response to Insurgent Criticism

It is apparent that conservative opposition remained the primary impediment to any type of fundamental party reorganization. Most old guard strategists rejected the progressive Republicans' explanations of the party's defeats. In fact, the increasing calls for reform seemed to solidify the old guard's ranks, with most conservatives believing that normal electoral patterns continued to be skewed by federal relief expenditures.

Predictably, GOP conservatives sought to associate themselves with the increasingly popular issue of party rehabilitation. A few days after the 1934 election Chairman Fletcher acknowledged that repeated defeats had brought on a crisis that threatened the extinction of the party. He recognized that new issues had to be developed lest party electoral efforts break down entirely. At the same time, however, the national chairman argued that rebuilding the party would necessarily involve continual and systematic opposition to the New Deal.[66] In December, after the Borah speech in New York, Fletcher remarked:

> If there is a popular demand for the articulation of a new set of principles by the Republican party and the submission of a party program based upon these principles . . . no one wishes to prevent this. On the contrary, I hope it will be done. . . . If it is a change in the official personnel of the National Committee that is desired by those asking for a "reorganization of the party," their freedom of action is unimpaired.[67]

Like many eastern conservatives, however, Fletcher felt that the results of the recent congressional elections had been obtained by "the most cynical and shameless use of relief money to obtain votes," and he believed that the Republican party was not dead.[68] In his analysis, the National Chairman was supported by such old guard leaders as Charles Hilles of New York. After the Borah liberalization efforts began, Hilles sent a letter to fellow members of the Republican National Committee urging the party to stand firm on its basic principles. The GOP, he argued, should not "imitate the New Deal" and would be unsuccessful in efforts to "stagger to the left."[69]

The basic outlines of old guard strategy were emerging. Confronted with drastic electoral reversals and the renewed specter of western insurgency, old guardsmen were determined to maintain conservative electoral appeals and, above all, control of the party machinery. Although congressional majorities, and even presidencies, came and went, the important matter for party conservatives was to retain control of the Republican party's national committee. In this fashion, any subsequent disillusionment with the Democratic recovery program would result in the restoration of Republican hegemony under conservative auspices. Unconvinced that any fundamental change had occurred within the electorate at large, the old guard strategists responded in a manner that mirrored the response of party conservatives to the Bull Moose insurgency of 1912: the old guardsmen felt that the restoration of "normal" political conditions would eventually return party conservatives to power as it had in 1920.

By early 1935 it was clear that the party's western progressives had failed to convince their eastern colleagues of the need to refashion the party's appeals. Herbert Hoover summed up much Republican sentiment when he wrote to John O'Laughlin:

> I get a good deal of amusement out of all the kept newspaper writers who are propagandizing the country that the Republican party must swing to the left. It would seem to me that when forty four percent of the voters [referring to the total Republican congressional vote in 1934] had sufficient emotion on the subject to vote against the New Deal, they have given a fairly definite indication that the vast majority occupies a place in the social spectrum somewhere to the right.[70]

Other party conservatives spoke in a similar fashion. The prudent course, according to Senator Lester Dickinson of Iowa, was to await the later results of the New Deal, as its failure offered the only hope for the GOP.[71] Senator Daniel Hastings surveyed the condition of the party and concluded that the New Deal was a "dangerous disease which must run its course."[72]

Thus, Republican National Chairman Henry Fletcher found himself in a position to resist the demands of the party's western insurgents. In a final, strongly worded statement, Fletcher indicated that he had no plans for resignation or for calling a meeting of the national committee to discuss a reorganization in which there was little interest. He could be certain of this fact, he said, because he had been in communication "with all members of the National Committee, all Republican State Chairmen and approximately 2,500 County Chairmen."[73] He challenged the critics of party policy to proceed with the reorganization of the party on more liberal lines if they had the backing which they maintained they had. This, the National Chairman knew was plainly impossible, as most of the national party apparatus remained in the hands of old guardsmen and Hoover appointees.

In light of the results of the 1930, 1932, and 1934 elections, however, much of this debate over the future direction of the Republican party appeared to be taking on a bitter, yet lifeless, quality. Many members of the party's western wing remained openly supportive of the recovery efforts of the Democratic administration, while the party's eastern wing had been reduced by electoral attrition to an ineffectual minority. With the party unable to agree on a process of rehabilitation, lacking adequate funding, and deserted by substantial elements of its traditional constituencies, its electoral appeal seemed extraordinarily narrow and its future as a major electoral force was now persistently questioned.

The Erosion of the Republican Electoral Coalition, 1933–1934

This pattern of GOP electoral defeats only hinted at the degree of the Republican electoral dilemma. The party's basic interest-group structure had been badly damaged. By 1934 the pattern of early New Deal legislation was becoming clearly discernible, and one distinguishing feature was its effort to induce economic recovery through the use of the largest existing institutional structures capable of having an immediate effect. Thus, the New Deal's focus on large industry and agriculture resulted from a pragmatic desire to stimulate production and employment in a short period of time. The New Deal coalition sought to include all groups and classes and attempted to effect a kind of political truce that recalled the unity and cohesion of wartime planning efforts. The crisis politics of the administration sought the abatement of partisan political conflict for the sake of a broad national unity.[74] In Leuchtenburg's words, "Roosevelt presented himself not as the paladin of liberalism but as father to all the people, not as the representative of a single class but as the coordinator of a series of interests."[75] In March 1934 the president even declined to take part in the traditional Democratic celebrations of the birthday of Thomas Jefferson, saying that it would be a "fine thing" if nonpartisan Jefferson dinners were held with both Republicans and Democrats serving on the banquet committee. The point, he felt, was to minimize ceremonies that were unduly partisan.[76] Roosevelt wrote to one of his key early advisers, Colonel Edward M. House:

> Our strongest plea to the country in this particular year of grace is that the recovery and reconstruction program is being accomplished by men and women of all parties—that I have repeatedly appealed to Republicans as well as Democrats to do their part.[77]

The president's inclination to incorporate a wide spectrum of views within the government and to permit the inclusion of divergent interest groups in the early "all-class" coalition of the New Deal pointed toward his continued suspension of "politics as usual."

By early 1934 New Deal recovery policies had substantially strengthened the cooperative farm bureaus and the industrial trade associations conceived in the 1920s. Equally important, these traditionally Republican constituencies had been quick to seize the opportunities provided by the early New Deal's pragmatic approach to recovery.

Millions of farmers participated in AAA crop referenda, and the Agricultural Adjustment Administration quickly adopted production control agreements, which were enforced by farm groups themselves.[78] During the first six months of the NRA American industry developed codes of fair competition that covered most of American industry and trade. Within two years the NRA had established over 540 codes that directly affected some thirty-eight million workers. While the creation of the National Recovery Administration (NRA) was the result of a variety of reform impulses, the business community was in the best position to seize the initiative in the code-drafting process.[79]

It is important to recognize that the mechanisms for giving the federal government systematic control over a bureaucratized national industrial system simply did not exist in 1934.[80] Even if such governmental mechanisms had existed and been politically acceptable in the long run, it is questionable whether they could have brought to bear the focused attention and specialized expertise that industrial interests did to the code-drafting process. The creation of codes of fair competition offered business the powerful incentives of exemption from the antitrust laws, governmental enforcement of price control measures and relief from competitive practices deemed injurious to reasonable profit levels. In addition, the prior existence of industrial trade associations, and their ongoing efforts to focus concern on problems of overproduction and price stabilization, gave business the capacity to transform the aspirations of the industrial interests into political reality.

From the inception of the NRA, the process of the development of regulatory codes was dominated by elements of the very industrial groups to be regulated. To industry the results, at least in the first year, seemed to point toward industrial self-government under the auspices of an administration that enjoyed broad popular support.

The practical effect of the administration's incorporation of potential political opposition was felt throughout the Republican electoral coalition as 1934 dawned. Widespread approval by farmers of government limitations on agricultural production, and the substantial business support accorded to the NRA code-drafting process, further constricted the GOP base of popular political support, which had already been devastated by the events of 1929–1932.

Private GOP communications took on a kind of quiet despair. Ogden Mills confided to a friend:

> Do not think that I underestimate the seriousness of the situation from a party standpoint, or that I fail to recognize how completely disorganized we are. I see little chance, however, of building up a popular movement on the basis of the immediate issues. I think we must make up our minds that we are in for a long fight.[81]

Writing to Herbert Hoover during the first Roosevelt Congress, Senator Simeon Fess acknowledged, "It was also realized that the greatest obstacle lies within our own ranks. . . . The situation from this angle is not very promising."[82] William Allen White wrote to Mark Sullivan, political columnist for the *New York Herald Tribune:*

> With one or two exceptions, Republican opposition on the Hill seems confused and hesitant. Most of our fellows seem to feel they will be retired if they do not go along with the Roosevelt program so that I fear the next Congress may be even more under the executive thumb than the present one. . . . This makes the approaching congressional campaign most important and we seem to be going into it with divided leadership, distracted policies and temporizing expedience. . . . Do you think the Republican party will go the way of the Whigs?[83]

This inability to offer even a semblance of effective minority opposition reflected not only the dramatic political and psychological effects of the One Hundred Days period, but also the disaffection of substantial elements of the Republican middle and upper-middle class constituencies. While the initial collapse of the Republican electoral coalition reflected a protest vote that cut across all income groupings in the population, the

fact that political realignment into a weakly based class cleavage had not
yet occurred by 1934 has been subject to far less attention.

The all-class recovery efforts of the early New Deal appear, however,
to have further diminished the already depleted Republican electoral
constituency. While there is no elaborate polling data available for the
early New Deal period, the clear sampling bias of the *Literary Digest* polls
can serve as one index of attitudes towards the early New Deal on the
part of attentive middle class voters. The *Digest*'s sample again consisted
of a mailed ballot drawn from telephone books and automobile registration lists. Thus, it continued to sample the attentive middle class, not
the national electorate as a whole. Still, the *Digest*'s 1934 poll found 61.1
percent of its sample in favor of the "acts and policies of Roosevelt's first
year." The *Digest*'s figures noted a net approval gain of 5.3 percent in the
president's overall popularity since 1932 and when such gains were
analyzed by geographic area, they were found to be centered in such
previously Republican strongholds as Pennsylvania, Connecticut, and
New York.[84] A second *Digest* poll that analyzed sentiment toward the
New Deal broken down on the basis of occupation utilized the somewhat
hazy category of "businessmen," but the results were nonetheless noteworthy: "Businessmen" recorded a 56.2 percent approval rating of New
Deal recovery policies.[85]

Thus, by early 1934, many conservative elements of the country
seemed to support the concept of a governmental-business recovery apparatus in which business elites would continue to play critical roles.
Widespread popular concern about market failure had not prevented the
development of strong industrial influence within the NRA, and early
administration recovery efforts seemed to be taking a "responsible"
course. Walter Lippmann reflected much centrist sentiment when he
wrote:

> I may perhaps be permitted to say that I do not regard the Roosevelt
> program as directed to the establishment of a planned economy.
> The program does call for the planning of many activities and for
> the conscious management of many things, but so did Mr. Hoover's
> program when he advocated the planning of public works, when at
> the onset of the depression he pledged industries to wage, price,
> and capital investment policies, when he attempted to stabilize
> farm prices, when, through the Federal Reserve System, he at-

tempted to reinflate the price level through credit expansion. Mr.
Roosevelt has carried these principles further than Mr. Hoover did,
but that did not set up a "planned economy" in any true meaning
of the word.[86]

Thus the pragmatic nature of early New Deal recovery efforts had
resulted in the enactment of policies that often favored organized, established interest groupings, such as business constituencies. In the space of
a year, a diverse coalition of groupings had been drawn into an intricate
web of recovery programs that enjoyed broad national support. From the
standpoint of the Republican party, such developments were viewed with
alarm; the direction of events pointed toward the continued diminution
of the party's influence, and perhaps even to the establishment of another
era of "good feelings."

CHAPTER FOUR

1935: The Breakup of the All-class
Coalition of the Early New Deal

•

The Liberty League

There were few, if any, positive portents for the Republican party as 1935 dawned. The all-class coalition of the early New Deal had engendered political movement that had been almost entirely away from the Republican electoral coalition, and thus, by Downsian lights, the Republican party should have begun a process of movement at least to the political center.

On the other hand, however, by the end of 1934 it was apparent that the administration's efforts to maintain this all-class coalition of interests were beginning to break down. Business leaders were gradually becoming aware that the New Deal involved more than industrial self-regulation of recovery efforts. The Securities and Exchange Act, passed in March of 1934, had been badly received by business spokesmen and, just as important, it was followed quickly by other regulatory efforts. Such measures as the Communications Act—which empowered the Federal Communications Commission (FCC) to regulate the radio, telegraph, and transoceanic cable industries, the Railroad Retirement Act—which raised railway pensions substantially, and the Air Mail Act—which established additional controls on the awarding of federal contracts—had all been sources of consternation for particular business constituencies.[1] Even more disturbing to conservative interests was the mounting federal deficit. Congress had restored the spending cuts made in the Economy Act, while expenditures for relief and public works continued unabated. On August 30, 1934, Lewis Douglas, the administration's budget director and principal advocate of economic orthodoxy, resigned because of his concern over the direction of administration fiscal policies. In a harbinger of the florid conservative rhetoric to come, he wrote to President Roosevelt:

> I hope, and hope most fervently, that you will evidence a real determination to bring the budget into actual balance, for upon this, I think, hangs not only your place in history but conceivably the ultimate fate of western civilization.[2]

In the same month, it became apparent that a number of conservative elements were coming to define matters in similar terms. An exchange of letters between R. M. Carpenter, a retired vice president of the du Pont Corporation, and John Raskob, the former chairman of the Democratic National Committee, convinced the two that there was deep concern among conservatives over the evolving direction of administration policies. These letters were the initial step that led to the formation of the Liberty League in August 1934.[3] The League initially defined itself as an "educational" organization dedicated to

> teach[ing] the necessity of respect for the rights of person and property . . . and the duty of government to encourage and protect individual and group initiative and enterprise, to foster the right to work, earn, save and acquire property and to preserve the ownership and lawful use of property when acquired.[4]

Funded largely by conservative Democrats, its membership included such prominent Democrats of the previous decade as Newton Baker, Bainbridge Colby, John Raskob, and the party's 1924 and 1928 presidential nominees, John W. Davis and Alfred E. Smith. However, the presence of Republican members, such as Congressman James Wadsworth of New York and now-retired Congressman James Beck of Pennsylvania, enabled the organization to claim a kind of bipartisan stance. Still, their disaffection with the administration was real and often bitter. Newton Baker, mentioned prominently in 1932 as a Democratic presidential candidate had the Roosevelt effort collapsed at the convention, wrote Walter Lippmann:

> The trouble with this recognition of the class war is that it spreads like a grease stain, and every group formed around a special and selfish interest demands the same sort of recognition. As a consequence our government for the last three years has been the mere tossing of tubs to each whale as it grows bold enough to stick its head out of the water. The administration seems to me to have no philosophy and no principles and I doubt whether those who are responsible for it could give any better definition of their objective than the phrase "to secure a more abundant life." This object I am sure is the central thought of highwaymen as well as of philanthropists, and unless those who use it have something very real and direct in their minds they are very dangerous both to themselves and to the rest of us.[5]

In a similar vein, John W. Davis, the party's 1924 presidential nominee, wrote Lippmann:

> I voted against Hoover with enthusiasm in 1932 because I thought the Democratic platform and the pledges of its candidate guaranteed a return to sound economics and orderly government. How far my hopes have been fulfilled I leave to you to surmise.[6]

Initially, the League seemed to draw upon a rich variety of practical political experience, while giving organizational expression to growing conservative fears. James Beck hailed "this most promising movement to defend constitutional rights."[7] While the League had taken no part in the congressional campaigns of 1934, Beck wrote to a friend before the 1934 elections that the organization was simply "marking time" until after the election and then would rapidly move into "the coming struggle to preserve our Constitution."[8]

Other Republicans viewed the formation of the organization quite differently. Herbert Hoover wrote to John O'Laughlin that

> the responsibility for the outrages of which they complain lie at the door of Messrs. Shouse, Smith, Davis, Raskob and Du Pont. If this

group had kept to the truth during my Administration . . . the
country would not be writhing in this situation. . . . Their public
statements give entire emphasis to the property right. . . . The
right of property cannot be allowed to run unlimited in the hands
of individuals. . . . I am neither for the Wall Street model nor the
Pennsylvania Avenue model.[9]

Still, the initial formation of the League recalled a series of successful
twentieth-century conservative lobbying organizations, such as the American Anti-Boycott Association (designed to maintain the open shop), the
National Security League (designed to support Allied efforts prior to the
United States's entry into World War I), and the Association Against the
Prohibition Amendment.[10] John O'Laughlin wrote to Herbert Hoover in
one of his private political reports:

The League is expected to have surprising strength. . . . I understand the League plans organizations in every state and this is
possible because it is well financed. . . . There is little doubt
that the chance of a Republican comeback has been strengthened,
especially as it is the general opinion that Roosevelt, as a result of
the existence of the League, will be forced to move to the left.[11]

The Breakdown of a Business-Government "Commonwealth" in the National Recovery Administration

By 1935 it was apparent that disillusionment with New Deal recovery
measures was not confined to some prominent Democratic stalwarts of
the 1920s and individual conservative industrialists. Despite the apparent
success of American industry in structuring the National Recovery Administration at its inception to further trade association objectives, the
fragile unity of entrepreneurial groups within the NRA had broken down
by early 1935.[12]

Once the sense of panic of the 1932–1933 period passed, it gradually
became clearer to much of American industry that the price exacted for
exemption from the antitrust laws was higher than anticipated. The
administration's sympathy toward efforts to raise wage rates and encourage industrial unionism, as well as its ability to license business through
the NRA code-making process, limited the previous prerogatives of

industrial managers. Efforts to deny government contracts to companies that refused to allow National Labor Relations Board–style representation elections were viewed as an unprecedented regulation of industry. [13]

Some corporations felt that the NRA was overly sympathetic to the demands of industrial unionists, particularly after it frustrated efforts to include open-shop clauses in industrial codes. [14] In response, a number of corporations refused to allow collective bargaining elections for their employees, while others continued to maintain that the labor provisions of the NRA should allow for company unions or for proportional representation for workers who chose not to affiliate with the American Federation of Labor. [15] It was becoming clear to business leaders that the administration of the NRA apparatus involved input from groups, such as organized labor, that stressed political agendas beyond trade association control. [16]

Just as the potential for unfettered industrial self-government had gone unfulfilled, so the promise of stability with regard to such matters as pricing and production control had proved very difficult to achieve. It became obvious that efforts to achieve industry-wide stability involved far more than simply outlawing cutthroat competition, defining unfair business practices, and portraying recalcitrant corporations as "chiselers." [17]

A welter of conflicts within industries or between industries, between integrated and non-integrated firms, and between large industries and small ones had become readily apparent by 1935. [18] Business segments had utilized the NRA from the beginning in efforts to enhance the market control of their own firms, often at the expense of rivals or suppliers. For example, it was in the interest of larger firms to eliminate wage and price differentials and negate the advantages that often made them possible. Small firms often had offset disadvantages in such fields as advertising or economies of scale by offering lower prices made possible by lower regional wage rates, locations convenient to local markets, or specialization in product line. One scholar has concluded that most of the code-writing process in the NRA can be viewed as an effort to eliminate price differences offered by smaller regional firms. [19] Thus small business increasingly viewed the NRA's price stabilization program as an effort to negate their competitive advantages, and the result was a steady increase in criticism of the industrial codes and the NRA itself.

Price stabilization had proved to be a formidable task, even before the protests of small business brought its alleged deficiencies to the attention of the public. Pricing and production agreements slowly broke down in industries composed of a large number of units producing a variety of products, and they disintegrated even more rapidly in industries where prohibitions to entry were few. Cooperation proved difficult in industries with expanding markets, relatively simple technologies or potential for easily utilized substitutes for products.[20] Industrial "self-government" seemed increasingly to mean businessmen sitting in judgment of their competitors, and it was a rare code decision that did not involve direct losses to one group or another.

By early 1935 the idea that organized business should continue its collaboration with government was becoming progressively less attractive to most elements of the business community. The resignations of such prominent industrialists as Alfred Sloan, John Jacob Raskob, and Pierre S. du Pont from the business advisory council of the NRA were indicative of evolving business attitudes toward any continuation of the business-government "commonwealth." Ultimately, individual business enterprises had submitted only to a process that they felt they could control; when the rise of other political forces made this difficult, enthusiasm rapidly waned. Thus the pattern of government support so eagerly courted by business after 1930 was soon being reconsidered as the NRA experience unfolded.

The renewed concerns of business leaders were reflected in the proceedings of trade associations. Officials of the U.S. Chamber of Commerce and the NAM met at a Joint Business Conference for Economic Recovery in December 1934. Romasco indicates that participants included not only key trade association officials but also presidents of numerous major commercial and manufacturing enterprises. The conference resulted in severe criticism of administration recovery efforts. The NRA, by this view, should confine itself to the enforcement of industry-wide codes formulated solely by the trade groups concerned.[21] Provisions for proportional representation of nonunionized employees should be established. Code provisions, if adopted, should remain exempt from the antitrust laws. If industries declined to adopt particular code provisions, a right of "appeal" should be established.[22]

By early 1935, then, industrial leaders were proposing a restructuring of the NRA that would retain the advantages obtained by the removal of antitrust considerations, while sharply limiting the influence of both government and organized labor on the code administration process. Such demands were attempts to regain autonomy in industrial affairs, an autonomy that was felt to be increasingly threatened. Business was long accustomed to regarding itself as the primary overseer of the economic life of the nation. Estimates of market conditions, wage rates, and labor relations had been arrived at on a company-by-company and an industry-by-industry basis, tempered primarily by evaluations of what the consumer and labor markets would absorb. The experience of World War I had shown that there was a role for government in the marketplace, but at that time government was seen as essentially a benign helpmate of private efforts, surely not its master, nor even its equal. The persistence and severity of the depression had badly damaged the self-esteem of the business community shortly after the associationalist efforts of the 1920s had depicted entrepreneurial efforts in the best possible light. Now, with the depression far from abated, the New Deal seemed to assail the business community with measures that few corporate leaders had anticipated. The initiatives of the New Deal recovery programs seemed to rest disproportionately in the realm of government power in early 1935, and business criticism was to take on ever more strident tones.

The Evolution of New Deal Electoral Appeals: The Second One Hundred Days

The calls of industrialists for a "moratorium" on the entire process of reform occurred just as the president was considering a significant intensification of his reform efforts. Although Roosevelt had abandoned his efforts to maintain the New Deal's all-class coalition with clear reluctance, the needs of other discordant constituencies were becoming increasingly apparent by 1935. While the continued popularity of such individuals as Huey Long and Charles Coughlin, and the persistence of the Towsendite movement were now matters of clear concern to the administration, they also offered new opportunities for political maneuvering, and the president responded by proposing a series of reform measures designed to forestall the increased activity of critics to the left of the administration.[23]

In June 1935 Roosevelt abruptly put the legislative process into motion. Calling congressional leaders together, he insisted on the passage of a number of major pieces of legislation before the Seventy-fourth

Congress adjourned.[24] Among these were the Social Security bill, the Wagner labor proposal, a banking measure, and public utility holding company legislation. Shortly afterward, an additional measure, labeled by critics a "soak the rich" tax measure, was added. After several months of what most observers had seen as drift and indecision, the New Deal had suddenly burst forth again.[25] The call of conservatives for an abatement of the reform impulse and a return to the familiar patterns of industrial control had gone largely unheeded. Walter Lippmann wrote Arthur Holcombe at Harvard University:

> Apparently Roosevelt has determined to burn his bridges so far as the conservative Democrats go and to stake his chances for reelection on an appeal to sectional and class feeling. I put it baldly but that seems to me what it comes to. For if he were bidding for the support of people like Smith, Byrd, and the like he would, of course, have to make a very different popular appeal. The effect of that, it seems to me, is to create an immense and, I think, increasing opposition which is entirely inchoate, without principle and without common conviction. It would contain all ranges of opinion from the Borah type of agrarian progressives on the one side to the blackest type of reactionary Republican on the other. The fact that they have no common principles will mean, I fear, that they will appeal to passion and primitive emotions and if they win, which I think not at all unlikely, we may very well face a period of severe reaction.[26]

As these now discordant elements cast about for a mechanism through which to counter the (to them) disappointing evolution of the New Deal, they gradually came to focus on the moribund Republican party.

By early 1935 the Democratic-business entente of the early New Deal period had almost entirely collapsed. With the emergence of the political agenda of the "Second One Hundred Days," business grew progressively more hostile to the administration. This disaffection began a process that seemed to infuse Republican efforts with new life in 1935.

Former Republican Senator David Reed used the 44th Annual Meeting of the American Iron and Steel Institute to inaugurate appeals to conservative Republicans and Democrats to unite in support of candidates who opposed any continuation of the New Deal.[27] These sentiments were echoed by the action of a wide variety of business associations. In November 1935 the American Bankers Association named Orval W. Adams, a harsh critic of the New Deal, as its vice president. The association issued a strongly worded statement that endorsed "Republican" demands for a balanced budget and the restoration of conditions that facilitated business financing.[28] At the National Founders Association Convention (an association of primary industries such as oil and steel), the keynote speaker called for "permanent peace" from "the costly experiments of the last two years."[29]

At the annual convention of the U.S. Chamber of Commerce, Roosevelt's recovery program was roundly criticized in the same forum that had accorded him strong support only two years before. It was apparent that these energetic propagandists for, and principal advocates of, the original NRA legislation had dramatically reversed themselves.[30] Overwhelming opposition to recent federal legislative trends was registered in a referendum sponsored by the U.S. Chamber of Commerce to sample its various constituent bodies. The responses to such hostile questions as "Should the federal government at the present time exercise federal spending power without relation to revenue?" or "Should there be government cooperation with private enterprise for regulatory or other purposes?", had shown an average of 35 to 1 ratio against "the trends exemplified by the Roosevelt relief and reform program." The Chamber adopted resolutions that objected to such measures as the Social Security bill, the continuation of the NRA and the Utility Holding Company Act. In addition, it asked for the "withdrawal of governmental agencies from activities properly the function of trade associations."[31]

By December 1935 business leaders were calling directly for "industrial mobilization" in order to end the New Deal. The National Industrial Council, comprising representatives of regional manufacturers and trade associations, joined with the NAM in adopting a political platform that called unabashedly for the defeat of the administration's "new economic order." Casting aside any effort at nonpartisan appeals, principal speaker S. Wells Utley of the Detroit Steel Castings Company warned other industrialists that they must prevent the Republican party from fashioning a "liberal" appeal or industry would be without a political refuge.[32] Alfred P. Sloan told the NAM: "I am convinced that industry's responsibility can no longer be adequately discharged by mere physical production." Among the first responsibilities he defined for industry were the "liquidation" of the New Deal and the cessation of deficit spending by government. James A. Emery, general counsel of the NAM, noted that "judicial remedies are not sufficient. . . . They afford no remedy against unsound policy. It is our obligation to contribute a clear understanding of the deadly nature of these enemies of our economic and political progress."[33]

It appears then that for many conservatives and business groupings, "political progress" was being increasingly equated with the Republican party. In August 1935, the Republican National Committee was able to announce both the retirement of its deficit and a swift influx of funds under the auspices of "The United Republican Finance Company of New York City."[34] Simultaneously, National Committee Chairman Henry Fletcher expressed the view that the party's 1936 efforts would be well financed and that the party would be able to refashion a national party apparatus "at its former strength."[35] One month later these plans began to take form. Fletcher announced the establishment of a finance committee composed of prominent industrialists who had volunteered their services to the party. With W. B. Bell, president of the American Cyanamid Company, acting as chairman, its members included Sewell L. Avery of Chicago, president and chairman of the board of Montgomery Ward; Joseph N. Pew, vice president of Sun Oil Company; Herbert L. Pratt, former chairman of the board of Standard Oil; A. W. Robertson, chairman of the board of Westinghouse Electric Company; Silas H. Strawn, former president of the U.S. Chamber of Commerce; and Ernest T. Weir, chairman of the board of U.S. Steel Corporation.[36] Fletcher went on to remark of these individuals: "In these circumstances, the only effective method of preserving the American system is, so they are convinced, national political action. To this end, they have pledged their aid to the Republican party."[37] Likening Republican efforts to the massive industrial mobilization that had accompanied the party's efforts in 1896 against William Jennings Bryan, Fletcher pledged a thoroughness of effort and an expansion of the party's western headquarters in Chicago.[38] By the end of 1935 the revolt of the industrialists against a recovery structure that many of them had been instrumental in creating served to infuse the Republican party with newfound hope.

The gradual return of industry to the Republican electoral coalition bolstered a broader pattern of optimism that came to characterize Republican party efforts in 1935. Despite this, however, even the party's most conservative spokesmen were aware of the importance of revitalizing the party's national organization. The defeat of the liberalization efforts of western insurgents had kept the party apparatus in conservative hands, but had again demonstrated the sorry state of internal party affairs. Plans had to be developed to reconstruct the party's electoral coalition.

Increasingly, then, conservatives attempted efforts aimed at party restoration. As early as February 1934 National Chairman Henry Fletcher told an audience at Cooper Union that the Republican party was not controlled by "stand-patters" or "reactionaries." The national chairman maintained that it was imperative that the party acknowledge the evolution of modern political conditions and the emergence of new economic problems. Whatever changes in party appeals became necessary, however, could be made in accordance with Republican principles of "sound" economics, constitutionalism, and individualism.[39]

Governor Harold Hoffman of New Jersey told an audience of Young Republicans in Philadelphia that the party needed young, vigorous leadership. Such leadership, he hoped, would criticize the Democratic administration for carrying social experimentation "too far."[40] Ogden Mills saw party restoration as requiring the proclamation of "clear cut" alternatives to the New Deal by the Republican minority. The Republican party should state that its policy was the maintenance of "our American political and economic systems as developed over a century and a half of amazing progress," Mills remarked.[41] Herbert Hoover, breaking a two-year period of self-imposed silence on public political commentary, told a group of Young Republicans in March 1935 that the party "must furnish the rallying point in the battle to protect and maintain fundamental American principles. . . . To accomplish this, the country is in need of a rejuvenated and vigorous Republican organization."[42] Theodore Roosevelt, Jr., told the same gathering that a restored Republican party was the one vehicle that could prevent the "crippling of our liberal institutions" and the erosion of "the heritage of our people."[43]

It is evident that conservatives felt that party rehabilitation could be accomplished without any fundamental alteration of Republican electoral appeals, but instead involved the refashioning of state and regional organizations. Acutely aware of the breakdown of Republican efforts in the West since 1932, party regulars planned to concentrate their efforts there.

Kansas Republicans showed clear interest in cooperating in such ef-

forts. The state had reelected a Republican governor in 1934, Alfred
Landon, whom Kansas Republicans already regarded to be of "presidential timber." Also, the state's national committeeman, John D. M.
Hamilton, was highly regarded by party conservatives. Thus it was
logical that the young governor and popular national committeeman
would assume some influence in regular party efforts to reestablish the
Republican western electoral base.

In March 1935 a group of Republican leaders decided to call an off-
year convention of midwestern Republicans in order to plan for the
rebuilding of the party in that section of the country. Plans for the
session were drafted by John D. M. Hamilton, who hoped that the
session "would reach tremendous proportions and stir up the lethargic
east."[44] He added that the conference would demonstrate party regularity
and was intended to show eastern elements of the party that the spirit of
insurgency in the west was not as widespread as had been asserted.
Convention work would include the drafting of a platform and the raising
of money to support the projected establishment of a western party
headquarters. The entire initial planning process for the proceeding was
so dominated by conservatives that the *New York Times* speculated that it
was an effort by supporters of former President Hoover to enhance his
prospects for the party's nomination in 1936.[45] While John D. M.
Hamilton quickly denied this, he made it clear that the conference was
not part of a western effort to force the national organization to adopt a
set of liberal principles or to transfer control of the party to its western
elements.[46] Clearly, party regulars were making efforts to keep western
"rehabilitation" efforts orthodox. Thus, the midwestern convention was
fundamentally an effort to enhance western conservative opposition to the
New Deal, rather than an effort to refashion electoral appeals.

The idea of regional conferences spread rapidly among party conservatives in 1935. Republicans in New England and the Far West joined
their counterparts in the midwest in announcing regional conventions.
As the idea of regional GOP conferences began to spread, the Republican
National Committee found that its rapidly improving financial health
was enabling it to undertake additional efforts at party reconstruction.

National Chairman Henry Fletcher presided over a series of meetings
with Republican leaders from the five large states of New York, Illinois,
New Jersey, Ohio, and Pennsylvania in order to plan financial drives. He
remarked afterwards that, in contrast to his 1934 financial worries, "from

the reports I get, the prospects of the party are improving rapidly and very satisfactorily."[47] The next day the Committee announced plans for the establishment of publicity and speakers bureaus, expansion of the party's statistical division, establishment of a national Young Republican division and extensive hiring of new staff assistants.[48]

Republicans from six New England states gathered in Boston on May 1, 1935, to begin the first of the heralded regional rehabilitation meetings. Keynote speaker Theodore Roosevelt, Jr., attacked the New Deal for producing higher living costs through the NRA while increasing the national debt and retarding the process of normal recovery. Congressman Theodore Christianson of Minnesota called for reduction of government expenditures, a balanced budget, and "demobilization" of governmental bureaucrats. Christianson urged the end of government interference in the day-to-day decisions of businessmen, along with a "discontinuation of regimentation" as exemplified by the NRA. The goal of the Republican party, he felt, should be the reuniting of all its elements and rededication "to the construction of liberalism as exemplified by Lincoln."[49] In short, the New England assembly had provided strong support for the continuation of conservative electoral appeals.

On June 10 and 11 the important midwestern party conference convened in Springfield, Illinois. Nine midwestern states sent delegations to what was now referred to as a "grass roots" conference. An estimated seven thousand delegates and alternates were named to the proceeding. The *New York Times* remarked, "The object of the convention appears in the main to be like that of an old fashioned spring religious revival meeting."[50] Another *Times* reporter was struck by "the earnestness and determination of the delegates to revive the Republican party as a courageous, militant organization."[51] *Times* correspondent Turner Catledge wrote:

There was nothing of the worked up propaganda in evidence at any time. . . . Inspired by the fear that the Roosevelt administration plans to revise the American form of government to permit radical social and economic changes, these men and women have decided to fight for "preservation of the Constitution" and to rejuvenate the much demoralized Republican party for the 1936 campaign.[52]

Such determination was underscored by the rhetorical flourishes provided by the main speakers. Harrison E. Spengler, acting chairman, established the tone of much of the meeting when he charged the president with violation of the 1932 Democratic platform, failure to balance the actual budget, and disregard for the maintenance of a sound currency. Former Governor Frank O. Lowden of Illinois delivered a keynote address in which he called upon the party to salvage the federal system, while declaring that "the supreme issue of the hour is the preservation of basic principles of the Constitution."[53] The "Declaration of Principles" adopted by the grass roots conference was highly critical of the administration; it included planks advocating a return to the gold standard, the adoption of a policy of "economy and thrift" and the "prompt" attainment of a balanced budget. Additionally, the platform attacked administration efforts as "unsound, un-American . . . [,] unconstitutional . . . [and] promoted by demagogic methods."[54]

Despite the rhetoric employed, however, the document contained a certain number of important concessions to western Republicans. First, it avoided any direct reference to New Deal agricultural recovery efforts, particularly the Agricultural Adjustment Act; second, the document endorsed the principle of the old McNary-Haugen farm bill, which had been repeatedly rejected by Republican congresses throughout the 1920s. Third, the platform also promised additional assistance to farmers in order to give agricultural interests equality with industry under a higher protective tariff.[55] The document was, thus, illustrative of the conservative Republican dilemma; efforts to hold the party entirely to its conservative roots risked alienation of agricultural groupings deemed essential to the party's efforts to win back the west. The fact that such concessions were viewed as politically necessary was quickly reflected in the fact that both Herbert Hoover and Henry Fletcher expressed approval of the convention's work.[56] The *Literary Digest* was correct in pointing out that "orthodox Republicans have taken the first two rounds of the Republican rehabilitation fight."[57] Certainly, the Springfield conference had been very much of a "regular GOP affair." Harrison Spengler and Frank Lowden, although of western origin, were hardly representative of the party's insurgent western bloc. As such, it is tempting to dismiss the midwestern conference as simply another party gathering of doctrinaire conservatives. What this analysis overlooks, however, is the fact that the Springfield conference marked the beginning of serious old guard efforts to induce western Republicans to return to the party's fold. Party leaders at Springfield consciously directed appeals to the disaffected western faction of the GOP. While the convention's declarations on fiscal and economic policy reflected many of the nostrums of economic orthodoxy, the party's endorsement of the almost forgotten McNary-Haugen agricultural plan gave tacit approval to the continued existence of the AAA. It had become apparent to old guard leaders, such as New York Committeeman Charles Hilles, that national electoral success could come about again only through the restoration of the western states to the Republican electoral coalition.[58] Accordingly, eastern party leaders became more sympathetic to the possibility of a western presidential candidate in 1936, running on a platform that would reflect strong western influence. Such sentiments would become increasingly important to Republican electoral strategists throughout 1935.

Numerous regional meetings of Republican partisans were held during the year. In August Young Republicans held a two-day regional conference at Yellowstone National Park, and in October Young Republican representatives from eleven states gathered in California, where they heard a strong attack on administration efforts by the increasingly visible Herbert Hoover. In November Young Republicans from thirty states met in Des Moines to lay plans for an attack on "New Deal tyranny."[59] And in late October senior Republican leaders from eight western states came to Salt Lake City, where Senator Robert Carey of Wyoming, a party regular, referred to the administration in his keynote address as "the most disgraceful since the country was established."[60]

This was the pattern established by the series of regional conventions that were variously termed "grass roots" meetings, "rehabilitation" efforts or "crusaders" conferences. From the beginning party conservatives, of the eastern or western variety, were dominant. Two overall trends were noteworthy. First, most of the meetings involved considerably more strident attacks on the New Deal than had been characteristic of much Republican commentary of the 1933–1934 period. Second, despite this intensified criticism, it was evident that the conservative eastern wing of the party was attempting to win back the party's western elements in preparation for the 1936 presidential campaign.

In September of 1935 the establishment of a western headquarters in Chicago provided tangible evidence of Republican concern with recapturing the party's western base in 1936. Party conservatives increasingly viewed the support of the West as the decisive factor in Republican efforts to rebuild the party's electoral coalition and, in discussions among

national committeemen, the "farm question" began to receive considerable attention. Spokesmen from the western states persistently maintained that the party could not oppose the AAA and still expect the
return of the party's western votes. It was felt, however, that farm vote
would return to the Republican fold if a plan that was equally remunera-
tive to farm interests was endorsed.[61]

Thus Republican strategists increasingly came to regard the party's
chronic struggle with insurgent agriculturalists as the primary electoral
problem facing the party. Unwittingly, however, they were laying the
groundwork for a series of major "perceptual problems" in evaluating
electoral conditions that would plague the Republicans throughout 1936.

CHAPTER FIVE

The Breakdown of Republican

Electoral Evaluations, 1935–1936:

The Polarization of Party Appeals

•

The contemporary observer is likely to be struck by the differences that exist between private Republican correspondence composed in 1934 and that written by mid-1935. Correspondence in 1934 had often centered on the party's incapacity to obtain funds, along with a continual preoccupation with the effect of the "relief vote." Some bitterness and a kind of general acrimony were frequently evident as well. By the middle of 1935, however, correspondence among Republican leaders began to reflect a general pattern of optimism that in many cases did not abate until the month prior to the 1936 election. In a short period of time the half-hearted opposition to the electoral power of the New Deal, so characteristic of the traditional accommodating role of minority parties, gave way to a strident opposition unanticipated by models of vote-maximizing electoral behavior. In short, the "issue space" between the parties began to increase rather than decrease in a fashion that helped consummate the political realignment of the 1930s.

Ogden Mills, who in 1934 had foreseen a "long fight" for the GOP, typified this change in sentiment when he wrote to a friend in August of 1935:

> There has been a great change since I last saw you. Roosevelt has lost so much ground in the last few months that I am confident

that if an election were held today, he could not carry a single
eastern state. . . . From all accounts, the swing away from the
administration is marked in all sections.[1]

Walter Lippmann wrote Newton Baker with an air of almost clinical de-
tachment:

> I am becoming increasingly troubled about the Roosevelt adminis-
> tration and increasingly, since last spring, I have begun to feel that
> a situation might develop as a result of a kind of loss of balance
> where it would be absolutely necessary not to reelect Mr. Roosevelt.
> This feeling doesn't rest merely on disagreement with certain of his
> policies, but with anxiety that the strain of the office, particularly
> as he has administered it, has produced effects which raise serious
> doubts as to whether he can remain master of the situation which
> he is creating.[2]

What factors served to produce such sentiments among Republican
strategists and other contemporary observers in light of the electoral
devastation brought about by the 1930, 1932, and 1934 elections? In
order to understand the later evolution of GOP electoral strategy, it is
important to recognize the way in which Republicans came to view
political developments by 1935. It is argued that even the party's more
sophisticated strategists found accurate evaluation of political conditions
to be particularly difficult during 1935 and 1936. A reconstruction of
information then available to party strategists makes it possible, however,
to understand how these perceptual problems developed.[3]

To begin with, the progressive disillusionment of American business
with the New Deal by 1935 infused Republican campaign efforts with
enormous financial support. In contrast to the relatively even financial
resources directed towards each party in 1932, and the worsening financial condition of the Republican party through 1934, business now
increasingly directed its campaign contributions to the Republicans and,
in many cases, the amounts were staggering.[4] As any fundamental shift
in the basis of support for a political party must ultimately be reflected
in the sources from which it draws its funds, the figures are worthy of
clear consideration. Tables 5.1 and 5.2, which duplicate those prepared
by Louise Overacker, are highly indicative of some of the changed political conditions that had come about between 1932 and 1936.

TABLE 5.1

Distribution by Economic Interests of Contributions of $1,000
or More to the National Committee, 1932

Economic Interests	DEMOCRATS		REPUBLICANS	
	Amount	Percent	Amount	Percent
Bankers and brokers	$301,100	24.2	$335,605	20.5
Manufacturers	130,950	10.5	431,647	26.3
Mining and oil	54,000	4.4	158,500	9.7
Railroads, airways & public utilities	76,500	6.1	67,500	4.1
Professional people	152,043	12.2	121,800	7.4
Publishers, advertising	88,500	7.1	22,000	1.4
Retail stores	30,200	2.4	36,000	2.2
Unclassified	125,300	10.2	142,840	8.7
Unidentified	284,403	22.9	323,050	19.7
TOTAL	$1,242,996	100.0	$1,638,942	100.0

SOURCE: Louise Overacker, "Campaign Funds in a Depression Year," *APSR* 27 (October 1933): 776.

The disaffection of financial interests with the Democratic party during the period is quite apparent. Only 3.3 percent of the contributions of $1,000 or more to Democratic efforts in 1936 came from economic interests which Overacker classified as "bankers and brokers." Democratic contributions from this source declined from $301,100 in 1932 to $42,000 in 1936.

While "manufacturers" had provided the GOP with some support in 1932 (contributing $431,647), in 1936 their support was both robust and accompanied by fewer dissenting voices than in the past. As table 5.2 indicates, that year manufacturers contributed $1,162,934 to the Republican National Committee, almost one-third the total amount given by large contributors. It is also noteworthy that many of the large contributions to the Democratic party in the manufacturers category came from representatives of tobacco interests who operated primarily in the one-party South.[5] Compilations of individual large contributors, drawn from lists provided by Overacker, are also revealing. The generous individual contributors to the Democratic effort of 1932 often were not found on the Democratic list in 1936. Fewer than one-third of those who

TABLE 5.2

Distribution By Economic Interest of Contributors of $1,000 or More to National Committees, 1936

Economic Interests	DEMOCRATS		REPUBLICANS	
	Amount	Percent	Amount	Percent
Bankers and brokers	$42,000	3.3	$578,910	14.7
Manufacturers	173,600	13.6	1,162,934	29.6
Brewers and distillers	73,050	5.7	6,650	.2
Oil	88,250	6.9	86,650	2.2
Mining	—	—	119,942	3.1
Railroad, steamship lines and airways	9,500	.7	94,933	2.4
Gas and Electricity	23,500	1.8	43,600	1.1
Merchants: wholesale and retail	29,000	2.3	72,350	1.9
Lumber, cement, building materials and contracting	15,000	1.2	44,600	1.1
Real estate	20,000	1.6	59,200	1.5
Newspapers, broadcasting and advertising	33,250	2.6	128,925	3.3
Motion picture producers, theater owners	30,250	2.4	1,000	*
Professional people	161,507	12.7	170,724	4.4
Officeholders	160,902	12.6	—	—
Organized labor	129,979	10.2	—	—
Other classifications	31,000	2.4	200,700	5.1
Unidentified	254,245	20.0	1,152,840	29.4
Total	$1,275,033	100.0	$3,923,958	100.0

* Less than one-tenth of 1 percent.
SOURCE: Louise Overacker, "Campaign Funds in the Presidential Election of 1936," *APSR* 31 (June 1937): 485.

contributed $1,000 or more in 1932 assisted the Democratic effort in 1936.[6] What was equally significant, however, was the reappearance of a number of these names on the Republican list. Pierre S. du Pont, Edward S. Harkness, William Randolph Hearst, William K. Vanderbilt, and Gertrude Vanderbilt Whitney were among the best-known of these prominent party "switchers." Overacker reported that in a number of cases, persons contributing to the reduction of the Democratic deficit as late as 1935 had changed their financial and political allegiance by 1936.[7]

Thus, contributions from large corporations would favor the Republicans by a better than 3.5 to 1 ratio during the period from 1935 to 1936 and, if contributions from political officeholders, organized labor, and southern industrial interests are not included, the ratio was even higher. The consternation felt by many members of the business community over the direction of the Second New Deal was rapidly redounding to the advantage of Republican campaign efforts.

The "Break Up" of the Democratic Coalition in 1935

Models of rationalized party behavior assume essentially accurate evaluations of political conditions by party elites. Yet, political conditions in 1935 were increasingly chaotic as new political forces began to compete with the administration for popular acclaim. Republicans came to believe that the direction of events greatly improved the prospects for the party in 1936. Roosevelt's abandonment of efforts to maintain the all-class coalition within the New Deal had not only fueled the alienation of the business community but also intensified criticism of the president from members of his own party. By 1935 the Liberty League had dropped its formal stance of "nonpartisanship" in public affairs and entered into direct criticism of the administration.[8] As noted previously, the League was assisted by a formidable array of senior statesmen from the Democratic party. Among such conservative Democratic groups there was discussion of the formation of a conservative "Jeffersonian-Democratic" party to run in opposition to President Roosevelt in 1936.

Within Republican circles these developments were seen as major opportunities. In December 1934, after the defeat of Upton Sinclair in the California gubernatorial race, Herbert Hoover wrote to House Minority Leader Bertrand Snell:

There is something to be derived from our experience here in California, where my friends built a bridge with the sane Democrats and therefore not only out-flanked the radical Republicans, but brought about the defeat of Sinclair.[9]

Former Congressman James Beck, now a major figure in Liberty League activities, wrote to the former President in a similarly optimistic vein:

> I have just completed a swing around the circle—and I am deeply impressed with the rising resentment against the Roosevelt administration. . . . The next two years are likely to witness an extraordinary situation such as that in 1860. The Democratic party may split up. [10]

Herbert Bayard Swope, brother of General Electric president Gerald Swope and a well-known journalist in his own right, wrote Walter Lippmann:

> I think FDR is slipping fast. I told him so a couple of weeks ago when *he* kept *me* up to four o'clock in the morning talking and drinking. I think the country is reaffirming its innate conservatism. But he is stumbling in his efforts to change his pace. It's an axiom of our political system that no president, in whose term the economic curve points upward, is ever defeated. But there is another action I have observed. Few, if any, presidential candidates have ever won with business united against him {sic}. [Italics in original]. [11]

John O'Laughlin, in his continuing private political reports to Hoover, wrote:

> The net result is to strengthen the movement for a coalition of conservatives of both parties, and you may expect a drawing together in this respect of the southern Democrats, particularly of [Eugene] Talmadge stripe and the northern, especially the New England, conservatives. [12]

Nor were Republican hopes bolstered only by the thought of coalition with conservative Democrats. The growing discontent to the administration's Left was also viewed as providing the Republican party with clear opportunities. The continued disaffection of Senator Huey Long suggested the possibility of his undertaking a presidential bid in 1936, and a Democratic National Committee poll conducted in 1935 indicated that he had clear support outside the South.[13] While Long's assassination in September 1935 removed the prospect of his decreasing the strength of the New Deal coalition, the continued popularity of Charles Coughlin, and the possibility of Coughlin endorsing an independent presidential effort in 1936, served to suggest the potential for additional difficulties within the Democratic coalition throughout 1935.

There also remained the possibility of the formation of a national Farmer-Labor party to capitalize on the continuing agricultural discontent that was rampant in the West in 1935. While at first glance, radical agriculturalists reflected only a small, localized influence that profited primarily by focusing on particular grievances, their aggregate power was more difficult to assess. The success of Farmer-Laborites in Minnesota and Progressives in Wisconsin at least suggested the possibility of influencing events beyond the boundaries of purely local grievances.[14]

In short, throughout 1935 Republican strategists saw the Democratic party as threatened by a series of potential schisms that could affect the 1936 election. One, led by conservative Democrats, was thought to have the potential to bring about a formal or informal alliance with Republican efforts. Other radical appeals were also seen as possibly serving to factionalize the Democratic coalition in 1936. Against this backdrop, additional sources of confusion were to appear.

The restoration of Republican optimism was brought about by more than the renewed fidelity of American business or the possibility of third-party efforts that would divide the Democratic coalition by 1936. Disillusionment with the direction of the Second New Deal by 1935 was not confined entirely to senior Democratic statesmen and corporate spokesmen; their hostility was only part of a broader pattern of estrangement from the changing Democratic party agenda that affected a large element of the upper-middle class. As Sundquist writes:

> The early years of the realignment of the 1930's saw an almost entirely one way movement. As the Democratic party gained its massive infusion of working class Republicans who were ready for radicalism, it lost few of its previous adherents who were not. . . . Nevertheless, the net shift of voters to the Democratic side undoubtedly concealed some countermovement of conservatives.[15]

A sophisticated observer of electoral patterns, Arthur Holcombe of Harvard University's Department of Government, inadvertently commented on this class-based phenomenon in a letter to Walter Lippmann:

> The reaction against the Roosevelt administration is running strongly in this locality. Among my colleagues who for the most part have always been critical of the Roosevelt administration the volume and intensity of feeling against it grow very strong. I find myself growing more conspicuously a member of a minority in sticking to my view that it is too soon to desert the New Deal, but I expect to maintain this position for the present.[16]

It is argued here that this countermovement of conservatives to the Republican party was a highly visible feature of political events in 1935 and that Republican strategists continually overestimated its importance throughout the period.

Again, the very unrepresentativeness of *Literary Digest* polls taken *between* the 1932 and 1936 presidential contests (and not utilized since) can help clarify the electoral shifts that occurred in 1934–1935. It will be recalled that the *Digest*'s atypical sample had nevertheless accorded the administration a 61.1 percent approval rating in July 1934. The 1935 *Digest* poll, however, pointed toward substantial "erosion" of New Deal electoral support.[17] In contrast to the broad support that was offered in 1934, only 37 percent of those sampled in 1935 now approved of the administration's policies, while 63 percent registered disapproval.[18] This was a decline of over 24 percentage points in approval since the 1934 poll had been conducted. As the 1935 poll sampled 1.9 million individuals, it suggests that attentive middle and upper-middle income groups were concerned over the direction of administration policy throughout 1935.

Another underutilized piece of evidence on the shifts that occurred during this period can be found in the polls undertaken throughout 1935 on behalf of the Democratic National Committee by the party's pollster, Emil Hurja. While scant evidence remains to suggest the method by which Hurja chose his sample, it involved ballots mailed directly to individuals selected by Hurja in advance. (*The Literary Digest,* by contrast, simply polled its readership, relying on the size of its sample to establish the poll's validity.) Results were reported by Hurja in a fashion that suggests both regional and economic diversity in his sample, and

Hurja maintained one control of interest to researchers now: He deliberately selected his sample from individuals who had voted in the 1932 election, thus reporting only on the electorate who had participated politically prior to the surge in registation that accompanied the 1936 election. Hurja's polling data suggests erosion throughout 1935 of the coalition that supported Roosevelt's initial election effort in 1932, while also indicating limits to the political conversion of formerly Republican voters reacting to "hard times" by voting for Roosevelt in 1932.[19] Hurja attempted to measure the shifts occurring throughout 1935 by comparing the preferences of 1932 voters with their preferences of November of 1935. The key findings of the poll are reproduced below.[20]

The stillborn Republican "revival" of 1935 involved a series of real shifts to the Republican party as the American electorate realigned itself during the period along the lines of a weakly-based class cleavage. The complete misperception on the part of the Republicans of what these shifts represented in the electorate as a whole, however, requires explanation, in part because it is apparent from private correspondence that Republican strategists clearly felt that party prospects were improving throughout 1935.

Some Preliminary Explanations of Republican Misperception

Robert Lane, in a study of business attitudes toward government regulation, also noted an abrupt shift in business attitudes between 1934 and 1935.[21] Employing content analysis of selected business journals between 1933 and 1937, Lane found that the number of "completely unfavorable" references to regulation by these journals more than tripled between 1934 and 1935.[22] He attributes this increased stridency on the part of business groupings to a high "psychic cost" imposed on businessmen by the administration of the New Deal recovery program.[23] Lane argues that, while the regulation of the 1930's clearly involved a relatively low economic cost, it exacted a cost in terms of anxiety and frustration that bore little relationship to actual economic cost. Lane writes:

> First, the regulation challenged the businessman's belief system, profaning his idols and deprecating his myths. . . . Second, it denigrated the businessman himself, lowered his status in the community and allocated to him a role subordinate to the one he had

TABLE 5.3

National Inquirer Poll, November 1935

WHAT ROOSEVELT LOSES,
BY REGIONS . . .

**Of those who voted for Roosevelt
in 1932, we lose**

1.	New England States	28.25%
2.	Eastern Seaboard	20.77%
3.	Border States	20.15%
4.	Lake Belt States	25.78%
5.	Farm Belt States	23.57%
6.	Mountain States	16.97%
7.	Pacific States	15.99%
8.	Southern States	13.09%
	Total	21.29%

WHAT ROOSEVELT GAINS FROM
REPUBLICANS, BY REGIONS . .

**Of those who voted for Hoover in 1932 and now
are for Roosevelt:**

1.	New England States	10.69%
2.	Eastern Seaboard	11.49%
3.	Border States	12.13%
4.	Lake Belt States	13.92%
5.	Farm Belt States	12.95%
6.	Mountain States	19.18%
7.	Pacific States	20.22%
8.	Southern States	18.52%
	Total	13.68%

SOURCE: Emil Hurja Manuscripts, Election of 1936,
Roosevelt Presidential Papers.

enjoyed. . . . It aroused new anxieties and developed uncertainties in a time already tense with doubt and foreboding.[24]

In addition, Lane argues that even moderate economic regulation deprived individuals of choices to which they had become systematically accustomed, such as dealing (or not dealing) with unions, determining wage rates for overtime, and the actual pricing of products. The New Deal, by this view, induced a series of reactions that are not understandable by simple reference to the actual costs imposed on entrepreneurial activity. The Republican party, then, by suddenly recovering sizable elite business groupings which were responding stridently to an altered public policy environment, might have found Downsian vote-maximizing behavior difficult to undertake by 1935.

Richard Hofstadter lends support to this analysis by noting the reversal of ideological roles that occurred between liberals and conservatives during the New Deal period. Historically, most conservatives have emphasized the importance of institutional continuities, a reverence for process, and an awareness of the persistent dangers they associate with what Samuel Huntington has come to term "creedal passion."[25] During the New Deal period, however, Hofstadter points out that it was the conservatives (and by extension, much of the GOP) who represented the tide of moral indignation previously associated with the reform impulse. Hofstadter writes:

> If one wishes to look for utopianism in the 1930's, for an exalted faith in the intangibles of morals and character and for moral indignation of the kind that had been once chiefly the prerogative of the reformers, one will find it more readily in the editorials of the great conservative newspapers than in the literature of the New Deal.[26]

Also, much dialogue over political economy had taken on an apocalyptic quality throughout the early 1930s. Conservative Republican campaign appeals partially reflected the increased ideological polarization that was taking place on a cross-national basis. For example, the contemporary observer is likely to be struck by how little consideration is given to any "managed" economic course prior to the popularization of Keynesian economic thought in the United States and Europe.[27] Such otherwise diverse thinkers as Harold Laski, Sidney Webb, Sidney Hook, and F. A. Hayek all reflected the widespread tendency to dismiss the possibility of a managed capitalist order. The existence of a "middle way" seemed increasingly remote to a wide variety of observers during the period from 1930 through 1936 and Republican campaign appeals often reflected this.

The evolution of Walter Lippmann's attitudes toward the New Deal also serves as an index of the polarization that occurred during the period. Between 1933 and 1935 he moved from a position of eclectic support for most New Deal measures to one of broad condemnation of administration policy. His primary work of the period, *The Good Society,* drew heavily on the writings of such classical economists as F. A. Hayek and Ludwig von Mises, and was in many respects indistinguishable from their work during the period. Selections from Lippmann's "Declaration of Principles," written in cooperation with Lewis Douglas and circulated at the Democratic National Convention in 1936, best illustrate his embrace of the classical position prior to the 1936 election:

> We are perfectly well aware that if certain favored industrial interests are to enjoy privileges and immunities which enable them to exercise monopolistic or quasi-monopolistic control in the markets for goods and for labor, then as a matter of simple justice, similar privileges and immunities must be extended to farmers, to wage earners, and to other groups. But we hold that this course of policy, begun under the Republicans and continued under the Democrats, can lead only to the progressive impoverishment of the people and their liberties. . . . We believe that the New Era and the New Deal are two streams from the same source. The one fostered private monopoly in the name of national prosperity. The other has fostered state controlled monopolies in the name of the national welfare. We believe that both are an aberration from the basic principles upon which this nation has grown great and remained free.[28]

However, whatever the level of ideological polarization reflected within the restored elements of the GOP coalition, it is argued here that Republican party strategy after 1935 revealed a systematic pattern of rationality that broke down completely in 1936, primarily because it was predicated on patterns of political behavior that only recently had been overturned by the strengthening of class-based political alignments in the 1930s.

Views of the Political Universe in 1935: The Clash Between Sectional and Class Analysis of Partisanship

Before the development of elaborate polling techniques in the late 1930s, interpretation of partisan divisions based upon an examination of the divergent voting patterns of different sections of the country had been a popular and familiar frame of reference for political scientists.[29] While this "sectionalist" view did not deny the importance of economic interests in formulating voting behavior, it maintained that economic interests were identified primarily by geographic location, and that any subsequent economic conflict was essentially conflict between different dominant regional interests.[30] The group basis of partisanship was viewed as an expression of one's regional interests and, therefore, would not vary greatly on the basis of economic class within a single regional grouping. It was believed at that time that the expression of economic consciousness merged into a larger sectional awareness. In short, the previous methods of analyzing partisan alignments, which had emphasized the development of sectional coalitions, did not reveal the growing importance of differences in electoral behavior based primarily on class.

One of the most thoughtful students of the political strategies predicated on sectionalism was Professor Arthur N. Holcombe of Harvard University, who first developed his analysis of party strategies in his 1924 work, *The Political Parties of Today*. Holcombe divided states into political sections and identified each section with a principal agricultural or industrial interest. For both presidential and congressional elections, he identified states and districts as being Republican, Democratic, and "doubtful." In essence, Holcombe found: 1) that distinct geographic political regions existed and that electoral trends within these regions revealed persistent levels of support for one of the two major parties; 2) that victory in presidential elections was achieved by combining appeals to politically "sure" geographical regions with appeals to politically "uncertain" regions where the party could count on some clear support; and 3) that, in the final analysis, the balance of political power was held by those uncertain areas that fluctuated back and forth between the parties.[31]

By the 1940s, sectionalist theory was increasingly open to the criticism that it tended to underestimate the effect of nationwide influences on regional patterns. It was also evident by that time that regional patterns of political behavior had been affected by the movement of the electorate into a class-based cleavage that negated or strengthed many of the established geographical distinctions in voting patterns.[32]

What is useful today about Holcombe's observations, however, are their striking similarity to much private Republican analysis of political conditions by 1935. Republicans, along with many serious contemporary political commentators (for example, those featured in the *New York Times* such as Turner Catledge and Arthur Krock), continued to presume the existence of strong Republican "sections" in the New England states, New York, New Jersey, and Connecticut, with Pennsylvania regarded as the strongest Republican bastion in the country. Throughout 1935 most contemporary commentary presumed a massive GOP comeback in the industrial Northeast in 1936.[33] The challenge for Republican strategists, by this view, was the reconciliation of its now "resecured" northeastern base with the disaffected western states that had deserted the party's national effort in 1932. Thus the Republican response on a national level to the extraordinary electoral upheavals of the 1930s came to focus on nothing more than an effort to recapture a western electoral base—the party's perennial "problem" since 1896. The collapse of the all-class coalition of the early New Deal was seen as signaling the restoration of the Northeast to its customary place in the Republican electoral coalition.

It is fair to suggest that by 1935, before the development and legitimization of modern polling techniques, Republican evaluations of electoral conditions broke down systematically. As discussed earlier, the rise of Democratic voting strength in urban areas in 1928 had been attributed by Republican strategists to Al Smith's appeal to Catholic voters. This view that electoral dispositions had not changed fundamentally was maintained even in the aftermath of the 1932 election. That election, many Republicans felt, simply demonstrated the response of the electorate to the persistence of "hard times" and its disillusionment with an administration that had presided over them. Whatever the merits of this analysis, it contributed in 1934 to the party's failure to recognize the prospect of lasting, durable change within the electorate as a result of New Deal initiatives undertaken after 1932. It was a rare defeated Republican officeholder in 1934 who did not privately blame adverse results on the "relief vote."

In 1935 a series of relatively small shifts to the Republican party—as the American electorate realigned itself on the basis of class cleavages— were increasingly seen as a portent of the Republican party's overall rehabilitation.

Unless one argues that private Republican correspondence was deliberately inaccurate, it is clear that party strategists grew increasingly optimistic throughout 1935. This is not, however, simply a case of seeing what one chooses to see. The Republican party of the period was, above all, the party of the Protestants of northern America, whose denominations had been, almost from the beginning, organized along class lines. Isolated in fashionable schools, colleges, and clubs, upper-class individuals probably had less direct contact with other social classes than was the case in the less dispersed cities of the nineteenth century; consequently, rapid shifts in political allegiance on the basis of socioeconomic class could have been easily misinterpreted. The sudden return to the GOP of disenchanted and polarized business interests, as well as infusion of disaffected "Bourbon" Democrats, provided a source of misleading evaluations and false hopes by 1935.

The recurrent tendency of Republican party leaders and contemporary political commentators to view political conflict as a product of sectional considerations rendered the party's leadership incapable of recognizing a dynamic new series of class-based political realities. Increasingly confused by the overall direction of electoral trends and unfamiliar with cross-sectional, class-based patterns of voting, the party began to cast about for a means to reclaim the midwestern and western states that had once provided electoral victory. Thus the advent of political realignment served only to confuse the new minority party as it undertook efforts at rehabilitation in preparation for the 1936 election.

CHAPTER SIX

The Politics of Expediency v.

"Saving the Constitution":

The Presidential Campaign of 1936

•

The Nomination of Landon

Most scholarly interpretations of the Landon nomination and campaign in 1936 have viewed it as an effort to liberalize the party's electoral appeals, thus providing confirmation of the predictions of rationalized party models. However, Landon's easy march to the Republican nomination resulted less from attempts to liberalize the party's appeals than from efforts to reconstruct the east-west sectional coalition that was critical to the party's presidential successes prior to 1932. Only by evaluating party efforts in a retrospective fashion—and thus minimizing the importance of the sectional concerns discredited after the 1936 election—have later analysts been able to glean a liberalizing trend. Landon's personal liberalism, fundamentally that of a western progressive, fit neatly into the party's overall strategic design in 1936.

Throughout 1935 Republican strategists were preoccupied with efforts to regain the western states that had deserted the party's presidential candidate in 1932. It was felt that such efforts required the selection of a candidate from a western state who would also be acceptable to the party's dominant eastern wing.[1] By the summer of 1935 a number of western Republicans were the subject of presidential speculation. Senators Lester Dickinson of Iowa and Arthur Vandenberg of Michigan were mentioned, along with Senator William Borah of Iowa, the latter having figured so prominently in the earlier party rehabilitation controversy. Frank Knox, publisher of the *Chicago Daily News,* also attempted to increase his visibility through a series of speaking engagements. In addition, Herbert Hoover's reemergence into public life increased speculation as to his intentions for 1936.[2]

The activities of Kansas Republicans, however, gradually became the focus of national attention, in part because their governor, Alfred Landon, had been the only Republican governor in the nation reelected in 1934. The *New York Times* remarked, "As one of the few survivors of the Democratic deluge, he couldn't escape distinction."[3] As both a westerner and an available candidate, Landon became the subject of heightened presidential speculation. Above all, he seemed to offer the prospect of a candidate who might unite the divergent eastern and western elements of the party. A former Bull Mooser who had since maintained a record of party regularity, Landon could not be immediately identified as a candidate from one or the other of the party's warring factions.

The original Landon campaign organization was primarily drawn from a group of Kansas politicians and journalists. Its members ranged from National Committeeman John D. M. Hamilton, a conservative, to the relatively liberal columnist, William Allen White. Throughout 1935 this group worked to lay the groundwork for the nomination of a governor who was relatively unknown at the national level. Landon was portrayed as a fiscally conservative, common-sense governor who, nonetheless, had accepted some New Deal innovations, such as the AAA. William Allen White wrote to one conservative eastern journalist:

> He has certain Coolidgian qualities in that he makes a poor speech but gets lots of votes. . . . Whenever we talk over the New Deal, it is in these terms: The issue is economy, a sound currency and a balanced budget.[4]

Throughout 1935 the Landon forces attempted to build up the Kansas governor's prestige among eastern Republicans. After a visit to New England, Hamilton wrote to White, "As long as they [eastern Republicans] are obsessed with the western idea, we should certainly make the most of it."[5]

White reported clear success in his efforts to foster interest in the

Landon candidacy in the east in 1936. He wrote Landon from Washington.

> I think the Republicans of New York lean toward you because they
> think you are in a general way decent and intelligent. I gather that
> New England will let us write the platform and let you take the
> nomination. . . . It seems to be assumed here that you will win
> and everybody is eager to learn the truth about you.[6]

By the fall of 1935 the Kansas governor began to expand his own efforts to gain national exposure. In a speech before the Ohio Chamber of Commerce, he advocated fiscally conservative policies, while calling for the continuation of efforts to accord the American farmer better treatment.[7] Speaking to the Kansas Young Republican Club, Landon depicted the 1936 election as one of the "most important and historically significant we have ever known," as it offered a "final" opportunity to reverse an increasing "centralization of power."[8]

Still, the Kansas governor had to contend with the aspiration of other potential Republican nominees. Originally, the intentions of Herbert Hoover were a source of concern to the Landon camp, as they were to other Republicans presidential aspirants. The belief was widespread among party leaders that the former president desired renomination in an effort to achieve personal vindication.[9] Hoover's reticence about formally declaring his intentions in 1935 only increased such speculation. In response to a request by members of the Republican House Campaign Committee that he formally renounce any renewed presidential ambitions and confine his efforts to party reorganization, the former president cryptically replied that he was already engaged in efforts to strengthen the party.[10]

Finally, in September of 1935, Hoover informed the Republican National Committee that he was not seeking a third nomination and that his primary interest was the nomination of a candidate who was resolutely opposed to the New Deal.[11] There seems little doubt, however, that the ex-president remained privately desirous of the nomination.[12] Intensely proud, and more important, retaining influence over a number of former officeholders from his administration, Hoover would remain a potential rival to Landon in Republican councils.

An additional source of concern to the party's conservative element was Senator William Borah. While Senator Borah, in all probability, could not have secured the nomination, it was felt that an attempt on his part to do so would aggravate the existing conservative-progressive split within the party.[13]

Seventy years of age in 1935, the fiercely independent Borah indicated that he would enter the presidential race only if sufficient support developed in his behalf. Sentiment favoring him, however, remained largely confined to the party's western insurgents, with eastern party leaders making clear their opposition to any presidential effort on his behalf.[14] Thus the antipathy of both the party conservatives and the regular organization prevented the Borah forces from ever mounting an effective campaign for the nomination. But, as a prominent spokesman for party insurgents, Borah remained a potentially divisive force who could hinder conservative efforts to unify the party's eastern and western factions.

Frank Knox, the manager and editor of the Chicago *Daily News,* had been a consistent rival of Landon. His bitter attacks on the New Deal seemed to make him essentially a candidate of party conservatives, but his appeal in the critical western states was felt to be limited. He wrote his wife, "If I have any chance [to win the nomination], it will be only as a fearless spokesman of opposition to the whole New Deal."[15] But Knox was unsuccessful in his efforts to cut into Landon's growing strength in the Northeast by appeals to eastern party leaders.[16]

Senator Arthur Vandenberg was also a presidential possibility, but he never actively campaigned for the nomination. Believing the Landon effort to be unstoppable, the Michigan senator did little on his own behalf and, it quickly became apparent that he was more interested in the party's nomination in 1940 than in 1936.[17]

It was clear by the end of 1935 that Landon had gained a commanding lead among the possible Republican nominees for 1936. This simply reflected the continuing belief of eastern conservatives of the necessity of nominating a candidate who could recapture the West in 1936. No other presidential hopeful seemed to match Landon's potential appeal. Acceptable to eastern conservative Republicans, he appeared to be a candidate who would enable the party to again be competitive on a national basis. Evolving Republican electoral strategy continued to be concerned primarily with the specter of western insurgency, while assuming the security of the party's base in the Northeast. Moreover, these (mistaken) assumptions were about to be reinforced by conclusions Republican strategists drew from their examination of the 1935 off-year election results.

Republican Interpretations of the 1935 Election Results

In the off-year elections of November 1935, Republicans recaptured a majority within the New York State Assembly, after having lost control of it in the Democratic landslide of 1934. In Massachusetts and Ohio the party scored gains in municipal elections, and in Philadelphia the GOP reelected their incumbent mayor, despite major efforts by Democratic Senator Joseph Guffey to promote the challenger as a strong advocate of the national administration.[18]

Republican leaders predictably expressed jubilation at this relatively small series of victories in the East, suggesting that they were indicative of trends which pointed towards the party's rehabilitation in the eastern United States. Republican National Chairman Henry Fletcher saw particular significance in the vote in the eastern states and commented: "The Republican party is on its way back to power. New York, Philadelphia and Cleveland tell the story and point the way."

Senator Daniel Hastings, Chairman of the Republican Senatorial Campaign Committee for 1936 remarked: "The voice of the people in yesterday's election was a powerful rebuke to the New Deal."[19]

In this predictable and ritualistic commentary, however, Republicans were joined by a series of contemporary commentators who cannot be dismissed simply as Republican partisans attempting to influence contemporary results. In the aftermath of the election, Arthur Krock of the *New York Times* wrote:

> To most experienced observers, it appeared that the elections in Ohio, the eastern seaboard, New England and Kentucky meant these things: One year before the President's campaign for reelection, the landslide sentiment in his favor had disappeared in the territory east of the Mississippi and north of the Ohio Rivers. The election will be close, with the President relying on the south and west. . . . Democrats might as well admit the existence of a serious defection in the east and the midlands from the landslide sentiment of 1932 and 1934.[20]

Summing up Republican sentiment in Washington, *Times* correspondent Turner Catledge wrote:

> There has been a marked division in the Republican party, many members having supported New Deal policies in Congress. Now those favoring a frontal attack on the New Deal as the chief appeal next year see their position strengthened and the party throughout the country willing to take an uncompromising stand against experimental recovery plans and vast expenditures.[21]

Increasingly confident in the restoration of its eastern base, the Republican party became preoccupied with efforts to regain the western states in 1936.

The Pre-Convention Strategy of Eastern Conservatives

By 1936 the overall strategy of the party's conservative leadership had become apparent. The western United States was to provide a candidate with strong potential appeal in that section of the country, and he was to enter the convention with a majority of the western delegates pledged to him. In order to facilitate the choice of a western candidate, eastern leaders planned to prevent the emergence of a standard bearer from the East. As noted previously, in the wake of political developments since 1934, it was felt that the national ticket would run well in the East, but support in the West could be developed only by a nominee from that region. Old guard leader Charles Hilles remarked that western support was predicated on the nomination of an individual "indigenous to their soil and that we [eastern Republicans] must make an important concession to the west if we are to put together a winning combination."[22] For their efforts, eastern Republicans were asking for a free hand in the naming of the vice presidential nominee. William Allen White wrote to Landon during a visit to Washington: "I am sure that they [New England] should like to have the Vice Presidential end of the ticket."[23] In an effort to retain some measure of control, eastern conservative leaders planned to send to the convention "uninstructed" delegations, thereby retaining some freedom to maneuver during the proceedings. In this scenario, the western candidate who emerged would not be closely linked with eastern support prior to his nomination.

The overall strategy of party conservatives synchronized well with the expanded efforts of the Landon forces. Landon's associates devoted the remainder of 1935 to consolidating support in the West, while establishing important contacts among eastern party leaders.[24] Early in 1936 Landon moved into high gear. At the Kansas Day celebration in January 1936 Governor Landon delivered a speech designed to appeal to eastern Republicans; in it he called for a renewal of confidence in the national credit, a balanced budget, and an end to social experimentation that put reform before economic recovery.[25]

As the Landon forces began public endeavors to obtain the nomination, the establishment of a more elaborate campaign organization became a practical necessity. John D. M. Hamilton, the conservative Kansas national committeeman, was named campaign manager in March of 1936. Hamilton was considered successful in his dealings with eastern Republican spokesmen, and his appointment clearly reflected the interest that the Landon forces had in continuing friendly relations with eastern party leaders.[26]

Efforts on behalf of the Kansas governor now evolved simultaneously in several areas. An overall expansion of publicity on Landon's behalf was inaugurated with the help of the heavily Republican press. Hamilton's first pronouncements on Landon were illustrative of the general effort that would develop. Speaking over a national radio hook-up, he emphasized the governor's concern with governmental economy and budget-balancing. Landon was depicted as a successful businessman who recognized the importance of "paying debts as he went along."[27] At the same time efforts were undertaken to improve the candidate's standing in the West. During a Nebraska address Landon spoke of the continuing need for "remedial legislation" for agriculture, while lashing out at the establishment of a "partisan political machine."[28]

The Landon campaign strategy called for him to forgo Republican primary contests, except in his own state and other selected contests where it seemed certain he would win. The nomination could then be obtained, it was believed, simply through the support of the large uninstructed eastern delegations. His advisers believed that an open drive for delegates that attempted to circumvent organization leaders might risk alienation of conservative eastern elements.[29] The Landon movement, as a result of favorable publicity and growing support from rank and file Republicans, gathered momentum with relative ease.

The Republican party staged twelve primary contests in 1936. Five primaries resulted in the naming of favorite son candidates or unpledged delegations, five were won by Senator William Borah, and Governor Landon recorded victories in Massachusetts and New Jersey.[30]

The Landon pre-convention effort also received strong financial support. William Allen White concluded that "[f]rom reports I am receiving, there seems to be an unavoidable drift of eastern capitalists toward Landon."[31] By April the *New York Times* was reporting strong sentiment for Landon among Republican leaders in New York, New Jersey, Delaware, Pennsylvania, and Maryland.[32] Eastern leaders continued their cooperation by announcing the selection of a series of uninstructed delegations to the national convention.

The only systematic opposition to Landon came from Senator William Borah. Borah contested several primaries, but lacking regular organization support, was badly beaten in Illinois, Massachusetts, New Jersey, and Ohio. Nevertheless, he managed to win primaries in Pennsylvania, Wisconsin, Nebraska, West Virginia, and Oregon.[33] However, the eastern strategy of sending uninstructed delegations prevented even a minimal challenge in most states. Undaunted, Borah pressed his attacks on the Republican leadership, charging that the Charles Hilles—old guard group and powerful corporate interests were attempting to control the convention, select the presidential nominee, and shape the party platform. The future of the party, Borah maintained, depended on its ability to rid itself of "monopolistic" influence, and he reaffirmed his intention to carry such concerns to the national convention in Cleveland.[34]

Frank Knox, the only other active presidential aspirant, never presented a serious preconvention obstacle to Landon. Knox's candidacy continued to be based solely on militant hostility to virtually all the policy innovations of the New Deal, including the AAA. As such, his appeal was primarily confined to the East and conflicted with developing Republican electoral strategy.

As the convention drew near, Landon's lead grew increasingly apparent. His drive for the nomination had been aided decisively by the efforts of the party's eastern wing to fashion electoral appeals that would attract the party's disaffected western elements. After the election Landon confided to William Allen White, "I can say that I made less effort for the nomination than any nominee in our time."[35] The Landon forces and the eastern old guard had reached agreement on a grand strategy they felt pointed towards a broader rehabilitation of the party.

On the eve of the national convention in Cleveland Landon's campaign manager, John D. M. Hamilton, claimed enough delegate support in the form of pledges and assurances of support to nominate on the first ballot.[36] Representative Joseph Martin of Massachusetts, floor leader of the Landon forces, agreed that a movement to the Landon standard by uninstructed eastern delegations assured the Kansan's nomination early in the convention. The congressman predicted that all of New England would vote for the Republican nominee in November, and would lead the way in establishing opposition to the New Deal. "There is no hope for New England," he said, "as long as the New Deal is in the saddle; the people understand that."[37]

The Republican Convention

The Republican National Convention of 1936 was shaped by the rapprochement achieved between the eastern party conservatives and the Landon forces. Events at the convention reflected the convergence of interests that had come to exist between the two groups. The Landon forces arrived with the largest single bloc of votes, as well as the only available candidate who was both acceptable to eastern conservatives and also offered the prospect of regaining the party's lost western base. Landon strategist William Allen White reflected his awareness of the eastern strategic design when he wrote to a friend immediately after the convention that "if we had been opposed, we would have been licked to a standstill."[38] But since Landon already had the tacit approval of the eastern conservatives, this was never a serious possibility.

Even before the opening of the convention, uninstructed eastern delegates began to announce their support for Landon. Connecticut's old guard state chairman, William Rorabach, declared that the contest for the nomination was "all over."[39] Although the large New York and Pennsylvania delegations remained formally uncommitted in order to retain influence in the composition of the platform, their leaders were careful not to express any opposition to the Kansas governor.

The formal opening of the convention afforded few surprises, as the delegates heard a number of addresses that were strongly critical of the evolution of the New Deal. Contemporary observers were struck, however, by the serious tone adopted by the delegates. Arthur Krock detected a similarity to "a camp meeting of the evangelical denominations" and suggested that the delegates "really wanted to lay bold siege to Jerusa-lem."[40] Walter Lippmann sensed the undercurrent of frustration when he wrote "This is the convention of a party which has suffered a series of devastating blows. The party has been disrupted and almost uprooted by them."[41]

These sentiments were underscored by Herbert Hoover, who delivered a bitter and powerful address which reflected the depth of political divisions in 1936. Hoover stated:

Either we shall have a society based on ordered liberty and the initiative of the individual or we shall have a planned society that means dictation no matter what you call it or who does it. There is no middle ground.

The speech, which was interrupted repeatedly by prolonged demonstra-tions and applause, momentarily caused Landon strategists to fear a stampede of convention delegates to the former president.[42]

Although order was eventually restored, the emotional explosion that greeted Hoover's speech reflected the stridency that had come to seize much of the GOP by mid–1936. Again, Walter Lippmann perceived the extraordinary mood of the convention:

Now in attacking the New Deal, there is a formidable indictment to be drawn but, except in certain fine passages of Mr. Hoover's speech, that indictment has not yet been made effectively. It has been made hysterically. It has been made intolerantly. . . . The indictment has been drawn without even a pretense of attempting to weigh the evidence, to recognize the difficulties, to acknowledge the achievements. And as a result, the indictment has as yet not been made persuasively. No impression has been created, so it seems to me, that the Republican party itself possesses those quali-ties of sound judgment, thorough knowledge and clear principles, which the orators say, truly enough, are sadly lacking in Wash-ington.[43]

In private, however, Lippmann's own disaffection and stridency of tone were also great. In a note to former President Hoover he said, "I very much liked your Cleveland speech and I think the argument has gone home effectively. The reconstruction of the philosophy of economic liberalism remains to be done, and I hope sometime I may have the opportunity to talk with you about it."[44]

But once the actual nominating process began, the New York and Pennsylvania delegations gave their support to Landon and he emerged as the Republican standard bearer on the first ballot. Frank Knox, the persistent western critic of virtually all New Deal initiatives, was chosen for the vice presidential spot. Thus, despite the outpouring of sentiment for Herbert Hoover, it appeared that the Republicans remained committed to their strategy of uniting the party's eastern and western wings in a common cause.

The Party Platform

From its inception the Landon movement had progressed with the benign tolerance of eastern party leaders. With Landon's emergence, however, it became apparent that party conservatives had fostered a force that was not entirely under their control. This was reflected in the protracted wrangling that accompanied the construction of the party platform. While there was little pressure for liberalization of the party in the atmosphere of 1936, the various factions saw the importance of addressing in the platform the sectional schism so apparent in GOP ranks.

Thus all agreed that the document should concern itself with the reconciliation of the divergent views toward the New Deal held by the eastern and western wings of the party. The actual process, however, proved to be more difficult.

An original draft of Landon's views was submitted to the resolutions committee after his nomination, but it proved to be unacceptable to a majority of the committee's membership, the opposition being led by old guardsmen David Reed, George Moses, and Hiram Bingham. The original platform draft was, thus, subject to a series of amendments offered by representatives of the party's conservative wing. William Allen White, Landon's representative on the platform committee, fought vigorously for the original draft, but the results of the committee's deliberations were to leave the original document, in White's words, "badly mangled."[45]

The product of a number of divergent outlooks concerning both the New Deal and the political conditions that the party faced, the platform that finally emerged embodied compromises on many issues. It urged the continuation of several reforms inaugurated by the Democratic adminis-tration—notably in the areas of securities regulation, social security, and unemployment relief—while advocating their administration by local agencies. Predictably, it pledged the party to the maintenance of a broad program of agricultural support to be administered on a "nonpartisan" basis.[46] However, while the document endorsed a series of specific New Deal reforms, it strongly condemned the overall direction of national policy since 1932. Its preamble stated that "for three long years, the New Deal administration has dishonored American traditions." The doc-ument then criticized the "flaunt[ing]" of the integrity and authority of the Supreme Court. It maintained that a "vast multitude" of new offices had been created, resulting in a bureaucracy that continued to "harass our people," while public funds had been utilized for "partisan political purposes." In addition, the document argued that the powers of the Congress had been "usurped" by the president, while the policies of the New Deal had "bred fear and hesitation in commerce and industry." Although supportive of labor's right to collectively bargain, the docu-ment added the somewhat cryptic proviso that such efforts should be conducted "without interference from any source."[47] In an effort to win the support of conservative Democrats, all the planks omitted any direct reference to the Democratic party. In short, the party platform attempted a clear condemnation of the New Deal while quietly endorsing its policies in a number of situations where it was deemed politically expedient. The *New York Times* remarked, "Not in the many years of the history of the Republican party has there been such a melange of method and principle for the sake of a united political front."[48] Confusion over the general direction of political trends was, thus, reflected in the divergent planks of the Republican platform of 1936, and this confusion was to character-ize much of the campaign effort that followed.

Even before leaving the Cleveland convention, Landon began prepara-tions for the national campaign. John D. M. Hamilton, the Kansas national committeeman, was named Republican national chairman at Landon's request. Landon then requested a meeting with the vice presi-dential candidate, Frank Knox, Hamilton, and other key figures from the National Committee in Topeka, Kansas, on June 16.[49] The meeting was called to consider changes in the organization of the National Committee and to begin development of broad strategy for the national campaign. It quickly became apparent, however, that the old guard of the party retained a strong influence in party councils. Henry Fletcher, the deposed conservative national chairman who had figured prominently in the reorganization fight of 1934, simply took over John D. M. Hamilton's former position as general counsel to the National Committee. Fletcher's chief assistants, old guardsmen William Rorabach and Ralph Williams, retained their positions as vice-chairmen of the committee, while the overall composition of the National Committee remained substantially the same.[50]

Moreover, no agreement on comprehensive campaign strategy was forthcoming. It was thus determined to keep the approach to the campaign as flexible as possible, so the presidential candidate would be in a position to adapt to "changed conditions."[51]

One student of Republican politics has concluded that it was the Topeka meeting that produced the sharp disagreements over campaign strategy that enabled both Knox and Hamilton to deviate from the moderately liberal positions established in the early Landon campaign.[52] Yet it seems apparent that the potential for a discordant campaign would have existed in any event. While the original Landon effort had been heavily influenced by younger, more liberal elements within the party, Landon's easy march to the nomination had been the result of deliberate abstention on the part of the party's eastern conservative leaders. The party platform reflected a series of compromises that allowed widely varying interpretations and emphases. Both Frank Knox and John D. M. Hamilton were powerful personalities, and neither was at all reticent about expressing strong opposition to the New Deal.

Thus, as the Landon forces attempted to lay the basis for an effective, nationwide campaign, it became apparent that the remarkable first ballot victory and the acceptance of a platform with a liberal tinge had only masked fundamental divisions over political strategy, divisions that would plague the party throughout 1936.

Early Republican Efforts

Landon had planned not to begin his national campaign until after his formal acceptance of the nomination on July 23. However, Hamilton, the newly elected national chairman, undertook campaign endeavors of his own and, with Senator Arthur Vandenberg and several other party spokesmen, began a series of strong attacks on the administration before the beginning of the Republican presidential candidate's own efforts.

Touring the nation ostensibly to encourage the rejuvenation of state-wide organizations, Hamilton made a number of speeches that were highly critical of the administration. In New York he asserted that the fundamental goal of the Landon campaign should be educative: "The electorate has not been told the evils of the New Deal policies or what its continuation will mean to American institutions."[53] In Pennsylvania he maintained that the New Deal was leading to the "erosion of free political institutions." In Milwaukee he charged that the present administration had become largely "personal government" and the president, a "harried and driven candidate."[54] In Michigan Senator Vandenberg adopted a similar tone. Opening the state campaign, he remarked that "a vampire of bureaucracy in Washington threatened both our rights and economy." He appealed to "traditional Democrats" to join in efforts to oust the "Roosevelt party."[55]

Landon did not join in these endeavors until July 23, when he formally opened his campaign in a speech accepting the Republican nomination. Moreover, from the beginning he had rejected the view that the administration of the New Deal was resulting in any final subversion of American institutions. Long supportive of the administration's agricultural and conservation programs, he also endorsed the principle of social security, and favored labor's right to organize.[56] Landon wrote to Senator Borah, "None of my campaign appeal speeches will be merely an attack upon the opposition. I cannot criticize everything that has been done in the past three years and do it sincerely."[57] Fundamentally a western progressive, Landon had gradually come to the view that the New Deal increasingly reflected politicized responses to social problems, responses that retarded the achievement of its often laudable ends. He was sincerely convinced that constitutional government in the United States was imperiled by the possibility of a debased currency and by an increasing centralization of power that he felt had taken on dangerous momentum. Like many Progressives of his generation, Landon felt that a distinction could be drawn between the political and administrative functions of government. Accordingly, his early speeches, while critical of the New Deal, did not reflect the bitter denunciations characteristic of many other party spokesmen. Initially he spoke in terms of constitutional government, economy, and efficient administration. In his acceptance address Landon pledged continued federal unemployment grants, along with the mainte-nance of agricultural price supports.[58] In the wake of the polarization that accompanied the campaign of 1936, however, the expression of such sentiments were often not enough. Walter Lippmann wrote Lewis Douglas:

> I wasn't too badly disappointed by Landon's speech, though I do feel his inexperience and a certain lack of sureness even about his own convictions. Why, for example, holding the philosophy that he professes, did he have to announce a formula about trade unions? Would it not have been far truer to the implications of his principles as well as briefer, and very refreshing, if he had said in effect: "People come asking me what my policy toward trade unions will be if I am elected president. In my opinion, it is not the function of the president to get himself entangled in labor disputes, and my policy is to insist that these questions be settled by those concerned with them and not dragged to the door of the White House." [59]

The divergent nature of Republican electoral appeals became ever more evident. Shortly after Landon's acceptance speech Frank Knox declared in a Chicago address that the very "preservation of free enterprise was the issue of the campaign." He went on to condemn the New Deal in unequivocal terms. [60] Still, this may have reflected more than philosophical disagreements over the effects of New Deal measures. One Republican party leader in California wrote to William Allen White that he felt Knox was deliberately attempting to draw a contrast between his own speaking style and that of the more austere Landon:

> I am malicious enough to suspect that there may have been malice in Knox making his acceptance speech as great a contrast as possible to Landon's. He regards himself as a stronger and abler man than Landon, and my opinion is that he is not adverse to the country sharing that opinion. [61]

John D. M. Hamilton also continued to be highly visible in the early stages of the campaign. In California he declared that the Democratic administration would replace the Constitution with "some other mechanism." [62] Whatever their motivations, the combined Hamilton-Knox efforts gave the campaign a stridently conservative character even before Landon undertook his first major campaign tour. Consequently, it is not surprising that Landon was repeatedly advised to minimize the role of the national chairman in the campaign. Walter Lippmann wrote William Allen White, an intimate friend of Landon's:

> Is it such a good idea for the chairman of the National Committee to present himself to the country as the interpreter and even the spokesman of the Governor's policies? Somebody is bound to get up and say that since the Chairman is going to control the patronage and run the machine and collect the contributions, it becomes a very dubious business for him to be talking about matters of policy as well.[63]

Another observer wrote White: "Already comments are being made on the fact that Hamilton, who should be the executive manager of the organization part of the campaign, is stealing the electoral limelight instead."[64]

Landon's own endeavors began in August with carefully orchestrated efforts to expand the appeal of the campaign. On his first major eastern tour, Landon deliberately avoided contact with eastern party leadership; he restricted his personal staff to a group of western supporters and avoided the selection of any aides who had a close connection with the Hoover administration or the large manufacturing interests.[65] Landon's annoyance at the early direction of the campaign was reflected in his letter to William Allen White:

> I read in the morning paper where Bob Owthwaite is to be sent ahead as advance man in making preparations for my trip. This again is an illustration of getting too many businessmen . . . in our campaign organization. I am hearing again and again that the old guard is functioning too prominently in the picture.[66]

Landon's early speeches were also deliberately general in their appeal. Opening his first major tour at Middlesex, Pennsylvania, he advocated a return to "the American way of life," which he characterized as offering security and abundance "without sacrifice of the freedom of the individual citizen."[67]

Landon's attempts to emphasize themes that would distance him from the party's old guard occasionally generated confusion. For example, at

Chautauqua, New York, he delivered a speech on academic freedom and the importance of a free press and radio.[68] The relationship between these objectives and the current campaign were not made clear, however. In Buffalo he accused the administration of "creating an atmosphere that had made it impossible for it to restore economy in government expenditures," while at the same time maintaining that "the Republican party believes in being generous in the spending of money for relief and emergency purposes."[69]

During the early speeches Landon spoke in a direct, undramatic style that deliberately underscored his midwestern background. But the moderate nature of the campaign themes developed by Landon highlighted their divergence from the campaign appeals being presented by other spokesmen. Knox, Hamilton and the Liberty League continued to attack the New Deal in unequivocable terms. Even as early as the middle of 1936, many GOP strategists were finding it difficult to accurately evaluate electoral trends. In this they were not alone.

The Continuation of Perceptual Problems in 1936

President Roosevelt's overwhelming victory in November 1936 is an excellent example of a historical event that, by upstaging the uncertainties that preceded it, appears after the fact to have been inevitable.[70] Little seemed inevitable in mid–1936, however. Despite the removal of the threat posed by a possible Huey Long candidacy, political conditions continued to be subject to a wide variety of interpretations. The *New Republic's* "TRB" summed up much contemporary commentary in his September 1936 editorial:

> There are no exact precedents for the present campaign. Perhaps the closest is that of 1896, when Mr. William Jennings Bryan had the solid opposition of the owning class. . . . To be convincing, prophecies concerning the November election ought to start with an estimation of the public campaign activities of great corporations and their agents. Unhappily, facts are few and obscure.[71]

Nor was the situation at all clarified by the public opinion polls then in operation. In July 1936 the Gallup poll accorded President Roosevelt the support of only 51.8 percent of the electorate. This represented a drop of four points since Gallup's June poll.[72] When electoral sentiment was analyzed by the Gallup organization on a state-by-state basis, thirteen states, with a total of 99 electoral votes, were said to be "safely Republican." Even more significant was the fact that the Gallup organization credited Landon with leads in eleven additional states, representing a total of 173 electoral votes. If these analyses of "trends" were accurate, the Republicans would amass 272 electoral votes and win the election.[73] The now renowned 1936 *Literary Digest* poll, whose 1932 counterpart had come within a percentage point of forecasting the actual popular vote that year, continued throughout the campaign to predict a massive Landon victory.

Private Republican correspondence of the time reflected both confusion and optimism. Discussing the effects that improvements in the economy would have on the election, Landon wrote to William Allen White:

> You remember the other evening we were discussing what effect it would have on the campaign if business conditions in the country would continue to improve. . . . This time a year ago, the state [Kansas] was burned up; the farmers didn't think they had anything left, but with the improvement in crop conditions and finances, they feel they have some property now . . . so the waste and extravagant expenditures are shocking to them as property owners. This does not only apply to the farmers, but to the small businessmen who were going along with the crowd who didn't feel that they had any interest in the amount of money the government was spending.[74]

John D. M. Hamilton wrote to Ogden Mills in July: "The tide is running strongly in our direction."[75] Ogden Mills himself wrote to a friend that he was "more and more convinced that Landon will measure up to the task. . . . In my judgment, there is better than an even chance to beat Roosevelt."[76] Kansas Senator Arthur Capper wrote to William Allen White, "I believe it will be a Republican year. I think we can carry the November election for Landon, as well as for the entire state and congressional ticket."[77] John O'Laughlin, in one of his private political reports, prepared for former President Hoover, reflected the continuing tendency to overestimate both the importance of conservative Democratic defections from the party and the current political appeal of Al Smith. He wrote:

> The President and his advisers are feverishly endeavoring to find some counterstroke for his [Smith's] declaration for Landon. . . . They are asking what Tammany voters will do even though [the] hall would shift to Roosevelt['s] support . . . [and] whether the Democrats in Massachusetts, New Jersey, Pennsylvania, Maryland and other states will be influenced by the claim that the New Deal is not the Democratic party and cast their votes for Landon as Smith will do. . . . Another point worrying the President and his advisers is: "Will Smith place his long political experience at the command of Landon?" They do not discount the effect of such an action. Smith's political skill is thoroughly understood.[78]

Confusion over the direction of political trends was also frequently reflected in much serious journalistic commentary. Although the *New York Times* announced editorial support for Franklin Roosevelt, its electoral analysis continued to forecast a close, hard-fought election. Much of the material presented in the *Times*'s feature articles described the electoral contest in terms of regional or "sectionalist" analysis, that is, an alignment of the "Republican East" against the "Democratic West" and South.[79] Nor was confusion confined entirely to journalists and Republicans. On July 26 Roosevelt's campaign manager, James Farley, the accuracy of whose final prediction in the presidential election of 1936 has long been remembered, foresaw Democratic losses in the House of Representatives. Farley felt at that time that the presidential candidacy of Congressman William Lemke on the Union party ticket would diminish the level of Democratic support in many northeastern states.[80] Even the combative Charles Michaelson, director of publicity for the Democratic National Committee, commented somewhat defensively, "The Democrats might lose nearly, if not quite, one hundred seats and still retain a working preponderance in the House of Representatives."[81] Massive Republican congressional gains were predicted by the *New York Times* throughout the year.[82]

Arthur Krock hinted at one source of the prevailing electoral confusion when he wrote of public opinion polls:

Two of the four groups which will probably decide the election have hardly been sampled, if at all. These four groups are the new voters, the colored voters, labor and agrarian citizens; and it is doubtful whether it will be possible to produce an accurate representation of the first two mentioned. This is because their names are not so easily come by in the public records.[83]

Nevertheless, he went on to predict a close popular vote.

The September Maine Elections

While "perceptual problems" on the part of Republicans had been rampant throughout 1935 and 1936, they reached a high-water mark as a result of Maine's early election in September of 1936. Landon had campaigned extensively in the state and the Republicans had now recaptured the governorship, while regaining control of the state's three congressional seats.[84] Although Republican successes in Maine could be rationalized by the fact that the state was small and traditionally Republican, *New York Times* correspondents were also impressed by the fact that Republican voters in primary contests in both Massachusetts and Pennsylvania had come out in greater numbers than their Democratic counterparts.[85] This was seen as a portent of trends in major industrial states. Arthur Krock, writing under the headline of "Republicans Are Restored to Major Party Status," observed:

It is perfectly reasonable to conclude from the vote in Maine that eastern states of generally similar make-up, which are normally Republican, will return in November to their ancient mooring. But to assume that agriculturally dominated states in other parts of the country will do the same is violent indeed.[86]

Expanding upon this analysis three days later, the *Times* characterized the Republican party as "a highly competitive major organization in all parts of the country except the South," which had effected "one of the most rapid recoveries any political party has ever made." Political trends, according to the *Times* pointed toward strong Republican gains in the House of Representatives, with a close presidential vote in the disputed states.[87]

Thus, the ongoing diversity of electoral appeals made by prominent Republicans through September 1936 is best explained by the continuing difficulty that contemporary observers had in determining electoral trends. Without modern sampling techniques to rely on, Republican strategists quickly once again assumed the electoral security of their northeastern base and, after the results of the Maine election, concentrated primarily on restoration of their disaffected midwestern and western constituencies.

Western Campaign Strategy

After September Republicans directed their main efforts toward fashioning electoral positions that would appeal to western interests. The party's entire strategic design, as it had developed since 1935, hinged on the party's revival in that area. Accordingly, during his western tours Landon abandoned the more general appeals for economy and efficient administration that had been characteristic of his eastern tours in favor of specific policy proposals designed to gain the support of agricultural groups.

In a major address in Des Moines Landon proposed higher agricultural benefits in the form of direct cash payments, crop subsidies, and price supports. In Minneapolis he criticized as injurious to domestic farm production the reciprocal trade agreements negotiated by the Roosevelt administration.[88]

The Republican campaign in the West took on an increasingly opportunistic tone. In Milwaukee Landon criticized the new Social Security plan as "unjust, unworkable, poorly drafted and wastefully financed."[89] At the same time, however, he pledged to provide old-age pensions for needy American citizens over the age of sixty-five.[90] But political news from the West continued to be disquieting to Republican strategists. Of the major farm groups, only the conservative National Grange appeared to be critical of the New Deal. The September Gallup poll showed declining Republican strength in the western United States.[91] Clyde Reed wrote to William Allen White that farm sentiment, even in Landon's home state of Kansas, remained Democratic.[92]

Republicans were also largely unsuccessful in efforts to win back many Republican progressive leaders who had deserted the party throughout the early New Deal period. Senator George Norris again supported Roosevelt, as he had in 1932. Senators James Couzens of Michigan and

Peter Norbeck of South Dakota also renounced the Republican ticket. Senators William Borah, Hiram Johnson, Gerald Nye, and even Senate Minority Leader Charles McNary, simply took no part in the campaign, confining their efforts to statewide contests.[93] In September some progressive leaders announced the formation of a "National Progressive Conference" to facilitate Roosevelt reelection, with former Republican (now Progressive party) Senator Robert La Follette, Jr., figuring prominently in these efforts.[94]

The Advent of Despair: The Final Campaign

By October Republican efforts took on a desperate, occasionally even frenzied, quality. While the true dimensions of the electoral defeat that was to come were by no means apparent, it was evident that the Landon candidacy had not had the desired effect in the western United States. Even sympathetic observers began to express disenchantment. Dorothy Thompson, then writing for the staunchly Republican *New York Herald Tribune,* wrote to William Allen White, "God knows I've wanted to come out and root for your friend, the Governor. But he won't throw me even an inch of rope to cling to."[95]

In addition, disquieting signs were finally being widely recognized in the traditionally Republican Northeast. Arthur Krock, reversing the position he took a month earlier, noted that the effect of organized labor's efforts in the Northeast was of increasing concern to Republican strategists, while the party was also receiving reports of widespread defections by black voters to the Democratic ticket.[96] Furthermore, the potential effects of massive registration increases in metropolitan areas were increasingly evident, and the *Times* reported that "many observers" saw these increases as favorable to the Democratic cause.[97] Still, the dimensions of the Democratic victory to come remained largely unappreciated.

A special *New York Times* poll of twenty political newswriters, published on October 15th, still accorded an average of 157 electoral votes to Landon. The experts concluded that the popular vote margin would not exceed 3.625 million.[98] And only a week before the election the *New York Times,* while now predicting a Roosevelt victory, wrote:

> Governor Landon will receive a far larger popular vote than Herbert Hoover in 1932, while the Republican Party will automatically

restore the working party command to the area east of the Mississippi River. There will be good Republican gains in the House of
Representatives.[99]

Nor was such confusion confined to Republican councils. Emil Hurja,
the pollster for the president and the Democratic National Committee,
wrote in his final report to James Farley:

> The outstanding deduction of all polls and available data is that
> enough states are indicated as close to make an adverse swing
> dangerous to victory with a slight definite improvement, on the
> other hand, making a major electoral victory a distinct possibility.
> . . . It will be seen that fourteen states are between 52.8 and 47.9
> percent Democratic with five between 50.0 and 47.9 percent. One
> could readily take these five additional states without upsetting the
> predictive possibilities of the chart and approach 450 electoral
> votes, and again, we could skin through with only a state or two
> to spare.[100]

Hurja's late October report, a state-by-state average of his own National
Inquirer poll, the Crossley poll, the Gallup poll, and an "adjusted"
Literary Digest poll, projected an electoral vote of 271 for the president
and 260 for Governor Landon.[101] While Hurja rejected this final electoral
vote tally in his report, many polls remained a source of persistent
concern to the Democrats, even as late as the end of October 1936.[102]

With the breakdown of Republican presidential efforts, however, a
change seemed to come over Alfred Landon. His campaign speeches grew
increasingly embittered, while his attacks on the president took on a
more personal form. In Detroit he asserted that the Democratic administration "had started on the road that leads to dictatorship" and spoke of
the "autocratic powers" now given to the chief executive.[103] In California
he charged the administration with attempts to bring about a planned
social order that, in other nations, had resulted in the destruction of
freedom of speech, press, and conscience.[104]

Landon also became more direct in his public association with business
interests. In Detroit, he chose to publicly confer with the increasingly
eccentric Henry Ford; this decision was strongly criticized by William
Allen White because of its possible repercussions among Jewish voters.[105]

Further campaign efforts were discontinued in the East, as the Republican candidate made his final efforts on the West Coast. In Los Angeles Landon urged President Roosevelt's defeat "as a means of preserving the Constitution and the American form of government." [106] In Phoenix he stated that "regimentation of the individual and curbing of his liberties underlie every one of the New Deal plans" and concluded that a major change in our form of government was not remote. [107]

Thus, as the campaign drew to a close, Landon's speeches more and more reflected the stridency and bitterness often characteristic of the disaffected conservative Democrats and the business elements that had, by 1935, infused the Republican party with false hopes. While Landon had never been able to successfully restrain Knox, Hamilton, or the Liberty League speakers, his own early campaign had always been tempered by his awareness of the need to refashion the party's appeal in the western United States. Now, engulfed by the frustration that accompanied the breakdown of the GOP's overall western strategy, his appeals became indistinguishable from those of the individuals who had inspired the stillborn Republican revival of 1935.

Even so, on the eve of the election Republican strategists continued to see a basis for hope. The *New York Times* characterized Landon strategists as "divided between confidence and hope." [108] A strong showing in the industrial Northeast for the presidential ticket, coupled with clear congressional gains would at least provide the basis for party rebuilding in preparation for the 1940 election. The *Times* also reported that some Landon aides remained clearly optimistic because of the possibility of massive defections from the Democratic ticket by disenchanted "Jeffersonians." Nevertheless, the *Times* predicted a clear Roosevelt victory because of his retention of bases in the South and the West. [109]

It was now widely acknowledged that Republican efforts to recapture their western base, so critical to the 1896–1928 Republican presidential coalition, had failed. Moreover, the electoral assumptions that had been the basis of Republican strategy during that period were about to be dramatically refuted by the extraordinary 1936 landslide.

Little preelection analysis foresaw the magnitude of the Republican defeat in 1936. (It should be recalled that even James Farley had predicted the loss of congressional seats by the Democratic party.) Republican leaders, having anticipated at least the restoration of the party as a competitive, dynamic force, were now confronted with one of the most devastating electoral repudiations in American party history.

The Landon-Knox ticket succeeded in carrying only the states of Maine and Vermont and garnered over 45 percent of the vote in only four states: Maine, Vermont, New Hampshire, and Governor Landon's home state of Kansas.[110]

Overall, the Republican presidential ticket received only 36.5 percent of the popular vote. Republican electoral strategy had completely broken down throughout the nation. Landon received his strongest support in the Northeast, but that had amounted to only 43.4 percent of the vote.[111] Almost as distressing was the extraordinary ongoing weakness of the party in the western United States: it polled only 34.4 percent of the presidential vote, failing to carry a single state. It was also evident that Landon had not received substantial backing in urban areas; he failed to come close to carrying any of the nation's twelve largest cities.[112]

The election results were also devastating to the GOP's already decimated congressional contingent. In the House their numbers went from 104 to 89. Among those defeated were such spokesmen as A. Piatt Andrew of Massachusetts, Chester Bolton of Ohio, and Schuyler Merritt of Connecticut. In fact Connecticut and Rhode Island now had no Republicans in their congressional delegations. In Pennsylvania, formerly a bulwark of northeastern Republican strength, voters ousting seven Republican congressmen—for the first time since the Civil War—gave the Democrats control of both houses of the state legislature. In addition, the Republicans lost 27 of 33 gubernatorial contests nationwide.

Although only one-third of the Senate faced the electorate, this did not limit further crippling Republican losses in that body. Republican membership in the Senate dropped from 25 to 16. The conservative eastern wing lost Daniel Hastings of Delaware, Warren Barbour of New Jersey, and Jesse Metcalf of Rhode Island. Conservative casualties were not confined, however, to the GOP eastern wing: western conservatives Robert Carey of Wyoming and Lester Dickinson of Iowa both failed to win reelection and a Farmer-Laborite filled the vacancy left by the death of conservative Senator Thomas Schall of Minnesota.

Moreover, for the first time, several factors combined to also diminish the strength of western progressive insurgents in the Senate. Senator James Couzens of Michigan lost a primary challenge to a conservative Republican opponent, who was then defeated in the general election by a Democrat. Senator Bronson Cutting of New Mexico had been killed in an airplane crash in late 1935, and Senator Peter Norbeck of South

Dakota died shortly after the election. In addition, Senator George Norris of Nebraska had run successfully for reelection as an independent. These events further diminished the progressive Republican Senate bloc.

In the course of just one evening, patterns of electoral analysis that had guided Republican political strategists since 1896 had been abruptly overturned. Contemporary comments reflected both confusion and despair. As Ogden Mills wired to Herbert Hoover: "I don't quite see where and how we are to begin to rebuild."[113]

Postelection Evaluations

In the aftermath of the nationwide Republican electoral disaster, GOP leaders offered various assessments of the reasons for the party's massive electoral rejection. Those of the liberal wing, such as William Allen White, attributed the defeat to the "reactionary turn" of the later campaign. He wrote, "The reactionary turn, and it was pretty definite after Minneapolis [an October speech], gave the final *coup de grace* to the Republican campaign." He felt that Republican efforts had been compromised by the continued influence of "ultraconservative advisers," and also that the increase in large contributions to the party suggested that the wealthy had virtually "advertised their control of the party."[114]

Hoover, who had found party appeals discordant from the very start of the campaign, also held in contempt some of the individuals who had financially assisted the party since 1935. He wrote to William Allen White:

> When the Republican party starts out to mix populism, oil, Hearst, munitions and the Liberty League, it is bound to come to grief. . . . I was interested in what you have to say as to sound finance of the party. . . . If the money was taken from Du Pont, Pew and company, they would "sell the party down the river" and I am not sure that it had not been sold.[115]

Governor Landon felt that his own efforts had been compromised throughout the course of the campaign by the actions of party leaders who were far less moderate than he. He felt the Liberty League and militant conservatives spokesmen, such as vice-presidential candidate Frank Knox, had exerted a disproportionate influence. Clearly the efforts of these individuals and organizations had severely hindered the party's attempts to modify its 1936 electoral appeals. Throughout the campaign they had been responsible for caustic electoral appeals and misleading electoral evaluations. Several years after the election, Landon confided to Walter Lippmann:

> I knew you criticized severely my Minneapolis speech and I don't know as I could very much blame you. I would hardly go so far as to say it was reactionary—at least in the accepted sense of that word. . . . I felt that I had gone so far in that speech as I could, in view of the Republican platform and the attitude of so many of our candidates for Senate and Congress. After all, the head of the ticket in his campaign has to bear his fellow candidates in mind. . . . But you will remember I had a hard time with the Resolutions Committee at the Convention. I think it will be easier for the next candidate to take the Republican party further in the direction in which I think you believe, and in which I know I believe.[116]

Yet it is apparent in retrospect that very few Republicans in the spotlight—many of whom later decried the influence of large corporations or extremists—had seen fit to speak consistently about these matters during the course of the campaign. This simply highlighted the fact that Republican party leaders had never arrived at any agreement after 1935 as to the types of appeals that would be effective with the electorate. As late as September 1936 many Republican strategists, lulled by the results in Maine, remained fundamentally optimistic about the course of the campaign. And this was part of a broader pattern of optimism that had begun with the break-up of the all-class coalition of the early New Deal. The perceptual limitations of many party leaders effectively prevented any real modification of electoral appeals throughout 1936, and this problem was compounded by the analyses provided by many of the serious political journalists of the period.

Continually preoccupied by the party's long-standing "problem" with western insurgency (the existence of which was consistently evident in the GOP's congressional ranks), Republican strategists never really understood the political trends in the formerly Republican Northeast after 1932. Somewhat distanced from the extraordinarily harsh effects of the Great Depression, party strategists had based all their electoral calculations concerning the 1936 election on the assumption that the restoration of Republican strength in the Northeast would be among the easier of the party's tasks. But now, in light of the 1936 results, it seemed possible that the New Deal coalition had not only permanently detached the party's western base, but had also forged a northeastern coalition comprising organized labor, recent immigrants, blacks, women, intellectuals, and young voters. The strength and popular appeal of that coalition might possibly cause the disappearance of the Republican party from the ranks of serious electoral competitors.

The Landon campaign's conspicuous failure limited the ability of the Kansan to act as titular head of the party. After the November debacle many other Republican leaders, like Landon, were publicly silent. The few who spoke at all were vague about future GOP policies. National Chairman John D. M. Hamilton said only that he was "unconvinced" of the need for a basic redirection in party philosophy.[117]

At a prescheduled December meeting the national committee voted 74 to 2 to retain John D. M. Hamilton as chairman. Beyond this procedural undertaking, however, the committee was reluctant to rejoin the political wars. Unable to agree upon a future course of action, many committee members felt that responsibility for the development of party policy should rest with the remaining members of the Republican contingent in Congress.[118] Moreover, the national committee seemed to recognize its inability at that time to undertake the formulation of a systematic political program for these independently elected officials.

The confusion prevailing among Republicans during the period was summed up by Ogden Mills in a letter to Hoover:

I agree with you that the mess is pretty complete. If we attempt to overcome this situation by rebuilding the party with an eastern foundation, we shall probably alienate for good all of the middle western agricultural states, whose allegiance to the party seems already pretty well shaken, if not destroyed. How to revitalize the Republican party under such conditions looks almost impossible. So far as I can see, then, the only thing for us to do is to wait and see and to be guided in the immediate future by the course which events may take.[119]

Thus, Republicans appeared to have entered 1937 in much the same indecise and confused state that had been the fate of the party during the

One Hundred Days period. Charles Michael of the *New York Times,* so optimistic a year before, now likened the condition of the party to that of the Whigs in 1852–1856.[120] Certainly, there was little to suggest that the tiny Republican congressional minority would not engage in the same kind of divided, ineffectual response that had been characteristic of Republican reactions to the New Deal since the President Roosevelt's first emergency session in March 1933. The overwhelming electoral victory for the president and his party in 1936 suggested that he was the first really "national" presidential choice since the early days of the nation. The *New York Times* concluded that the dimensions of the electoral triumph would help to ease the factional conflict "which had long bedeviled public officials and broken up into blocs legislatures and congresses."[121] Even allowing for a measure of postelection hyperbole on the *Times*'s part, Roosevelt entered 1937 with a overwhelming congressional majority, tremendous popular charm, enhanced political experience, and the astonishing level of public support demonstrated by the 1936 election. Thus Republican strategists could hardly be blamed for open contemplation of what this extraordinary demonstration of national unity seemed to foreshadow for the future of their party.

PART THREE

The Republican Congressional Party
Confronts The New Deal

•

CHAPTER SEVEN

"The Old Signs and Portents Have
Disappeared": The Republican Party
in the "First One Hundred Days"

•

Just as the evolution of Republican electoral strategy has been under-chronicled, the Republican congressional contingent remains the forgotten element of the famed Seventy-third Congress. With the exception of studies of the party's insurgent western elements, little scholarly attention has been paid to the party's overall reaction to the legislative initiatives of the period. Yet an understanding of the divisions that rapidly emerged during the first session of that Congress is central to an appreciation of the political and electoral dynamics of the New Deal period, particularly since the persistent resurfacing of regional schisms within Republican ranks would be a source of consternation to the party's congressional leadership throughout the session.

Even more important, the GOP's propensity to analyze the electorate in sectional rather than class or ideological terms grew out of the party's experiences in both the Seventy-third and Seventy-fourth Congresses. Preoccupied with its efforts to reunite its eastern and western wings, the party never appreciated the emergence of modern urban electoral power until after the 1936 election.

A brief discussion of the Republican congressional party's key members is presented here along with a short analysis of the confusion and uncertainty within minority ranks as the session approached. Then, in order to understand the patterns of congressional party response, the key bills of the session are analyzed on the basis of Republican support or non support, rather than in chronological order. In this fashion the changing character of Republican responses, along with the demoralization within party ranks, can be more readily perceived. Briefly put, the session of the Seventy-third Congress was, for most of the GOP, less a period of renewed hope than a time of prolonged reexamination undertaken amidst continual political setbacks.

The Republican congressional contingent that would confront the newly arrived Roosevelt administration had been drastically shrunk by the far-reaching results of the 1932 Democratic landslide. In the Seventy-third Congress that convened in 1933 there were 35 Republican senators and 117 representatives, but this minority contingent was far from homogeneous. The eastern old guard remained firm in its conviction that the impulse to reform that arose out of the despair of the depression was not worth the cost of the damage it would do to the social and economic precepts that had guided the nation in the past. In contrast, their western counterparts, many of whom had openly broken with the Hoover administration, viewed the new Roosevelt administration with empathy. Long at odds with eastern party leaders over farm relief, western Republicans viewed much early New Deal legislation as not inconsistent with their own earlier progressive goals. I shall show that the major divisions within the Republican congressional minority would continue to be largely regional and were, at least initially, an extension of the previous decade's conflict between eastern conservatives and western progressives.[1]

Sixteen senators and sixty-seven representatives composed the dominant, conservative eastern wing of the party.[2] The eastern senators, traditionally allied with the financial and industrial interests of the Northeast, were led by David Reed of Pennsylvania, Frederick Walcott of Connecticut, Daniel Hastings and John Townsend of Delaware, Frederick Hale of Maine, Phillips Goldsborough of Maryland, Hamilton Kean of New Jersey, and Henry Hatfield of West Virginia.

In the House the conservative eastern congressmen rallied around the leadership of Bertrand Snell of upstate New York.[3] Their numbers included an articulate core group comprising New Yorkers Hamilton Fish, Jr., Clarence Hancock, Daniel Reed, John Taber, James Wadsworth, and Robert Bacon; Pennsylvanian James Beck; and Robert Luce, Joseph Martin, and Allen Treadway of Massachusetts.

The western wing of the party was composed of nineteen senators and fifty congressmen. As a group they represented the insurgent bloc within the party that had become so disaffected during the Hoover presidency, but it was a considerably less homogeneous group than its eastern counterpart. One subgroup, consisting of about twelve senators, had formed a long-standing insurgent bloc within the party. Prominent among these individuals were Robert M. La Follette, Jr., of Wisconsin, Hiram Johnson of California, George Norris of Nebraska, William Borah of Idaho, Gerald Nye of North Dakota, and Arthur Capper of Kansas. The Republican House contingent also contained a strong progressive bloc composed of about twenty-seven members, including George Blanchard and James Frear of Wisconsin, John Cooper of Ohio, Everett M. Dirksen of Illinois, Lloyd Thurston and Fred Gilchrist of Iowa, and William Lemke and James Sinclair of North Dakota.

A smattering of party regulars were also in the western delegation that assembled in 1933; they included Senators Arthur Vandenberg of Michigan, Simeon Fess of Ohio, Charles McNary of Oregon, and Lester Dickinson of Iowa. Some of their House counterparts were Chester Bolton and John Hollister of Ohio; Joseph Hooper of Michigan, and Oscar De Priest and James Simpson of Illinois.

Bitterness over the factional divisions that had plagued Hoover's reelection campaign was immediately evident as the Republican congressional delegation assembled quietly in Washington during the critical days of March 1933. Senator David Reed announced that he would sponsor a movement to bar, both from party caucuses and previous (seniority-based) committee assignments, the four Republican senators who had openly supported Franklin Roosevelt.[4] This measure was originally directed at *all* party insurgents, but it floundered because of the difficulty of defining "party regularity"—support of Herbert Hoover in 1932 becoming the only test that could be agreed upon. Although Reed's proposal was never acted upon by the minority caucus, it is illustrative of the schisms that continued to plague the GOP as it assumed minority status in 1933.

A more immediate problem, however, was the general uncertainty and confusion that surrounded the delegation's efforts to decide upon a course of action as the new Congress convened. The massive Democratic victories had swept away much of the party's congressional leadership: both Senator James Watson, the former majority leader and Senator George Moses, the former president pro tempore, had been defeated in 1932. Finally agreeing to confine themselves initially to the bare necessities of organization, senate Republicans selected Charles L. McNary of Oregon as the minority leader. With a long-standing interest in agricultural problems, an easygoing manner, and a history of party regularity, McNary was to prove a good choice. In the House, the Republicans again elected Bertrand Snell of New York as minority leader.

The Republican Party and the First One Hundred Days

The trouble is that we are voyaging on an uncharted sea; the old signs and portents have disappeared, or are useless.

—Herbert Bayard Swope to Walter Lippmann, June 7, 1933[5]

Few events in modern political history can compare with Franklin Roosevelt's initial coming to office. The ringing invocations of his inaugural address combined with the intimacy of his "fireside chats" served to rekindle hope and soothe fears. With consummate personal skills, Roosevelt appealed to mass concerns, thus providing meaning and hope to a nation grown weary of political paralysis. Roosevelt's personal presence, political popularity, and mammoth electoral majorities all profoundly affected members of Congress. Yet these advantages alone were all subordinate to the extraordinary persistence of the Great Depression. Emotional and psychological reactions to the national crisis had been building up for some time, and it was clear that in 1933 there had to be some kind of turning point. In March 1933 fourteen million people were jobless, and business bankruptcies continued unabated.[6] Such statistics, however, were no longer necessary to demonstrate the level of distress now existing throughout much of American society. Without ever having agreed as to what should be done, by 1933 the American people clearly felt that the subordination of individual interests for the sake of a more harmonious pattern of broad national action was a fundamental prerequisite to an effective recovery. Walter Lippmann wrote Felix Frankfurter at Harvard University:

The doctrine of powers that I have been preaching in the last few weeks does not arise from any doubt as to the value of discussion, reflection, criticism and persuasion as conditions for wise action, but out of a conviction that the character of this crisis requires extraordinary methods. That extraordinary methods are very dangerous and can become a habit I vividly realize, but I think we must not be afraid to resort to them if we realize the dangers and are clear about the necessities.[7]

The crystallization of such sentiments had, for the moment, severely limited the scope of partisan opposition by the Republican minority.[8] Also the pace of the session would be greatly speeded by the adoption of closed rules that restricted amendments to and debate on virtually every major piece of legislation. No minority party in this century has entered a legislative session with fewer resources.

Legislation Supported by the GOP: Glass-Steagall and the Economy Act

On March 9, 1933, the Seventy-third Congress convened in special session at the request of the president. The first measures considered received rather broad "regular" Republican support. These measures have generally been viewed by historians as conservative ones with substantial support in the financial community. The Glass-Steagall Banking Act was designed to remedy speculative abuses engaged in primarily by commercial banks prior to the stock market collapse. The bill prohibited such banks from purchasing securities for their own accounts and had the effect of separating commercial and investment banking, thus ending the considerable involvement commercial banks had in the marketing of securities.

Roosevelt's banking message was read as newly elected congressmen milled about trying to locate their seats.[9] The session was conducted in an atmosphere of "wartime crisis" and the forty minutes alloted for House debate reflected this sense of urgency. The lack of debate makes reconstruction of attitudes difficult but we know that Minority Leader Snell declared:

Of course, it is entirely out of the ordinary to pass legislation in this house that, as far as I know, is not even in print at the time it is offered. . . . The house is burning down and the President of the United States says this is the way to put out the fire. And to me at this time, there is only one answer to this question and that is to give the President what he demands and says is necessary to meet the situation.[10]

The House promptly passed the Glass-Steagall Banking Act by a voice vote. In the Senate, the bill was also quickly passed by a vote of 73 to 7.[11]

Some western Republicans disagreed sharply with the provisions of the measure. For example, Senator Borah wrote to a constituent that the measure was "laying the foundation for the creation of a financial dictatorship with headquarters in New York."[12] Other western insurgents expressed similar concerns over the control that eastern banks would exercise within the national banking system.[13]

Conservative Republicans, in contrast, had found the proposal to be a very acceptable measure. Roosevelt's criticism of bankers in his inaugural address had suggested that he might countenance radical reform, including even the nationalization of the banking system.[14] Instead, the Glass-Steagall Act also extended government assistance to the private banking structure that enabled many banks to resume operations. William Leuchtenburg notes that the bill was drafted largely by former officials of the Hoover administration and, as such, had broad conservative support.[15] And since it was a major proposal of the Roosevelt administration, it also enjoyed Democratic backing. In response to criticism from Felix Frankfurter over the hasty passage of the measure, Walter Lippmann wrote:

> I recognize fully the *potential* danger of too hasty, too ill-considered reorganization, but what would you have done in the circumstances of the last two or three weeks? Do you really think, for example, that I should have urged Congress to consider carefully and attempt to understand thoroughly the provisions of the banking bill before passing it, or was it right to call upon Congress to take the thing on faith, suspending debate, suspending the process of education, suspending the deliberative method? I faced that choice honestly in my own mind, and I am prepared to risk the potential dangers which you point out for the sake of averting the much more actual dangers which were right upon us.[16]

TABLE 7.1

East-West Breakdown of Republican Senate
Vote: Glass-Steagall Banking Act

	EAST	WEST
Yes	13 (92.8%)	10 (66.7%)
No	1 (7.2%)	5 (33.3%)

As noted above, the House passed this measure on a voice
vote thus providing no data for analysis.

It was now fully appreciated on both sides of the aisle that this was no ordinary session.

Minority party approval was also evident the next day when Roosevelt introduced his second measure to the Congress. The Economy Act requested sweeping presidential powers to limit the payment of veterans' benefits and to reduce the pay of federal employees.[17] In Roosevelt's orthodox phrase, "Too often in recent history, liberal governments have been wrecked on the rocks of loose fiscal policy."[18] The bill reflected the early influence of such conservative Democrats as Budget Director Lewis Douglas who was determined to balance the federal budget. Despite the persistent strength of the veterans' lobby, the bill received much conservative Republican support. Seventy-two House Republican votes made possible the passage of the bill despite the strong opposition of rebellious Democrats.[19]

Again Republican commentary had a strong bipartisan tone. Congresswoman Edith Nourse Rogers of Massachusetts stated:

> The bill as I see it is not a Democratic bill, it is not a Republican bill; it is exactly what it says—a bill to maintain the credit of the United States government. . . . It is a question that transcends all personal obligations to any class and concerns the whole population of the country as to whether or not we are to maintain our standard of government or become a bankrupt nation.[20]

A few days later the Senate passed the measure easily over the opposition of a small bipartisan coalition of western progressives.[21] These westerners had hoped that the Roosevelt administration would embark upon a program of monetary expansion that would result in increased purchasing

TABLE 7.2

East-West Republican Senate and House Votes: Economy Act of 1933

| | SENATE | | HOUSE | |
	East	West	East	West
Yes	14 (87.5%)	5 (33.3%)	50 (78.9%)	22 (44.9%)
No	2 (12.5%)	10 (67.7%)	14 (21.9%)	27 (55.1%)

power; instead, they argued, the overall effect of the Economy Act was deflationary. The absence of systematic "regular" Republican opposition to both the banking and economy acts simply reflected the conservative nature of these early administration proposals. Walter Lippmann noted this pattern of bipartisan approval of the bill when he wrote to Felix Frankfurter:

> I feel that you are vividly and properly aware of the influence of wealth and vested interests in government policy, but that you do not give sufficient weight to the effect on government by the pressure of organized minorities like the veterans, the prohibitionists, the farmers, etc. The government is subject to distorting influence from a relatively small class of wealthy people and from the distorting influence of a very large class of people who are not wealthy but equally selfish and dangerous. . . . Let me just say that my plea for concentration of authority for Roosevelt was not made until I had been satisfied as to the essential wisdom with which he would use such authority.[22]

Under the leadership of a Democratic president, economic orthodoxy had rapidly won victories that would never have been possible under Hoover.

Still, the Republican minority was uneasy. For one thing, the political momentum of the new administration was striking. On Thursday, March 9th, the Congress adopted the Glass-Steagall Banking Act and on Saturday, March 11th, it approved the Economy Act. Within one week, it had also disposed of the formerly intractable issue of Prohibition.

Moreover, through the vehicles of newsreels and radio "fireside chats," Roosevelt was continually more visible to the electorate than previous presidents had been. Walter Lippmann spoke to some of these concerns on a bipartisan basis when he wrote:

Of course the means are rough and, to a degree, irrational, but the process of reason in public affairs is necessarily a very slow process, and in an acute emergency you have either the choice of means that will procure the end or forgo attaining it." [23]

The lack of a spokesman of stature or authority comparable to the president was increasingly evident to the Republican congressional minority. It was also apparent that the New Deal would propose some measures that would be departures from the policies of the Hoover administration. Senator David Reed of Pennsylvania reflected the ambivalence of early Republican attitudes toward the new administration when he wrote to former President Hoover:

Most of us were willing to cooperate on the Banking Bill and the pending Economy Bill, but we served notice yesterday that cooperation would cease if he [Roosevelt] tried to pass any of the wild schemes for farm relief with which he has been flirting. [24]

In the eyes of the regular Republican minority, "wild schemes" were about to be undertaken.

Farewell to Orthodoxy: The GOP and the Passage of the NRA, the AAA, the TVA, and FERA

As noted, both the Glass-Steagall Banking Act and the Economy Act were conservative measures that reflected the influence of economic orthodoxy, so it is not surprising that they received substantial regular Republican support. However, that was not the case with most of the measures considered by the Seventy-third Congress, and the bipartisan consensus of the early days of the session rapidly disappeared. Moreover, the Republicans found themselves not only unnecessary to the passage of legislation but also hopelessly divided.

The National Industrial Recovery Act

The National Industrial Recovery Act was the cornerstone of the New Deal recovery program, an effort to restore industrial production through the exercise of positive government intervention. It was perhaps the most important legislative measure considered during the session. The proposed National Recovery Administration [NRA] was to give various industries the opportunity to establish prices, determine wages and hours, and decide other details of production appropriate to the industry in question.[25] Once established, industrial codes were to have the power of law; that is, their violation would subject individuals or firms to criminal prosecution. Trade associations, such as those developed during the 1920s, were to serve as clearinghouses for the coordination of concerns common to the members of a particular industry and were to work to make that industry more efficient without running afoul of antitrust laws. While many expectations and assumptions were factors in the drafting of the legislation, the overall thrust of the proposal suggested a framework to stimulate economic recovery.

It was felt that the famed labor provisions of Section 7-A of the act would increase employment and wage levels, thus expanding the existing purchasing power of wage earners.[26] Increased wages would benefit the entire economic system by initiating an increase in employment that would then gain momentum. In addition, it was felt that the elimination of predatory price-cutting would stabilize profit levels and encourage the expansion of business operations. The reform of "cutthroat" practices would thereby encourage economic recovery. A spirit of volunteerism was to be maintained by making initial acceptance of industry-wide codes volitional on the part of businessmen.[27] The act was a mixture of economic theory, political eclecticism, and psychological exhortation—a rapidly devised search for a way to encourage both increased employment and broad participation at a time when the social order seemed under severe threat.

From the beginning conservative Republicans were divided on the merits of the legislation. Some old guard spokesmen bitterly criticized the legislation. Congressman James Beck of Pennsylvania, solicitor general under Warren Harding, characterized the legislation as an effort "to transform a representative democracy into a virtual dictatorship in the vital matter of industry."[28] Suggesting that the bill's provisions made the federal government the effective arbiter of hours of labor, maximum output, and minimum wages, he equated such enforcement with "economic slavery, an abridgement of the freedom of individuals to engage in lawful occupations."[29] Representative Allen Treadway of Massachusetts warned that the measure could be employed by particular industries interested in obtaining competitive advantages:

> I tremble to think what the cotton manufacturers of New England might do to southern textile manufacturers if a precedent like this is established and upheld by the courts. We can say to the cotton farmer, "Neither you nor anyone for you, shall work more than three hours, or five hours, or six hours a day; you shall not pay your hired hand less than $3.00 per day—if you do it will be a crime to transport the cotton you raise in interstate commerce."[30]

Yet some conservative Republican congressmen were sympathetic to the measure. Congressman Richard Kelly of Pennsylvania admonished James Beck for preaching "a counsel of despair." Characterizing the Recovery Act as a measure that enjoyed broad support, Kelly said, "The United States Chamber of Commerce has joined hands with the Federation of Labor which most eloquently proves that neither wrote this bill but that its provisions are fair to both." Kelly thought the federal role should not be that of a dictator but that of a "guide and umpire", and he suggested that business viewed the measure as an effort "to meet the problem of destructive competition in fair and lawful manner."[31] Representative Harold Knutson of Minnesota, the ranking Republican on the Ways and Means Committee, pointed out the broad bipartisan support which the measure had attracted in committee hearings. Summing up many industrialists' views of the measure, he remarked, "This legislation will be made effective through voluntary codes and agreements entered into by groups engaged in the same industry or trade. It is designed to prevent cutthroat competition and unfair trade practices."[32] A number of Republicans introduced into the *Congressional Record* the testimony of Harry Harriman, president of the U.S. Chamber of Commerce, speaking strongly in favor of the measure.[33] The dilemma of Republican representatives over the measure basically showed that the NRA concept was indeed receiving strong support from some business sectors. In May 1933 particularly, the NRA could be seen as suggesting little more than an unprecedented peacetime collaboration between industry and government, one designed to induce economic recovery.[34] To many business leaders in 1933 the "reform" aspects of the NRA were eclipsed by the assistance it offered in avoiding antitrust problems. Throughout 1933 evaluation of the potential value of the NRA varied widely among business groups, but the U.S. Chamber of Commerce was indeed in the forefront in promoting the NRA. Romasco writes: "It [the Chamber] performed the varied roles of principal advocate of the original legislation, energetic propagandist in persuading industry to cooperate in the venture, and chief monitor of its administrative development."[35]

The NAM, by way of contrast, was concerned over the NRA's labor provisions and guarded its endorsement; it saw the Act as a product of political forces that were not sympathetic to business.[36] Thus, while sentiment against the measure was still strong among eastern Republicans, the benign outlook towards the NRA adopted by some business groups appears to have had some effect on the Republican House delegation.

In the Senate a diverse coalition of Republicans waged a desultory campaign against the measure. Even the severest critics of the NRA concept recognized the support that existed within the business community for the measure. Senator David Reed of Pennsylvania, an unreconcilable foe of the legislation, acknowledged:

> I have been approached by such concerns as big steel manufacturing companies, saying that they had thought it over and, in spite of all the theoretical disadvantages which I have been urging, they think it is going to be a good thing for the industry.[37]

Old guard Senator Simeon Fess professed to be "annoyed" at the messages of support for the legislation that had come to him from industry leaders throughout the nation.[38] He continued to object to the broad general authority to be conferred on the code-making apparatus and the potential for legal sanction against violators:

> The code which is indeterminate [and] indefinite . . . is to be established as the standard; it is written into law under an administration whose party has always, from the beginning, stood for no encumbrances on the individual.[39]

Senator Henry Hatfield of West Virginia chastened manufacturers who endorsed the measure as "shortsighted and unconscionable and only fa-

vor[ing] it as an evasion of anti-trust laws which protect the consumer."[40]
He depicted the NRA as an agency whose activities would only increase
wages and, therefore, the cost and prices of individual goods.[41] If, to
many Republican conservatives, the major issue under consideration was
the expansion of government power, to progressive Republicans such as
William Borah the problem with the NRA was the cooperation it would
encourage between the federal government and the "trusts and monopo-
lies" of the country. Borah became the leading progressive critic of the
bill, especially of its provisions for suspension of antitrust proscriptions.
Quoting from the writings of Louis Brandeis, he alleged that the measure
would result in nothing more than further concentration of wealth and a
consistent bias in favor of established industrial interests.[42] Borah wrote
to a friend at the time:

> The masses will pay for it in the end. There may be a temporary
> revival, but the price fastened upon the great body of the people
> will amount to nothing less than a crime.[43]

In the end, however, Borah received little help from other progressive
GOP senators. Although a few expressed displeasure with the NRA, the
fact that a sympathetic president was courting their approval was not lost
on these progressive Republican senators; with the exception of Borah,
all voted for the bill when it was presented for final passage on June 9.[44]
Senate party regulars, however, remained in consistent opposition to the
measure with only Charles McNary and conservative Arthur Robinson of
Indiana joining Republican insurgents in support of the bill.

When it became apparent that the measure would pass without fundamental revision, the NAM joined the Chamber of Commerce in an
appeal to American industry to give wholehearted support to NRA efforts to promote economic recovery.[45] During the six months following
the act's passage codes of fair competition were negotiated that covered
the vast proportion of American industry and commerce. An effort
to create what Ellis W. Hawley has termed "a government-sponsored
business commonwealth" was underway and the early consequences would
be disastrous for the party historically associated with American business.[46]

TABLE 7.3
East-West Breakdown of Republican Senate and House Votes: National
Industrial Recovery Act

	SENATE		HOUSE	
	East	West	East	West
Yes	0	10 (62.5%)	22 (33.8%)	34 (70.8%)
No	14 (100%)	6 (37.5%)	43 (66.2%)	14 (29.2%)

The Agricultural Adjustment Act

In the same fashion that the passage of the NRA formalized the tentative incorporation of sizable Republican industrial constituencies into the early New Deal recovery structure, the enactment of the new administration's farm program inaugurated a process of incorporation within agricultural groupings. Recent analysis of early New Deal farm policy has stressed the importance of continuous interaction between state administrative capacity and farm groups to the development of New Deal agricultural policy, and the political power of this coalition immediately split the GOP along regional lines.[47]

The Agricultural Adjustment Act [AAA] proposed by the administration provided for restrictions on the amount of acreage that could be brought into production, the reduction of farm mortgage rates, and the payment of fees to farmers who agreed to deliberately limit production. The measure could properly be viewed as a hybrid of a series of farm production control efforts and proposals that dated back to the Populist period.[48] The bill was designed to achieve an equilibrium between production and consumption of farm products, an equilibrium that had never been achieved through voluntary cooperative efforts. The control of production under force of law was the measure's major departure from Republican farm policies of the 1920s.

Upon the bill's introduction, the House Republican leadership made clear its intention to oppose the measure, with Minority Leader Snell indicating that Republican representatives would subject the entire plan to close scrutiny.[49] He admitted, however, the difficulty of fashioning consistent opposition to the legislation when he characterized the party's western representatives as "ready to jump at anything that appeared to be at the rainbow's end."[50]

The divided sentiments of the minority were evident throughout the debate on the measure. Regular Republicans made major criticisms of the concept of agricultural planning, price controls, and the potential for coercion that they depicted as inherent in the measure. At the same time, Representative Clifford Hope of Kansas declared:

> Is there any man in the cotton industry today who has the ability, knowledge and training to supervise the growing, marketing, processing and distribution of the great cotton crop of this country? . . . Under the terms of this bill, we must secure men able to supervise every branch of agricultural activity from producer to consumer.[51]

Representative Fred Britten of Illinois depicted the measure as a tax on the consumer of agricultural products, saying "You are going to pass a bill which will tax every man, woman and child $16 to $110 per year. . . . It is a tax on the essentials of life and nothing else."[52] The effect of the measure, Representative James Wadsworth of New York charged, would be the creation of an immense bureaucracy controlling the economic activity of millions.[53] Representative James Beck of Pennsylvania suggested the unconstitutionality of Congress's efforts to regulate agricultural production not engaged in interstate commerce. In a thoughtful (albeit acrimonious) speech he remarked, "I think of all the damnable heresies that have ever been suggested in connection with the Constitution, the doctrine of emergency is the worst."[54]

Such criticisms, however, did not reflect the overall Republican reaction to the AAA. Farm state Republicans defended the measure in a fashion that recalled their support of McNary-Haugenism in the 1920s. Representative William Lemke of North Dakota stated:

> The farmers of this nation are in desperation. . . . In my state and in numerous other states, mortgage foreclosures are now being stopped by force by enraged farmers who are driven to desperation in defense of their homes.[55]

Representative Roy Woodruff of Michigan felt the measure would bring about an overall rise in the agricultural price level. He added, "The people of this country have given a mandate to President Roosevelt. They want him to do whatever he can to bring relief to our people everywhere. I concur in this belief and am going to vote to give him that opportunity."[56] Representative Leroy Marshall of Ohio addressed the dilemma that many Republicans confronted when he indicated that he could not support the measure were it not for the extraordinary conditions that existed in the nation's agricultural regions. Under prevailing conditions, however, he saw no alternative.[57]

Thus, in spite of the opposition to the bill that continued among the party's eastern congressional leadership, Republican lines broke down in the end. In the House final roll call, the AAA gained the support of thirty-nine Republicans, thirty of whom came from the West.

In the Senate Republican objections were not dissimilar to those raised in the House. Senator David Reed depicted the measure as a tax on industrial workers and the consuming public generally.[58] Senator Simeon Fess characterized the legislation as a direct attack on economic liberty, "limiting him [the farmer] in his ability to care for his own business by the sale of his own product without first entering into an agreement under authority from Washington." In a preview of future arguments before the Supreme Court, Fess opined that the administration of the act involved the broad delegation of unspecified administrative authority.[59]

Again, however, regional divisions emerged. Senator Arthur Capper characterized the measure as an effort to establish some degree of security for farmers who were confronted with extraordinary conditions that antedated the depression.[60] Capper argued that the measure simply accorded to agriculture advantages that had been previously granted to industry. The regional nature of Republican reactions was again reflected in the Senate's final roll call on the measure, at which fifteen Republicans (all westerners) voted for the farm relief bill offered by the Democratic administration. Their ranks included the ten insurgent Republican Senators plus western party regulars Charles McNary, Lester Dickinson, Arthur Robinson, Thomas Schall, and Frederick Steiwer.[61] The inability of the minority party to arrive at a cogent overall response to administration's initiatives was becoming increasingly evident.

The Federal Emergency Relief Act and The Tennessee Valley Authority Act

The passage of both the Federal Emergency Relief [FERA] and the Tennessee Valley Authority [TVA] Acts again demonstrated the diffi-

TABLE 7.4

East-West Breakdown of Republican Senate and House Votes:
Agricultural Adjustment Act

| | SENATE | | HOUSE | |
	East	West	East	West
Yes	0	15 (78.9%)	9 (13.7%)	30 (60%)
No	15 (100%)	4 (21.1%)	57 (86.3%)	20 (40%)

culty of resisting the emerging power of the New Deal, along with the persistent regionalism now so evident in Republican responses. FERA provided for grants to the states (not loans, as had been the case under the Hoover administration) for the direct relief of the unemployed. While the proposal was entirely foreshadowed by Roosevelt's presidential campaign, it nevertheless elicited strong old guard Republican opposition. Supported by most of the eastern Senate bloc, Simeon Fess of Ohio led the hopeless campaign against the measure. Arguing that the bill could divorce the power to spend from the necessity to tax, he remarked:

> When we start out with a direct appropriation out of the Treasury, we have started something that vary [sic] with the degree every state will seek to fill its obligations, and the calls which will come to Washington wherever there is unemployment will be beyond count.[62]

Senator Phillips Goldsborough of Maryland stressed considerations of federalism, arguing that states that had successfully met relief burdens within their own borders "would now be required to pay in federal taxes sufficient funds to make up the sums which have gone and will go to borrowing states."[63] A minority of House Republicans voiced similar objections, while also arguing that federalization of relief efforts would discourage private charitable contributions.[64] House Republicans speaking in opposition to the measure took the general position that federal money utilized for relief should be granted as loans to the states—in short, a continuation of the Hoover administration policies.

In the end, however, the vocal protests of conservative Republican spokesmen only temporarily masked the deep divisions within their own party as to the proper response to the unfolding recovery measures of the

TABLE 7.5
East-West Breakdown of Senate and House Votes:
Federal Emergency Relief Act

	SENATE		HOUSE	
	East	West	East	West
Yes	0	13 (72.2%)	33 (51.5%)	41 (83.6%)
No	12 (100%)	5 (27.5%)	31 (48.5%)	8 (16.4%)

New Deal. Senator Arthur Robinson of Indiana, a dependable party regular, responded to Simeon Fess' pleas for continued local responsibility to the administration of relief:

> The counties cannot collect their taxes. . . . Municipalities cannot sell their bonds. The states have reached the end of their resources but, thank God, the credit of the United States is still good, and the first duty of any government is to keep its people from starving. . . . The Senator from Ohio fears it may increase taxes. . . . Let us increase taxes and get money into the treasury with which to feed the people who are starving to death.[65]

Most Western progressive Republicans, however, did not participate in floor debate on the measure, and the efforts of conservative Republicans to maintain consistent minority opposition to FERA disintegrated completely. Forty-one of forty-nine western Republican members of Congress supported the measure on the final roll call vote, and a slim majority of the eastern representatives joined them, to the consternation of the party's leadership.

The Tennessee Valley Authority

By April 1933 it was apparent to the progressive Republican bloc that this was no ordinary legislative period, and that all kinds of legislative proposals that had been previously rejected now stood an excellent chance of being adopted.[66] Of all the projects proposed unsuccessfully since 1920 by the Republican progressives, one in particular symbolized their frustrations under three Republican presidents: year after year George Norris and other progressives had fought without success for government operation and development of the Muscle Shoals area of the Tennessee River. Republican progressives felt that such a project would provide economic stimulation and capital improvement, while boosting the region's economy and increasing enormously the nation's supply of inexpensive electrical energy. Joining in these sentiments were the Democratic party's southern members of Congress, despite their historic opposition to federal intervention in the region's affairs.

As presented to the Congress in April 1933, the TVA proposed the construction of multipurpose dams that would control floods while also generating inexpensive, readily available hydroelectric power. It was also felt that such an operation might serve as an indicator of what would be a "reasonable" rate for a privately operated power company to charge. The TVA would also manufacture fertilizer, dig navigable channels, engage in conservation efforts, and generally cooperate in a host of more minor experiments in such areas as architectural design and library construction.[67]

Many accounts of the decline of the domestic New Deal have stressed the opposition that arose within the southern planter and manufacturing groups to federal interference with local governmental structures. Such resistance was sparse, however, in 1933, as the South joined in a common cause with western progressives and endorsed the creation of the TVA. The extraordinary severity of the depression combined with the crisis atmosphere of the period to overcome traditional reluctance toward federal efforts in the region.

Continuing its early pattern of incorporating potentially dissident groups, the administration proposed to rely on state and local administrators to manage the TVA's operations in the South and the West. Early TVA projects focused on such matters as river navigation and the introduction of low-cost fertilizer, along with the development of small-scale industry in rural areas. While these operations were designed to minimize interference in state and local politics, they nevertheless suggested the potential for more comprehensive intervention in the future.

To conservative Republicans of the period the entire plan hinted at a kind of utopianism run wild. More fundamentally, they objected to the precedent of government entering into the production of electric power in competition with the private power companies of the region. Representative Charles Eaton of New Jersey remarked:

TABLE 7.6

East-West Breakdown of Senate and House Votes:
Tennessee Valley Authority Act

	SENATE		HOUSE	
	East	West	East	West
Yes	0	14 (73.6%)	2 (3.1%)	16 (32%)
No	15 (100%)	5 (26.4%)	62 (96.9%)	34 (68%)

If we are to have the government in the fertilizer and power business, there is no reason why it should not go into other industries which are imbued with as much, or even more, of a public interest.[68]

Representative John Taber of New York warned that the entire project involved not only competition with industry, but additional taxation of business during a period of economic depression.[69] Senator Jesse Metcalf of Rhode Island argued that there was little need for government to embark on a series of new efforts in the midst of economic crisis.[70] In addition, six of the eight Republican members of the House Military Affairs Committee signed a minority report asserting that the creation of the TVA committed the nation to a program so sweeping and vague that it threatened the credit of the United States.[71]

Although eastern Republicans voiced most of the opposition to the creation of the Tennessee Valley Authority, the vote on the measure remains one of the few instances during the first One Hundred Days where, for the most part, the House minority party united. Only eighteen of the GOP House members voted for the legislation. House Republicans from districts outside of the regions directly affected took little interest in the measure, regarding it as special interest legislation that placed the government in competition with private industry.

In the Senate, however, the progressive bloc exhibited considerably more cohesion, with fourteen western Republicans voting for passage.

Despite the stridency of conservative Republican criticism in 1933, the more innovative period of TVA operations did not begin until 1939, when the agency became the centerpiece of the drive for southern industrialization.[72] For the Republican party, however, the effect of the establishment of the TVA was more immediate; the legislation both hastened and deepened the party's regional split between eastern conservatives and western progressives.

The Interregnum of Despair: The GOP in the First One Hundred Days

At the conclusion of the first session of the Seventy-third Congress, House Minority Leader Snell criticized the administration severely for its failure to balance the budget, its creation of an atmosphere of "uncertainty," its bureaucracy, and for the hectic pace with which it had rushed legislation through both houses of Congress. The New York representative claimed that the minority had avoided resorting to "capricious criticisms" even when it "violently disagreed" with administration proposals; on the contrary, it had registered its disagreements in a "dignified and parliamentary manner."[73] Clearly this was a highly partisan appraisal, one which minimized the fact that the large Democratic majorities in Congress precluded any effective GOP criticism. More important, Snell's statement masked the internal divisions between the western and eastern wings of his own party that now all but foreclosed any concerted action. Given the underlying bitterness between the discordant elements of the party, Republicans had little choice but to pursue a policy of restraint. Senator Simeon Fess expressed this feeling in a letter to Herbert Hoover in California:

> My deepest concern grows out of our failure to have taken definite steps in the reorganization of our party to ratify the action of those pseudo-Republicans who took themselves out of the party in the last election. Our party should have ratified that action and kept them out insofar as we could go here in the capital.[74]

At the conclusion of the One Hundred Days session on June 16 the dominant eastern wing of the Republican party seemed to have been simply overwhelmed by the sheer momentum and rapidity of events. In the space of one short session an unprecedented number of major measures had been written into law. The nation had quickly become committed to an unparalleled peacetime program of government-industry cooperation, adopted a farm program that had been consistently rejected throughout the 1920s, accepted federal responsibility for the administration of relief, dramatically expanded public works, and had finally disposed of the divisive issue of Prohibition.

President Roosevelt, in Leuchtenburg's words, "had directed the entire operation like a seasoned field general."[75] An individual previously viewed as a kind of amiable, moderately progressive governor of patrician background, Roosevelt now appeared to be a supremely confident leader who had restored hope to American life. Little in the president's prior career had enabled the Republican minority to anticipate the extraordinary congressional and mass political cooperation that Roosevelt was able to elicit during the First One Hundred Days.

Republican correspondence during this period alternately reflects bitterness, confusion, and despair. Many of the early Republican reactions to the emergency period are apparent in letters written to former President Hoover, who had now left the Waldorf-Astoria to take up residence in Stanford, California. Their tone is reflective of the dismay within party ranks. Representative James Beck of Pennsylvania wrote, "You have been much on my mind this session of Congress, which now seems to me to mark the end of our form of government. . . . I know you must view with grief, as I do, all that has happened."[76] Senator Simeon Fess confided to Hoover the frustrations of the GOP in attempting to formulate any systematic response to the legislative initiatives of the One Hundred Days period:

> It is not an easy situation to take to the floor . . . surrounded by men who are anxious for you to sit down and embarrassed because of your advocacy of fundamental principles. It is exceedingly disheartening. I do not know what is to be the outcome. . . . [I]f the President should send a message asking for a suspension of the operation of the Constitution for the time being, the message would be overwhelmingly passed by both Senate and House.[77]

Ogden Mills, Hoover's secretary of the treasury, wrote to the former president, "Politically there is no change. It is still too early to oppose or to criticize. . . . I see no signs of returning strength in the Republican party, and I see nothing about it until next fall."[78]

Hoover responded to Mills by remarking, "The large question is whether this program is simply an emergency program not a social program."[79] Senator Warren Austin of Vermont bitterly condemned the political behavior of business during the One Hundred Days session in a long letter to the former president, saying of them:

> These men are not thinking in terms of government for the long run, and are not concerned for the fundamentals of American institutions, but they are concerned with what is to happen right away from day to day.[80]

Still, not all Republican reaction was so uniformly pessimistic. Senator George Norris wrote friend that "Roosevelt is the first president we have had for a great many years who sympathizes with the underdog. . . . I am with him in his fight."[81] William Allen White wrote to Harold Ickes, "How do you account for him [Roosevelt]? Was I just fooled in him [sic] before the election or has he developed?" Having supported Hoover in the 1932 campaign, White concluded, "I have been a voracious feeder in the course of a long and happy life and have eaten many things, but I have never had to eat my words before."[82] In the aftermath of the One Hundred Days legislative period, perhaps the only matter upon which the Republican minority could agree was the surprising dimension of Franklin Roosevelt's leadership.

Second Session of the Seventy-Third Congress

As the second session of the Seventy-third Congress approached, Republican responses continued to be characterized by the factionalism that had marked the first session. Acknowledging this, Senator McNary and Representative Snell decided at a strategy meeting not to undertake a specific course of action. It was judged wiser to simply respond to the policy initiatives of the administration. "It is not the part of the minority to offer a legislative program, and therefore we will not have an affirmative program," Snell remarked.[83] Senator McNary adopted a similar position. While announcing a Republican Senate Caucus for January 2, 1934, McNary made it clear that no attempt would be made to define a systematic program for the minority party. Further, no efforts would be made to pledge Republican senators to attacks on Democratic recovery policies.[84] Clearly, McNary had rejected any thoughts of systematic assaults on administration recovery legislation. Robert Allen White wrote to William Allen White:

McNary is strongly opposed to any general flaying. I had [a] private talk with him. . . . His attitude [is that the] Republicans ought to lay low, cooperate where possible and let [the] Democrats have full responsibility for [the] record.[85]

McNary's predispositions aside, it is important to recognize that the overall lack of forthright policies on the part of the minority was primarily the result of the inability of the Republicans to agree on a position toward the administration's recovery program. Republican leaders, increasingly wary of exacerbating unresolvable divisions among themselves, simply agreed to let the eastern and western factions of the party each determine their own course.

The Gold Recovery Act of 1934

The measures to be considered here from the second session of the Seventy-third Congress concerned monetary policy and regulation of the securities market. The debate surrounding the Gold Recovery Act of 1934, the first important act of the session, is revealing of the theoretical limitations of Republican economic analysis during the early 1930s period. Prior to the popularization of Keynesian analysis after 1936 (and the later contributions of the Chicago school), regular Republican leaders often had little to offer save the "sound money" platitudes reminiscent of the campaign of 1896. In addition, the effects of inflation in Weimar Germany clearly weighed heavily on the minds of Republican leaders after 1930. Thus virtually any proposal for monetary expansion in the early 1930s was viewed negatively.

As a result, when the president requested the authority to devalue the gold content of the dollar as part of a tentative monetary inflation program, responses to the measure were reminiscent of the controversies of 1896. Financial leaders and business journals criticized the president for currency manipulation, while proponents of inflation in the South and West rallied to the president's support.

Republican reactions echoed earlier regional divisions. Eastern Republicans criticized the proposal on a number of grounds. To conservatives such as Senator David Reed, devaluation was an act of "immorality and dishonesty."[86] Representative Robert Luce of Massachusetts said, "We shall deprive part of the citizens of this country of a huge amount of

TABLE 7.7
East-West Breakdown of Republican Senate and House Votes:
The Gold Recovery Act of 1934

	SENATE		HOUSE	
	East	West	East	West
Yes	0	11 (52.3%)	34 (52.3%)	37 (78.7%)
No	13 (100%)	10 (48.7%)	31 (47.7%)	10 (21.3%)

property, by compelling them to turn it over to the government of the United States."[87] Congressman Hamilton Fish, Jr., of New York characterized the bill as "repudiation, confiscation and capital levy" on the wage earners of the nation.[88]

Senators David Reed and Frederick Walcott, along with Representatives Bertrand Snell and Robert Luce, issued a joint statement criticizing the administration's proposal as "the first step on the German road to ruin" whereby the administration could "resort to the printing press and the issuance of fiat currency."[89]

Republicans also objected to the supervision of the entire gold devaluation process by the office of the secretary of the treasury. While recognizing the power of the national government to reclaim gold through the power of eminent domain, they argued that this transferred much of the nation's wealth "into the maelstrom of partisan politics" from which it might not emerge.[90] By this view, a highly politicized authority (the secretary of the Treasury) was supplanting an agency less subject to political pressure (the Federal Reserve Board). But the Republicans quickly became aware that efforts to prevent devaluation would be fruitless and accordingly, shifted their focus to attempts to restrict the management role of the Treasury Department. In cooperation with conservative Democrats, such as Senator Carter Glass of Virginia, Republicans sought to have the entire devaluation process placed under the direction of an independent board. In a rare show of partisan unity, twenty-nine Republican Senators supported an unsuccessful amendment designed to establish such a board.[91] On the final roll call concerning devaluation, however, the regional character of party responses was again determinative. Eleven Republicans, all westerners, voted for the act, viewing it as a measure that would increase regulation of eastern financial interests. In the House the objections of GOP leaders were apparently unpersuasive, as seventy-one Republican members supported the measure. It was clear that much of the congressional minority was showing little interest in arraying itself against the politically popular New Deal, even on less salient issues.

The Securities and Exchange Act of 1934

The second major piece of legislation proposed in the session arose out of congressional investigations into fraudulent securities transactions in the 1920s and involved consideration of greater and more stringent federal regulation of securities transactions. The Securities and Exchange Act would empower the Federal Trade Commission [FTC] to supervise the issuance of new securities, require the publication of certain financial information on each stock issue, and make issuers liable for any misrepresentation which occurred.[92] The measure occasioned delight among some progressives who believed that Wall Street wielded disproportionate power over the national economy, and had certainly been partially responsible for the onset of depression.

The bill seemed, however, to be at odds with the administration's early philosophy of a government-business commonwealth and drew sharp criticism from regular Republicans. Representative Schuyler Merritt of Connecticut argued that the first prerequisite of industrial recovery was increased business confidence, and that the widespread uncertainty about the effects of the measure could only retard industrial activity.[93] The bill, in his view, was not primarily a means to control stock market abuses, but rather a crippling regulatory measure. In the words of Representative Carroll Beedy of Maine:

> The bill imposes upon the vast business interests concerned the obligation of complying with such additional requirements . . . as are deemed necessary for the protection of investors in the pure discretion of the Federal Trade Commission.[94]

Representative Merritt also charged that undeniable stock market abuse was being used as an excuse to impose costs on and exert control over every manufacturing and corporate interest in the nation. Congressman Charles Bakewell, also from Connecticut, argued that the burden of reporting requirements would be felt disproportionately by smaller com-

TABLE 7.8

East-West Breakdown of Republican Senate and House Votes:
The Securities and Exchange Act of 1934

	SENATE		HOUSE	
	East	**West**	**East**	**West**
Yes	0	15 (83.3%)	8 (12.5%)	20 (42.5%)
No	11 (100%)	3 (16.7%)	56 (87.5%)	27 (57.5%)

panies and would inhibit industrial innovation.[95] Summarizing the Republican case, Representative Everett Dirksen of Illinois asked, "Are we going to load additional impediments, additional obstacles, additional burdens upon the slim thread of recovery at the present time?"[96]

In the House of Representatives Republican opposition to the measure was relatively firm, as the bill seemed to depart from the concept of business-government cooperation. Only twenty-eight House Republicans voted for the measure. In the Senate, however, the minority again split along regional lines. Fifteen Republican senators, all of them from the West, supported the regulatory measure, while all eleven eastern Senators opposed passage. Once again the Republican minority was wracked by its own internal schisms.

The Republican Party in the Seventy-Third Congress

The initial Republican reaction to the New Deal was shaped by the factionalism that beleaguered the party throughout the 1920s. While the divided, demoralized character of party responses was undeniable, several distinctive patterns emerged. The most important was the ongoing regional conservative-progressive schism that had plagued the party's congressional delegation even during its majority days. This was a far more visible problem in the Congress than was the diminution of support from upper-income constituents (which could be blamed on "hard times").

Thus, from the dominant eastern wing of the party, there was a consistent disapproval of most New Deal legislative efforts. In the Senate, this hard core of opposition followed such old guard eastern stalwarts as David Reed of Pennsylvania, Frederick Walcott of Connecticut, Daniel Hastings of Delaware, and Frederick Hale of Maine. Generally allied with them were a few conservative midwestern and western Senators,

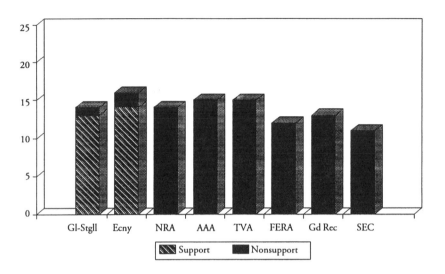

FIGURE 7.1
Seventy-third Congress: Eastern Senate Republicans

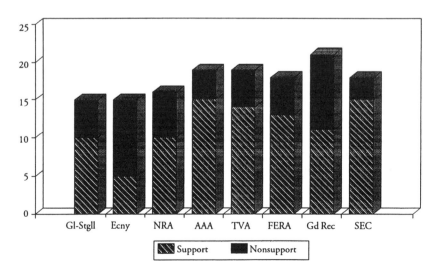

FIGURE 7.2
Seventy-third Congress: Western Senate Republicans

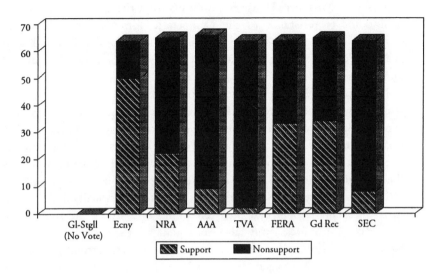

FIGURE 7.3
Seventy-third Congress: Eastern House Republicans

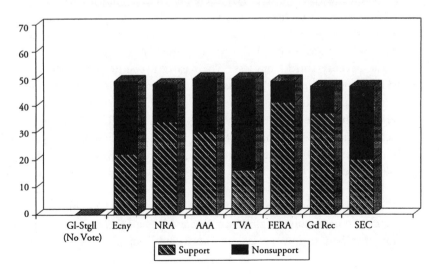

FIGURE 7.4
Seventy-third Congress: Western House Republicans

such as Simeon Fess of Ohio, Lester Dickinson of Iowa and Roscoe Patterson of Missouri. House Republicans from the East also provided a focal point of resistance to the Democratic administration, centering primarily around the leadership of House Minority Leader Bertrand Snell of New York and other members of the New York, Pennsylvania, and Massachusetts delegations.

In the party's western delegation, however, efforts to present a systematic response to New Deal initiatives had failed completely. The western wing of the party simply did not have the consistent hostility to New Deal programs evident in the East. Of all the GOP factions, the progressive western senatorial contingent had shown the least antagonism toward the emerging New Deal, their support being based on both progressive ideology and regional self-interest—the latter specifically reflected in their votes on agricultural and relief measures. Western Republican members of Congress were also consistent in their support of many New Deal measures, due primarily to the particularly strong progressive influence in the Wisconsin, North Dakota, Michigan, Iowa, and Pacific Coast states' delegations.

While aggregate Republican voting patterns reflected greater opposition to, than support of, the new Democratic administration, these statistics obscure the persistent nature of the regional schisms so apparent within the party throughout 1933. Figures 7.1 and 7.2 summarize the east-west voting patterns of Republicans during the Seventy-third Congress and illustrate quite clearly these persistent regional divisions.

The immediate effect of the One Hundred Days period was to split the party wide-open along regional lines. The eastern senatorial contingent had averaged only 24.5 percent approval of the legislative initiatives of the Seventy-third Congress. Their eastern counterparts in the House had supported New Deal proposals 34.6 percent of the time. In contrast, western Senate Republicans had supported the administration 65.9 percent of the time, while their colleagues in the House had voted for Democratic recovery efforts 58.8 percent of the time. Generally speaking, Republicans in the Senate seemed to feel freer to express dissent than did their colleagues in the House, all of whom would face the electorate in 1934.

At bottom, the nation and much of the Congress had consented to an exercise in mass politics, dramatic leadership, and economic experimentation that had simply passed by the Republican party. Unprepared for their rapid descent to minority status, most of the party's congressional members had either been swept along by events or were simply obstructionist. Little party-wide strategy had been developed by the Republican minority during the session. Aware of the widespread feeling that the economic cycles predicted by the old orthodoxy had stopped moving, many Republicans had willingly accepted a secondary role during the congressional session.

CHAPTER EIGHT

"Defending the American Way of
Life": The Republican Party in the
Seventy-Fourth Congress

•

Whereas the Seventy-third Congress met in an atmosphere of national crisis that limited Republican criticism, circumstances had changed by the time the Seventy-fourth Congress convened in January 1935. Partisan criticism was again legitimate and the 1935–early 1936 period would see Republican strategists and leaders increase the "issue space" between it and the Democratic party in a fashion that led to the consummation of the realignment of the 1930s. While recent literature examining the passage of social legislation has emphasized the important role of political elites during the 1935–1936 period, the importance of GOP reactions remains underappreciated.[1]

The administration's legislative proposals to the Seventy-fourth Congress presented a different kind of challenge to the Republican minority than was the case with the Seventy-third Congress. New Deal efforts in the Seventy-fourth Congress moved beyond the initial utilization of large industry and agriculture to foster economic recovery, into a broader concern with overall social reform. The Seventy-third Congress considered only a few measures, such as the Economy Act and the Glass-Steagall Banking Act, that reflected the influence of economic orthodoxy. The Seventy-Fourth Congress however, sought to interpose the power of the federal government to bolster industrial unionism, establish social insurance, and alter patterns of taxation and the organization of utility companies.

In the context of the heightened partisan battles of 1935 many of the measures considered in the session appeared to many Republicans as unprecedented in both effect and scope. As in the Seventy-third Congress, however, party responses continued to be shaped by the regional divisiveness that was becoming such a source of concern to the GOP's electoral strategists.

The Republican minority of the Seventy-fourth Congress had suffered further attrition in the 1934 congressional elections and now numbered only 104 representatives and 25 senators. Although severely weakened, eastern conservative leadership remained in nominal control in both houses. In the Senate the 10-member eastern wing of the party was composed of: Frederick Hale and Wallace White of Maine, Ernest Gibson and Warren Austin of Vermont, Daniel Hastings and John Townsend of Delaware, Henry Keyes of New Hampshire, Jesse Metcalf of Rhode Island, Warren Barbour of New Jersey, and James Davis of Pennsylvania. This eastern contingent was joined by a western faction of 6 "regulars" that included Arthur Vandenberg of Michigan, Lester Dickinson of Iowa, Robert Carey of Wyoming, Frederick Steiwer of Oregon, and Thomas Schall of Minnesota.

With the exception of Robert La Follette, Jr. (who had taken on the Progressive Party label), the party's entire progressive wing in the Senate had been returned intact. Its members again included Gerald Nye and Lynn Frazier of North Dakota, Hiram Johnson of California, William Borah of Idaho, Peter Norbeck of South Dakota, James Couzens of Michigan, Bronson Cutting of New Mexico, Arthur Capper of Kansas, and George Norris of Nebraska. However, the 9 insurgent senators and the sympathetic Charles McNary of Oregon continued to constitute a minority—within the minority party.

In the House conservative Republicans predominated. Of the 51 eastern House Republicans, most were extremely conservative, with the Bertrend Snell—led group from the New York, Massachusetts, Pennsylvania, and Connecticut delegations at the forefront. The western House Republican contingent totaled 53, but its insurgent component had been reduced by electoral attrition and by defections. The progressive Republican element in the House now numbered no more than 15, and its membership was scattered among several western states. Prominent among its ranks were William Lemke of North Dakota, Lloyd Thurston of Iowa, and Karl Stefan of Nebraska.

The Legislation of the Seventy-Fourth Congress

No attempt has been made here to examine the legislation of the Seventy-fourth Congress through an additional typology. The landmark social legislation of the session generally met with strong regular eastern Republican opposition, while the party's regional groups operated with renewed force. The only exception was the Social Security Act, where the failure of a recommit vote produced a rush to support the legislation on the final vote. The vehement Republican congressional criticism of the session underscores the confusion among party leaders over the interpretation of political trends at that time.

The Public Utility Holding Company Act

James Patterson notes in his study of congressional conservatism within the Democratic party that the debate over the utilities holding company legislation was an important event: "For the first time, moderate as well as irreconcilable Senate Democrats voted against an important New Deal measure."[2] In short, the bill became an early benchmark vote in the evolution of the conservative congressional coalition. In the case of the GOP, however, the act was simply one of several that party regulars opposed during that session, as the "issue space" between the parties began to increase.

The Public Utility Holding Company Act, which engendered broad conservative criticism, had two primary components. The first simply provided for federal coordination and integration of such holding companies along more efficient lines. But the second contained what quickly became a controversial "death sentence" provision.[3] The provision empowered the Securities and Exchange Commission (SEC) to take steps to simplify the complex structure of holding company operations in the field of electric power production. While it was hoped that utility companies would cooperate with SEC efforts at simplification, the bill nevertheless authorized the SEC to compel the dissolution, by 1940, of all holding companies that could not demonstrate to the commission a sound economic rationale for their existence.[4] Even before the "Second One Hundred Days" program, the president had shown interest in efforts to break up the complex nature of utility company organization. This reflected not only the influence of Brandeisian liberals within the administration, but also the widespread publicity given to a series of abuses attributable to the holding company structure.[5] Popular outrage had followed from investigations of some power companies' efforts to influence state legislatures and avoid state regulation.

The "death sentence" section of the legislation became a rallying point for Republican opposition to the bill. Conservative Republicans focused their strongest criticism on the effect that they predicted such legislation would have on economic recovery. Senator Daniel Hastings of Delaware warned

> We shall find that fear of the effect of this bill will cause, indeed has caused, people to go headlong into their broker's offices or to their bankers and insist upon disposing of their utilities' stock. . . . That of itself is disturbing to them, disturbing to the country and, in my judgment, does not add anything to the progress of the nation.[6]

Hastings also defended the economies of scale that, he argued, the holding company structure produced:

> It became necessary for the holding company—for instance, in order to develop a new industry or to enlarge an old industry—to offer the public a diversification in the investment which it made. This could only be done through the holding company. The fact that the holding company . . . has since that time, because of the greed which runs throughout human nature, permitted certain abuses to grow . . . is not a good reason why one should say it is in the interest of the public to get rid of the holding company as an institution.[7]

Moreover, the specter of systematic federal control of private sector organizations increasingly came to concern Republican spokesmen. Senator Lester Dickinson of Iowa remarked:

> I have here the record only for the year 1928, but it shows that in that year there were 573 active corporations listed on the recognized

stock exchanges, of which 487 were holding companies. I wonder whether or not in now setting the precedent in this field in which the government is going to assume control, we are opening the way for federal control of types of businesses other than public-utility corporations.[8]

Senator Wallace White of Maine, speaking in the immediate aftermath of the *Schechter* decision, concluded:

Congress here seeks to pass on to the Commission [SEC] almost plenary powers of regulation and control, with no adequate definition of those to be regulated, and no definite or definable rule to guide or control the Commission in its task.[9]

Again, however, the party's western insurgents sharply disagreed. Senator George Norris of Nebraska stated:

The absurdities into which the holding company system leads . . . [affect not only] the consumers of electricity, but also the honest investors in securities. . . . In all the years of my investigations, I have been unable to find a single instance where a holding company in the second degree is of any benefit to society.[10]

Referring to the strong lobbying effort that utility interests had mounted against the measure, Senator Norris said:

We are hesitating now because through their power they have covered this country with a network of propaganda never before known or equalled . . . which [is] coming every day now in the shape of telegrams and letters to the members of this body to save the "poor investors." Unless we pass some bill such as this to prevent this kind of depredation against the people, the whole [holding company] structure will ultimately collapse.[11]

Conservative House Republicans voiced objections similar to those of their colleagues in the Senate. Congressman Pehr Holmes of Massachusetts charged that the proposal would adversely affect economic recovery and was "reform conceived in prejudice."[12] Holmes's colleague from

TABLE 8.1

East-West Breakdown of Republican Senate and House Votes:
The Public Utility Holding Company Act

| | SENATE | | HOUSE | |
	East	West	East	West
Yes	0	9 (64.2%)	7 (13.7%)	20 (39.2%)
No	10 (100%)	5 (35.8%)	44 (86.3%)	31 (60.8%)

Massachusetts, Charles Gifford, characterized industry as prepared to "proceed with recovery if the government would relax its heavy hand."[13] Congressman Schuyler Merritt of Connecticut suggested that the development of a pattern of centralized political control over the private sector was gaining inexorable momentum.[14] Congressman Carl Mapes of Michigan foresaw the possibility of confiscation of property "without due process of law" that would lead to the demoralization of both business and the investing public.[15]

On the final roll calls, eastern and western conservative Republicans in both houses opposed the Public Utility Holding Company Act quite solidly. In the Senate, however, the conservative-progressive split maintained its old strength, as all nine members of the party's insurgent westerners voted for the act.[16] In the House, by contrast, only twenty-seven Republican congressmen voted for the act; seven eastern and twenty western congressmen made up this total.[17] Despite the increasing stridency of the Republicans, party unity remained an elusive goal.

The National Labor Relations Act (The Wagner Act)

The depth of the disaffection of Republican regulars was again demonstrated during the debate over the landmark Wagner Act. The National Labor Relations Act, as it was officially called, placed the power of the national government squarely behind the right of labor to bargain collectively, while compelling employers to accede to peaceful efforts to unionize their plants. A National Labor Relations Board [NLRB] would be empowered, not only to recognize collective bargaining units, but to issue "cease and desist" orders against employers whose actions were defined as unfair to labor's bargaining units. While the right to unionize had been recognized previously, the Wagner Act strongly asserted the right to organizational efforts, ending the earlier "benign neglect" that had been characteristic of national policy.[18] Both the passage and the later implementation of the Wagner Act were bitterly resisted by all types of business and industry groups, and enforcement of its policies became a serious concern in the face of systematic employer resistance.[19]

It should come as no surprise that conservative Republicans displayed little enthusiasm for the National Labor Relations Act. Unfortunately, a complete reconstruction of Republican congressional sentiment is difficult. In the whirlwind of the Second One Hundred Days, Congress passed the measure after limited debate and only a few roll calls; indeed, final House passage was accomplished without a roll call vote.[20] There is evidence, however, of the overall nature of Republican attitudes. Senator Daniel Hastings of Delaware took up much of the time alloted to minority speakers and focused his objections on giving federal legal support to the "closed shop":

> Is it not true that the individual worker should be free to decline association with his fellows? In what condition do we find the worker who is in the minority? . . . If the employer so desires and the majority of the labor union so desires, they may make an agreement whereby no one may be employed in the establishment unless he belongs to that union.[21]

Congressman John Taber of New York followed up this line of reasoning by offering an amendment that would have limited NLRB authority to create single labor bargaining units within plants, but his amendment was quickly defeated by a voice vote of 78 to 43.[22] Walter Lippmann was equally disaffected, and in the midst of the controversy he wrote:

> It is a bad bill. It extends the scope of the government's responsibility beyond the government's power to discharge that responsibility. It sets up undefined rights and proposes to enforce them by the cumbersome process of litigation and prosecution. It distorts the decisive elections by the untrue assumption that elections will show a clear majority. . . . The bill should, I believe, be scrapped, and wholly a different bill drafted. It should be limited to a relatively small number of large industries that are unmistakably interstate in

character. For those industries government intervention backed by legal compulsion should be limited to the conduct of free elections. Beyond that the government should make no effort to use compulsion to promote unionism or collective bargaining, but should confine itself to mediation and conciliation. This much it might hope to do effectively. To attempt more than it can do effectively is to create trouble for everyone.[23]

In contrast, Senator George Norris of Nebraska saw the measure as redressing a fundamental imbalance in the employment relationship: "The employer has almost unlimited economic power in dealing with the affairs of the employee." In addition, he spoke of the long time use of the judicial injunction against labor's efforts to organize: "The history of these injunctions shows that the general trend was to construe the laws as capital wanted them to be construed."[24]

Despite the absence of a recorded vote, House Republicans were afforded more opportunities during debate on the measure to express their opinions. The recently announced *Schechter* decision, in which the Supreme Court ruled against the improper delegation of "legislative authority" under the NRA to the executive branch, provided the basis for some Republican objections. Representative Robert Rich of Pennsylvania, referring to the decision's recital of limitations on federal control of goods not in interstate commerce, said:

It is clear to me that a dispute between employer and employee about plucking poultry . . . is a dispute not in commerce but in production. . . . As in other acts, the relation of an employer and employee engaged in manufacture or local service also has no direct relation to interstate commerce.[25]

He likened the proposed National Labor Relations Board to "a gigantic police court, for employers may be summoned from every part of the United States on any kind of petty dispute . . . and this would breed strikes as fast as a fish lays eggs." Finally, Rich maintained that the Wagner Act would work only to the benefit of a small minority of workers who were represented, while generating industrial strife that would substantially impede economic recovery.[26] Representatives Frederick Lehlbach of New Jersey and Charles Halleck of Indiana also argued

TABLE 8.2
East-West Breakdown of Republican
Senate Vote: National Labor
Relations Act

SENATE

	East	West
Yes	3 (30%)	10 (83.3%)
No	7 (70%)	2 (16.7%)

As mentioned previously, passage in the House was by
voice vote.

that, in the aftermath of the *Schechter* decision, there was no constitutional basis for the enactment of the measure. Halleck said, "We have no moral and no legal right to enact any law in contravention of the Constitution.[27] Representative Rich added that the act would simply promote industrial strife while lowering the overall wages paid within industries.[28] The only Republicans who commented favorably on the measure were Representatives Vito Marcantonio of New York and William Ekwell of Oregon, neither of whom delivered complete addresses.

In the Senate's final roll call on the bill, thirteen Republicans supported the measure. Senators Warren Barbour, James Davis and Wallace White joined ten western insurgents in voting for the bill.[29] Once again, eastern conservatives took the lead in expressing the bitter opposition of the GOP (and its industrial allies) to the measure. Little thought was now given to rapprochement.

The Wealth Tax Act of 1935

President Roosevelt also jolted conservatives in both parties with the introduction of the Wealth Tax Act of 1935. The measure called for major revisions in the tax code that included increased taxes on gifts, inheritances, and high incomes. The proposal also levied an excess profits tax and raised the graduated corporate tax rate.[30] The measure reflected the changed political sensibilities of the "Second New Deal." Its submission, in Leuchtenburg's words, "raised an outcry from business and the press such as had greeted none of the President's previous recommendations."[31] While the proposal stopped far short of efforts to redistribute

national wealth, it did reflect presidential disillusionment with the steadily rising tide of business criticism, and it was a tacit recognition of the
now persistent political appeal of Huey Long.[32]

The Republican congressional delegation was sharply critical of the
measure. The bill, in Senator Arthur Vandenberg's words, was a "tin foil
measure which snipes inconclusively at wealth, but which will neither
produce revenue commensurate with our spending nor achieve any useful
social purpose." While the measure was not designed to increase taxes on
middle or lower incomes, Vandenberg argued that the "workers may
never see a tax bill, but they pay, in deduction from wages and in
increased costs of what they buy or in broad cessation of employment."[33]
The ultimate effect of the proposal, he maintained, would be to drive
"wealth out of dynamic industrial investments and into static, tax-
exempt bonds."[34] Senator Warren Barbour of New Jersey argued along
similar lines: "Excessive taxes do not distribute wealth. They destroy it.
Wealth vanishes as the proceeds of taxes are collected and spent."[35]

In the House Representative Allen Treadway of Massachusetts argued
that the amount of money raised by the increased levels of taxation would
be insignificant. He also maintained that the redistributive features of
the measure would be minimal: "If the three hundred million of additional receipts were divided among the entire population, it would mean
only about two dollars and twenty-five cents per capita."[36]

The mere consideration of the measure provoked strong Republican
response. Senators Charles L. McNary and Daniel O. Hastings offered
a motion to adjourn the Congress until November of 1935 without
consideration of the Wealth Tax measure.[37] The defeated motion, designed primarily to embarrass the administration, read, in part,

> Further resolved, that between the day of adjournment and Novem-
> ber 18, 1935, the proper committees of the two houses are re-
> quested to study the financial condition of the government as to
> income and expenses and make such recommendations as they find
> necessary to balance the budget and begin the reduction of the
> national debt.[38]

The Republican members of the House Ways and Means Committee
also issued a minority report that portrayed the proposal as a "political
gesture" that, in their judgment, "came at a time when the administra-

TABLE 8.3

East-West Breakdown of Republican Senate and House Votes: The Wealth
Tax of 1935

| | SENATE | | HOUSE | |
	East	West	East	West
Yes	0	7 (36.8%)	3 (6.1%)	16 (30.2%)
No	10 (100%)	12 (63.2%)	46 (93.9%)	37 (69.8%)

tion's popularity and prestige were rapidly on the decline." The report
went on to quote such conservative Democrats as Carter Glass and Lewis
Douglas on the effects of the measure.[39] Representative Hamilton Fish,
Jr., of New York characterized the bill as one that would "drive surplus
capital away from private industry and charitable institutions into tax-
exempt securities."[40]

Business was unremitting in its opposition to the tax measure. The
NAM, the U.S. Chamber of Commerce, and the American Mining
Congress, among others, denounced the plan as one that would prolong
the depression while harming millions of investors in industry.[41] Thus,
while the plan may have been an effective political appeal for the administration in the increasingly uncertain political climate of 1935, it also
spawned vehement, systematic protest from conservative groups throughout the country. Eastern Republicans cooperated with conservative Democrats in a successful effort to remove the intercorporate dividend tax, to
reduce the increases in proposed graduated corporate tax rates, and to
otherwise water down the measure in committee hearings.[42]

In the end, Republicans were uncharacteristically solid in opposing
the measure's final passage. In the Senate only seven western insurgent
Republicans voted for the measure.[43] Only nineteen House Republicans
supported final passage, sixteen of them western representatives.[44] The
tentative, uncertain responses of the Republicans of the Seventy-third
Congress were now far less in evidence. The breakup of the earlier all-
class coalition of the New Deal was restoring a measure of combativite-
ness to the GOP.

The Social Security Act of 1935

Despite its regressive financing provisions, the Social Security Act of
1935 constituted a milestone in American social and political history.

The act established a national system of old-age insurance in which both employers and employees were required to participate. It revised historical assumptions about the nature of social and individual responsibility and codified the principle that the individual had certain basic claims before society.

From the beginning, there was strong conservative Republican opposition to both the principle and the administration of the proposed system.[45] Major opposition came from eastern conservatives and a few western party regulars. Senator Daniel Hastings of Delaware argued that the social security fund would be subject to a variety of demands that would prevent its retention in a separate fund established for retired workers: "Does anybody believe that such a huge sum of money, accumulated for any purpose, could be preserved intact?"[46] The fund would be dissipated by Congress, he maintained, and the increasing cost of the program paid for out of general revenue.[47] Hastings wrote to Ogden Mills concerning a speech that Mills had given in New York:

I am delighted that you left out a thing that is appealing to so many people, namely, social security. I am satisfied that we can never rebuild the Republican party with that as a part of its foundation.[48]

Senator Charles McNary, however, sharply disagreed, remarking:

It must be evident to the most determined individualist that in most instances, old-age dependency in the United States is not due to individual maladjustment, but to social and economic forces which the individual cannot hope to govern.[49]

In the House Republicans portrayed the measure as an additional burden on business. Representative Allen Treadway of Massachusetts noted that "the taxes imposed will be collected from business operations in the red as well as those fortunate enough to make a profit." He also maintained that the measure would retard capital formation: "Not only is business going to be affected by the direct burden imposed upon it, but it is going to feel the effect of reducing the purchasing power of employed individuals."[50] Representative Harold Knutson of Minnesota also portrayed the measure as retarding economic recovery, remarking:

I am convinced that at this time the annuity and unemployment conditions constitute a serious threat to recovery because they impose two distinct payroll taxes, one of which falls entirely upon the employer and the other jointly upon the employer and employee.

Repeating a now familiar Republican refrain, Knutson maintained: "The prime need of the hour is recovery, not social reform. . . . There is no compelling reason for taking [these questions] up at this time."[51] Representative James Wadsworth of New York felt that the effects of the undertaking of minimum income guarantees by a democracy would be economically disastrous, arguing that "once we pay pensions and supervise annuities, we cannot withdraw from the undertaking no matter how demoralizing and subversive it may become."[52] Other House Republicans indicated their disapproval of the measure in a minority report issued by Republican members of the House Ways and Means Committee.[53] In the Senate Daniel Hastings of Delaware proposed an amendment that would have limited the payroll tax on small businesses, an amendment that was decisively defeated.[54] A last-ditch effort by the Republican House leadership to recommit the measure to committee for further study was also voted down by a margin of 253 to 149.

Despite the overall tenor of most Republican commentary as presented in the *Congressional Record,* it then became apparent that there was no way to prevent final passage of the act.

The final roll call on the measure demonstrated the unwillingness of many conservative Republicans to actually cast votes against the legislation, which passed by a margin of 372 to 33 in the House and 77 to 6 in the Senate.[55] The *New York Herald Tribune* commented: "There was a general rush to go on record for social security legislation."[56] As a result, an accurate index of Republican attitudes toward the legislation is reflected in the Senate vote on Daniel Hastings's amendment to limit payroll taxes and in the effort of the House Republican leadership to recommit the bill. Both have been considered here in lieu of the final, lopsided vote on passage which does not reflect the true opposition to the measure. In both tables below a "yes" vote should be interpreted as an antiadministration vote. Thus, even the politically popular Social Security Act—in many ways an extension of earlier Progressive Era statewide legislation—engendered substantial Republican opposition in the atmosphere of 1935. Despite the continued existence of the party's eastern

TABLE 8.4
East-West Breakdown of Republican
Senate Vote: Hastings Amendment to
Social Security Act of 1935

| | SENATE | |
	East	West
No	2 (20%)	6 (60%)
Yes	8 (80%)	4 (40%)

TABLE 8.5
East-West Breakdown of Republican House
Vote: Motion to Recommit:
Social Security Act of 1935

| | HOUSE | |
	East	West
No	2 (2%)	0
Yes	50 (98%)	53 (100%)

conservative-western insurgent split, Republicans effectively closed ranks in the House on the motion to recommit.

The Soil Conservation and Domestic Allotment Act

While the problem of industrial-governmental relations was the central focus of the Seventy-fourth Congress, agricultural questions also received attention. Early in 1936 the Supreme Court held the processing tax of the AAA unconstitutional.[57] The effect of this decision was to limit severely the ability of the federal government to disburse subsidies to farmers, forcing the administration to find a new mechanism to distribute such subsidies without incurring further Court disapproval. The Soil Conservation and Domestic Allotment Act provided payments to farmers for not planting certain soil-depleting crops and for growing soil-enriching grasses and soybeans.[58]

Eastern Republicans were almost uniformly hostile to the proposal, viewing the measure as an unnecessary delegation of power to an administrative agency. Representative Charles Tobey of New Hampshire maintained:

> We are shortly to raise by taxation one-half billion dollars to be placed in the hands of the Secretary of Agriculture, and the only limitations curtailing him are confined to what the Congress sets forth the object of the bill to be.[59]

In addition, the minority portrayed the measure as an effort to influence elections in agricultural regions. Congressman Tobey further suggested that the bill be retitled an effort "to continue the flow of government checks to the vast voting agricultural population" in anticipation of the 1936 election.[60]

Republican attitudes also showed the influence of particular sectional farming interests. Continued opposition to the measure came from congressional Republicans representing livestock and dairy farmers; these constituents felt that the bill completely ignored their interests. House Minority Leader Snell, an upstate New York Representative, summarized this view when he remarked, "Your favored farmers in the south and west receive government checks and our farmers help to furnish the money to make these checks good." Representative Snell also felt that the measure would simply result in increased competition for eastern farmers:

> This bill threatens to undo recent progress by the dairy farmer. . . . Land now producing cotton, wheat and corn will be taken out of production . . . and there will be a greatly increased production in dairy products and livestock.[61]

Thus, Republican reaction embodied both broad philosophical objections and the influence of particular regional constituencies. Accordingly, in the end large portions of both wings of the party voted against the agricultural measure. Eastern Republicans continued to object to government "interference" in agriculture and the administration of price supports in general. Some western Republicans remained unhappy with production restrictions, and others viewed particular provisions of the bill as unfavorable to their own local agricultural interests. In the Senate Republican support consisted of the votes of only six western insurgents.[62] In the House only twenty-one Republicans, twenty of whom were from the west, voted for the measure.[63] Thus the party's preoccupation with recapturing the western United States often mixed uneasily with its newfound stridency.

TABLE 8.6
East-West Breakdown of Republican Senate and House Votes:
The Soil Conservation and Allotment Act of 1936

	SENATE		HOUSE	
	East	West	East	West
Yes	0	6 (46.1%)	1 (2%)	20 (39.2%)
No	9 (100%)	7 (53.9%)	49 (98%)	31 (60.8%)

The Republicans in the Seventy-Fourth Congress

As the Seventy-fourth Congress took place, the "issue space" between the parties began to increase. The chief characteristic of the session was the opposition of the GOP's dominant congressional elements to the general direction of most New Deal reform. Congressional debates and roll calls demonstrate the persistence of conservative Republican opposition even in the face of electoral reversals. Still, the stridency of Republican opposition was not a sign of a reconciliation of the party's divergent eastern and western wings. The strongly unified antiadministration minority party responses that would characterize the later conservative coalition had not yet been achieved.

Eastern House Republicans in the Seventy-fourth Congress supported New Deal initiatives 6 percent of the time on the roll calls considered in this chapter (a substantial decline from the 34.6 percent of the Seventy-third Congress), while their eastern counterparts in the Senate supported New Deal measures only 10.2 percent of the time (a decline of more than one-half from the 24.5 percent of the Seventy-third Congress).

In contrast, western Republican senators voted with the administration 53.5 percent of the time (as opposed to the 65.9 percent of the Seventy-third Congress); this reflected both continued progressive support in the Senate and the departure of many western old guard Senators in the 1934 election. Western House Republican approval of New Deal initiatives during the Seventy-fourth Congress averaged 27.1 percent (a substantial decrease from the 58.8 percent of the Seventy-third Congress); this change represented a mixture of responses that, nevertheless, still diverged from those of their eastern counterparts. However, a number of progressive western Republican members of Congress had been replaced by Democrats, thus leaving the remaining GOP contingent more unified and more conservative.

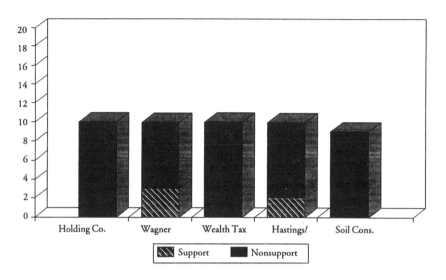

FIGURE 8.1
Seventy-fourth Congress: Eastern Senate Republicans

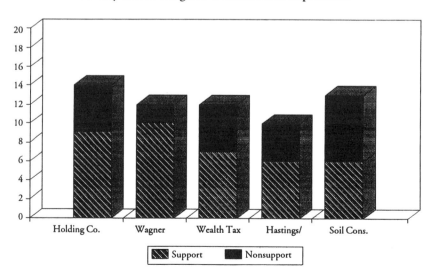

FIGURE 8.2
Seventy-fourth Congress: Western Senate Republicans

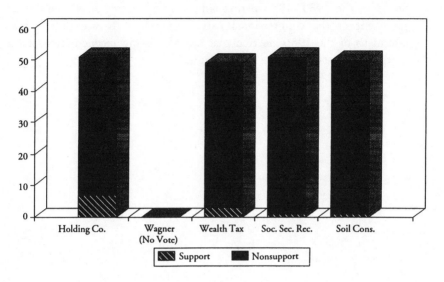

FIGURE 8.3
Seventy-fourth Congress: Eastern House Republicans

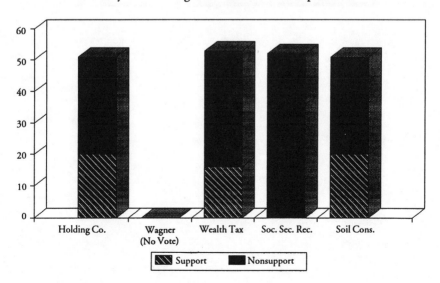

FIGURE 8.4
Seventy-fourth Congress: Western House Republicans

Nevertheless, the focus of party strategists on the western United States in the 1935–1936 period simply reflected the most visible and persistent of the congressional party's problems. It was only in the aftermath of the 1936 election that a more lasting reconciliation of the party's congressional wings would begin.

CHAPTER NINE

Republican Politics of Restraint and

the Genesis of the Congressional

Conservative Coalition: 1937–1938

•

The formation of the congressional conservative coalition in response to the continuation of the domestic New Deal has long been regarded as one of the benchmarks in the study of presidential-congressional relations and the history of domestic reform. Considerable scholarly attention has concentrated on the changing components of the Democratic party during the 1930–1936 period and the tensions that developed within the party's enlarged congressional contingent. The focus of these studies has usually been on the uneasy relationship between the party's vastly expanded northern-urban wing and its electorally secure southern-rural base.

The disaffection of many of the Democrats' southern representatives with executive branch initiatives, and the renewal of Republican partisanship led to the conservative coalition that would severely limit the prospects of the domestic New Deal, even after the 1936 election.

Most studies of Democratic party factionalism take the abrupt renewal in 1938 of unified Republican congressional responses as a given, despite the fact that the Republican party's earlier reactions to the New Deal had been deeply affected by regional and ideological divisions. Yet it was the rapid abatement of the Republican party's previous western progressive–eastern conservative schism, so evident in the Seventy-third and Seventy-fourth Congresses, that was the numerical prerequisite to the formation of the conservative congressional coalition. The neglected topic of the party's increasingly homogeneous responses and the lasting modification of its electoral appeals undertaken after 1936 are the central concerns of this chapter.

The surviving Republican members of Congress assembled in January 1937 for the opening of the Seventy-fifth Congress. Included in their senatorial contingent from the East were conservatives Warren Austin and Ernest Gibson of Vermont, Frederick Hale and Wallace White of Maine, John Townsend of Delaware, and James Davis of Pennsylvania. And, despite the dimensions of the 1936 landslide, Henry Styles Bridges of New Hampshire and Henry Cabot Lodge of Massachusetts had been elected to the Senate in their respective states.

Representing the party's "regular" senatorial group from the West were Arthur Vandenberg of Michigan, along with Charles McNary and Frederick Steiwer of Oregon. Weakened by deaths and electoral attrition, the GOP progressive bloc in the Senate was now composed of Lynn Frazier and Gerald Nye of North Dakota, William Borah of Idaho, Arthur Capper of Kansas, and Hiram Johnson of California.

In the House forty-five of the eighty-nine Republican members of Congress were from eastern districts. Coming primarily from rural areas in the Northeast, they remained strongly conservative; they continued to follow the leadership of Minority Leader Bertrand Snell and retained among their numbers such conservative stalwarts as Daniel Reed, Hamilton Fish, Jr., John Taber, and James Wadsworth of New York; Robert Luce, Joseph Martin, Allen Treadway, and Richard Wigglesworth of Massachusetts; and Robert Rich and William Ditter of Pennsylvania.

The forty-four western GOP representatives were gradually adopting an ideological complexion not unlike that of their conservative House colleagues from the East. Six conservative western Republicans had succeeded in gaining election to the Seventy-fifth Congress. In addition, the western progressive element had shrunk as a result of losses to Democratic candidates in the 1936 landslide. Western progressives maintained substantial representation, however; included were Cassius Dowell and Fred Gilchrist of Iowa, William Lemke of North Dakota, Clifford Hope of Kansas, and Karl Stefan of Nebraska.

Recognizing that the party had been reduced to skeletal representation in both houses, and aware of the internal divisions that had plagued earlier efforts to address New Deal legislation, party leaders decided against the presentation of any formal legislative proposals. Any effectiveness that might be developed, it was felt, would depend on the growth of disagreements within the majority party.[1] As William Allen White wrote, "I don't see where we can get enough cohesion to stand for another victory, unless the President hands us an issue. . . . Nothing that we can do to him is going to help much."[2] What the demoralized Republican minority did not know, however, was that they were about to be handed just such an issue.

Two well-known developments benefited the minuscule Republican minority in the Seventy-fifth Congress. The first was the controversy that rapidly arose over President Roosevelt's Supreme Court reorganization proposal, and the second was the "Roosevelt recession" of 1937. The fight over reorganization of the Court enabled Republicans members to recover a degree of organizational and tactical cohesiveness, while the onset of recession in 1937 encouraged the return of a measure of partisan combativeness.

The Supreme Court Reorganization Proposal and Its Effect on Republican Congressional Tactics

From the very beginning of the New Deal the framers of the Roosevelt administration's legislative proposals had been concerned with the possibility that recovery measures would be struck down by the Supreme Court. These concerns had proved to be well founded. In addition to striking down the NRA, the Court had invalidated the AAA processing tax measure, the Guffey Coal Act of 1935, and, in the spring of 1936, a New York minimum wage law.[3] Concern over possible Supreme Court reaction to impending recovery legislation was regularly reflected in congressional debate in both houses after 1933. It appeared possible that the Court would continue to strike down New Deal proposals despite their clear legislative support and popular appeal.

By December 1936 Roosevelt had settled on the idea of enlarging the Supreme Court in an effort to modify its ideological composition.[4] In February 1937 Roosevelt asked for congressional authorization to appoint a new judge whenever a federal judge with ten or more years of service failed to retire within six months after his seventieth birthday. Roosevelt also requested the appointment of up to six new justices on the Supreme

Court as well as authorization to expand, to a lesser degree, the number of judges serving in other federal courts.[5]

The announcement of the president's plan came as a surprise to all but a few close associates. Despite Roosevelt's early criticisms of Supreme Court decisions, the issue of court reform had not been raised during the 1936 election campaign.

Almost immediately the president's proposal sparked an emotional outcry from many quarters. Even discounting the predictable criticism of conservatives, it soon became apparent that there existed a broad, widespread reverence for the Supreme Court as an institution.[6]

Within a few weeks organized opposition to the proposal (much of it, to be sure, originating from individuals and organizations already critical of the president) had become a political crusade. Senator Capper wrote to William Allen White: "The protests reaching Washington from all sections of the country have been overwhelming. We have seen nothing like it in many years."[7]

Although the intensity of conservative reaction was predictable, it quickly became clear that a broader, bipartisan opposition was coalescing, and that the court proposal was rapidly becoming one of the most potentially divisive controversies in recent American history.[8]

The enfeebled and divided Republican minority watched the rapid unfolding of events with astonishment. As soon as he perceived the dimensions of the controversy, Senate Minority Leader McNary gathered Republican senators into conference. Predictably, some conservative Republicans—such as Senator Vandenberg—were already preparing strong partisan attacks on the "court-packing" measure.[9] Moreover, McNary found that Senator Borah and other Republican progressives were also strongly opposed to the president's plan. Thus, for the first time since they found themselves in the minority, the party's senatorial contingent had actually arrived at agreement with respect to a legislative proposal. However, given the party's small numbers, it was determined, after a stormy conference, to say virtually nothing on the issue.[10] In Senator McNary's words, "Let the boys across the aisle do the talking. . . . We'll do the voting."[11]

Appeals for silence on the issue were also sent to House Republicans and other national party spokesmen by Senate Republicans. Both Herbert Hoover and Alfred Landon were persuaded to refrain from issuing public statements or making speeches criticizing the plan.[12] While this silence was initially a tactic used to gain time by a party now weary of oratory, it quickly became established party policy on the issue. Until the court plan was actually defeated in July 1937, Republican senators maintained a discreet silence. Arthur Capper wrote to William Allen White: "We are letting Wheeler [Senator Burton K. Wheeler of Montana], Burke [Senator Edward Burke of Nebraska] and other Democrats do most of the fighting." [13]

The "strategy of silence" undertaken during the court fight led to a a broader change in the party's legislative strategy. Aware that their lack of numbers now prevented them from exercising any systematic influence, GOP members of Congress began to cast about for other strategies by which to make their presence felt. They began attending bipartisan conservative meetings and devising strategies in conjunction with conservative Democrats. [14] Gradually the Republicans began to consider patterns of overall response to Democratic legislative initiatives, something they largely failed to do in the Seventy-third and Seventy-fourth Congresses. William Allen White wrote to Charles McNary: "Now we must be opportunists. We must take counsel of expediency. We must turn and duck and dodge to survive as an opposition." [15] The adoption of this attitude on the part of Republicans was to prove crucial to the formation of the congressional conservative coalition.

The Recession of 1937

For all of the administration's troubles with the nascent conservative coalition up until the fall of 1937, it had still been able to make one indisputable claim: Overall economic conditions had consistently improved since 1933. This had been a particularly difficult argument for Republicans to counter. Unemployment had been reduced while industrial activity had steadily increased. In the most direct fashion, the administration could correctly maintain that the New Deal had worked. In mid-1937, however, the economy of the United States went into a steep decline. Industrial production dropped sharply, and stock prices plummeted in the wake of increased business failures. While economists continue to debate the origins and causes of this economic dislocation, of one historic fact there is no argument: The recession of 1937 had arrived. [16]

What might have occurred in Congress without this abrupt change in economic conditions must remain conjectural. In fact, the recession changed political circumstances considerably. Republicans unsurprisingly labeled it the "Roosevelt recession" and sought, as their Democratic counterparts had earlier, to define the issue in partisan terms. But the main point is that the 1937 depression was a decisive factor in the growth of overall congressional conservatism, regardless of party. Suddenly the president appeared confused and indecisive and this perception eroded some of his political prestige while weakening the unity and resolve of the New Deal coalition. The economic downturn also served to restore some legitimacy to strong Republican criticism of the administration. Thus, Frank Knox wrote to Alfred Landon: "The fight on Roosevelt's leadership is to be renewed with increased vigor in the session just beginning." [17] Above all, the predictable tendency to hold incumbent administrations responsible for economic conditions now hindered the Roosevelt administration's ability to work effectively with Congress. By 1937 the New Deal was no longer novel and its inability to abate recession damned it in the eyes of many congressional leaders. This revival of confidence among conservative critics was to facilitate the task of Republican leaders throughout the 1937 legislative session.

Although the emotionally charged debate over the court reorganization and the economic downturn were damaging blows to the president's congressional coalition, they were far from the only controversies that developed during the Seventy-fifth Congress. The dramatic expansion of the Democratic coalition in the wake of the electoral collapse of the Republican party had transformed the old Democratic party of the 1920s, principally through the addition by 1937 of a vastly expanded urban base. In the 1937 session 46 percent (153) of the House Democrats represented urban districts, compared to 29 percent in 1931. [18] In all probability, therefore, the very size and diversity of the Democratic membership in 1937 would have created some divisions within the party's coalition, even if the court-packing controversy had not arisen. Throughout the Seventy-fifth Congress, Republican strategists strived to exploit the urban-rural and sectional divisions that were increasingly apparent in the reconstituted Democratic party.

Congressional Voting Patterns

The issues discussed below are those that were selected by James Patterson to illustrate the divisions within Democratic ranks during the

Seventy-fifth Congress. They also reveal the altered dimensions of minority party behavior. Included are a variety of domestic issues that culminated in final roll calls on passage of the measure or resolution discussed, and they represent issues over which there existed not only interparty differences but also division between administration and antiadministration legislators in the president's own party. They reveal both the strengths and limitations of the conservative coalition in 1937 and the changing patterns of Republican responses.

The Fair Labor Standards Act

The Fair Labor Standards Act authorized Congress to establish minimum wage scales and maximum work schedules. The bill also called for the establishment of a labor board that would have the authority to increase minimum standards if collective bargaining efforts broke down.[19] Again a split in Democratic ranks heartened the Republican minority. Southern conservatives feared the elimination of the south's competitive manufacturing advantages that were due to lower regional wage rates. Republicans, adopting a strategy of restraint (as opposed to complete silence), said little when a split among Democrats over the measure developed on the Senate floor. As a result, a full reconstruction of Republican attitudes toward the measure is difficult, but it is clear that the broad grant of authority proposed for the labor board was a matter of concern to many Republicans.

Senator Vandenberg of Michigan argued that the measure suggested the possibility of determination of wage rates through political mechanisms, the advent of which would be a threat to the independence of *both* industry and labor.[20] Senator Styles Bridges of New Hampshire suggested that the bill, as drawn, would make the proposed labor board a virtual "czar of industry."[21] Senate Republicans devoted their energies to drafting and proposing amendments that would have the effect of crippling the measure, in hopes of attracting bipartisan support. Senator Vandenberg offered an amendment that would have limited the jurisdiction of the proposed labor board, and Senator Henry Cabot Lodge of Massachusetts offered another that placed quotas on foreign imports. Both amendments were defeated, however. Several Democrats sponsored amendments, seeking wage exemptions for specific categories of workers, that were defeated. Finally, a motion to recommit the entire measure went down to defeat by a vote of 48 to 36. Confronted with the fact that the administration had the votes necessary to pass the measure, some previously recalcitrant Democrats returned to the administration's side, and the measure passed by a roll call vote of 56 to 28.[22]

Several factors accounted for the administration's final triumph in the Senate. First, the final bill contained numerous exemptions from proposed wage and hour requirements, and that had weakened southern Democratic opposition. Second, since it was obvious that the measure would face a difficult time in the House, many southern Democratic senators felt it unnecessary to place themselves in implacable opposition to the president on the Senate vote. Finally, in the aftermath of the court fight, it was evident that many Democrats desired to work toward some kind of genuine reconciliation within their own party.[23]

While the bill revealed a sectional split within the Democratic party, the fact that there was considerable unity within the previously divided Republican ranks passed almost unnoticed. Only Republicans Henry Cabot Lodge of Massachusetts and James Davis of Pennsylvania had supported the measure. Davis was highly sensitive to labor pressure in the wake of the 1936 results, and both Lodge and Davis were supportive of efforts to stem the flight of heavy industry from the Northeast.[24] The rest of the Republican senators, including the entire progressive insurgent bloc, voted against the measure. As the congressional session unfolded, it would become apparent that many western progressives were coming to view the increasingly urban orientation of the New Deal in a different light.

In the House, the Fair Labor Standards bill ran into almost immovable opposition. A Republican–southern Democratic coalition successfully prevented the measure from reaching the floor of the House during the first session.[25] When, in the midst of strong administration pressure, the measure finally reached the House floor in December 1937, it was recommitted by the House in a close vote of 216 to 198.[26] A conspicuous factor in this bipartisan opposition was the unity again achieved by the Republican minority. Eighty-one of the party's eighty-eight congressmen had voted to recommit the measure and, thus, defeated efforts to pass the Fair Labor Standards Act in 1937. In this endeavor they were supported by 135 Democrats. As previous studies have noted, House Democratic divisions were coming to reflect many of the urban-rural sectional antagonisms that had already begun to surface within the majority party in the

TABLE 9.1
East-West Breakdown of Republican Senate
Vote: Fair Labor Standards Act

SENATE

	East	West
Yes	1 (14.2%)	1 (11.1%)
No	6 (85.8%)	8 (88.9%)

TABLE 9.2
East-West Breakdown of House Vote Motion to
Recommit—Fair Labor Standards Act

HOUSE

	East	West
No	2 (4.5%)	5 (11.3%)
Yes	42 (95.5%)	39 (88.7%)

A vote for recommittal, in this instance, should be interpreted
as an antiadministration vote.

Senate.[27] For the beleaguered Republican minority, however, the direction of events finally pointed toward the restoration of political opportunities.

The Dies Sitdown Resolution

Even before the announcement of the court plan, labor-management problems had become a national preoccupation. This was attributable in part to organized labor's use of "sitdown strikes" during a series of major industrial disputes in the 1930s. Aware of the strong support offered to the Democratic ticket by organized labor in 1936, a number of conservatives held the administration—and, by extension, the president—responsible for the Congress of Industrial Organization's (CIO) new militancy. Even though this was an unfair characterization of President Roosevelt's attitude toward organized labor, the sitdown strike crisis did provide an occasion for the expression of bipartisan conservative disapproval of the new tactics of organized labor.

TABLE 9.3
East-West Breakdown of Republican
House Vote: Dies Sitdown Resolution

HOUSE

	East	West
Yes	43 (97.8%)	35 (79.5%)
No	1 (2.2%)	9 (20.5%)

As with the Fair Labor Standards recommit vote, a "yes" vote
indicates an antiadministration vote.

In March 1937 Martin Dies, a Democratic congressman from Texas, offered a resolution calling for a full-scale "investigation" of the sitdown strikes. The administration, while striving to maintain a centrist position with regard to the sitdown controversies, made known its opposition to the resolution. After an unruly session on April 9, 1937, the Dies motion was eventually defeated in the House by a vote of 236 to 155.[28] Still, the vote revealed considerably broader sentiment against the administration than might have been expected in the wake of the 1936 election. A relatively unknown House member from Texas had obtained the support of 155 representatives in an effort to investigate the CIO and its ties with the national administration. Seventy-eight of the supporters of the resolution had been Democrats; 78 of the 88 House Republicans had joined this group, again displaying a far stronger partisan unity than had been evident in the Seventy-third or Seventy-fourth Congresses. When acting in cooperation with conservative Democrats, Republicans appeared to be growing comfortable with muted expressions of clear partisanship. Since the Dies resolution was never considered by the Senate, Table 9.3 provides a breakdown of Republican voting patterns on this motion only in the House of Representatives.

Byrd Amendment to Wagner Housing Act

The questions of housing improvement and slum clearance had long been concerns of northern urban Democrats. Soon after Senate passage of the Fair Labor Standards Act Senator Robert Wagner of New York sponsored a bill which would have authorized loans to municipalities for the construction of low rent housing.[29] Upon reaching the floor of the Senate,

TABLE 9.4

East-West Breakdown of Republican
Senate Vote: Byrd Amendment to
Wagner Housing Act

SENATE

	East	West
Yes	7 (100%)	8 (100%)
No	0 (0%)	0

A "yes" vote represents nonsupport of the administration's,
because passage of the amendment effectively crippled the
Wagner Act.

the bill ran into vigorous opposition from a bipartisan coalition led by Democratic Senator Harry F. Byrd of Virginia. This group, hostile to the growing level of expenditures directed towards urban areas, sponsored an amendment which limited per unit construction costs so decisively that the bill's proponents claimed that the result would be little, if any, construction.[30] After debate characterized by almost complete Republican silence, a bipartisan conservative coalition succeeded in passing the amendment by a vote of 44 to 39. In support of this key amendment twenty-nine Democrats had joined the entire Republican senatorial contingent.[31] In a fashion similar to the Fair Labor Standards bill, opposition to the housing proposal demonstrated the political power that could be exercised by a unified Republican minority acting in concert with a minority of Democrats who had been galvanized by both sectional and urban-rural splits within the majority party. Once again a Republican-conservative Democratic coalition had demonstrated the ability to decisively influence the substance of legislation. Since it was the adoption of the amendment that crippled the Wagner Housing Act, only the amendment vote is reproduced here.

Executive Reorganization

Plans for reorganization of the executive department had predated the New Deal.[32] Therefore, when a proposal to enable the president to restructure agencies had first been presented in early 1937, it encountered little opposition. Few individuals then seriously questioned the need for reorganization of various bureaus, particularly in light of the expansion of government activity since 1933. Yet it quickly became apparent by late 1937 that congressional opposition to the plan had come to exist for a variety of reasons. Republicans feared extensions of civil service would give permanent seniority to Democratic appointees, thus politicizing the administration of bureaus.[33] Some Democrats and Republicans feared the measure would limit opportunities for congressional patronage. More important, this opposition quickly came to reflect a number of truly bipartisan concerns on the part of many congressmen who desired to protect long-established and previously beneficial relationships with particular agencies and personnel. It was a rare congressman who had not dealt extensively in the past with one or more agencies of particular importance to his district, and reorganization seemed likely to disrupt these established channels. Also, many congressmen came to view the plan as simply another demand for increased presidential power. In the aftermath of the court battle the reorganization effort could be viewed as an additional step toward the "centralization" of power. Increasingly aware of congressional hostility, the administration had not even attempted passage of the bill by late 1937. But careful modification and limitation of some of its provisions suggested its passage in 1938 was a possibility.[34]

However, it soon became apparent in 1938 that even the modified measure was unacceptable to a broad coalition of Republicans and conservative Democrats. Early that year Republicans, though now displaying more overt partisanship than in 1937, nonetheless took a secondary role in congressional discussion of the measure. Senator Borah and his colleague, Burton K. Wheeler of Montana, developed a strategy for derailing the measure that was similar to the one employed by conservative forces during the Supreme Court controversy.[35] Republicans were to confine themselves to brief commentary on the measure, leaving the burden of most debate to dissident Democrats. Senator Vandenberg of Michigan suggested in a brief speech that the measure would lead to no substantial economies and could only point towards "centralized one man government in the United States."[36] Senate Minority Leader McNary confined his public efforts to the insertion of hostile articles about the measure into the *Congressional Record,* and Senator Austin of Vermont spoke only of the institutional prerogatives that he maintained Congress would lose if the measure passed.[37] These criticisms were echoed by the party's progressive wing. Senator Borah characterized the entire measure

as "a universal grant of power" amounting to "virtually unlimited delegation of authority."[38] Senator Capper of Kansas rose only to submit a list
of farm organizations opposed to the measure.[39] As the final vote approached, it appeared that a bipartisan senatorial coalition might have
gathered enough support to defeat the bill. Yet a motion to recommit
was defeated by a vote of 48 to 43, and the bill itself passed the Senate
by a vote of 49 to 42.[40] However, on the vote for final passage, all
fifteen Republicans and more than one-third of the Democratic party
membership in the Senate had again opposed the administration.

The Republican role in the Senate debate was widely criticized by
administration supporters. Democratic Senator James Byrnes of South
Carolina remarked in a floor speech:

> The galleries must suppose you gentlemen [Republicans] have no
> minds at all, since you are entirely dumb on the question before the
> Senate. I know that's wrong. I know you have minds but your
> minds are entirely on the 1940 election.[41]

Moreover, it was apparent that the measure would encounter extreme
difficulties in the House. Faced with clear, widespread opposition, the
administration sought to compromise on the reorganization measure by
exempting a number of agencies from the bill's provisions, while also
accepting a series of amendments introduced in the House.[42] All the
administration's efforts proved unavailing, however; after a rancorous
session, the House voted to recommit the bill by a vote of 204 to 196.[43]
Thus, the executive reorganization measure had been effectively killed.
The vote gave a clear indication of the kind of diverse coalition that had
come to confront Roosevelt. The successful total of 204 votes included
the unanimous support of all 86 Republicans who were present to vote
on the measure.[44] The Republicans had been joined by 110 Democrats
and 8 representatives who had run as members of the Progressive or
Farmer-Laborite party. The unanimous GOP stand demonstrated the
systematic cohesion that Republicans had developed by the end of the
Seventy-fifth session. The most conspicuous factor manifested by this
newfound Republican unity was the lack of western progressive defections
that had been so characteristic of the party's efforts in the previous
two Congresses.

The reorganization defeat reflected the fact that the loose conservative

TABLE 9.5
East-West Breakdown of Republican
Senate Vote: Executive
Reorganization Bill

SENATE		
	East	West
Yes	0	1 (12.5%)
No	8 (100%)	7 (87.5%)

TABLE 9.6
East-West Breakdown of House Vote: Motion
to Recommit—Executive Reorganization Bill

HOUSE		
	East	West
No	0	0
Yes	42 (100%)	44 (100%)

The motion to recommit here represents an
antiadministration vote.

coalition had now achieved a kind of durability on certain types of issues.
Unlike the court bill, it could not be maintained that the administration's defeat on executive reorganization was due to any hastily devised
tactics; nor is it entirely fair to blame the provisions of the reorganization
bill itself. As Patterson points out, the simple fact is that—unlike
relief spending, farm price supports, or labor standards legislation—the
concept of governmental reorganization simply failed to interest the New
Deal electoral coalition. Once the lack of any popular clientalistic pressure was apparent, individual congressmen had found it more politic to
oppose a reorganization measure that had produced little positive constituent interest.[45] However, Patterson's observation also points out a fundamental weakness of the conservative coalition as it existed in 1937. Most
of its successes were on measures, such as court reform and executive
reorganization, that had attracted little support from the powerful liberal
coalition which had proven so effective in the 1936 election. Measures
that succeeded in mobilizing influential elements of the liberal coalition
could still amass enormous congressional support. This was reflected in

the administration's efforts to obtain approval for the "pump priming" measure of 1938.

The "Pump Priming" Bill of 1938

Roosevelt's efforts to find a remedy for the sudden onset of recession in 1937 had been slowed by contradictory advice from his aides. In April 1938, however, the president announced a sweeping, multi-million dollar spending program to ease the depression.[46] The plan anticipated the expenditure or utilitzation of some $6.5 billion of federal funds. The money would be released both through New Deal agencies and relaxed reserve requirements within the Federal Reserve system.[47]

From the beginning many Republicans had little sympathy for the plan. Doubtless encouraged by the administration's recent legislative reversals, they intensified both their visibility and their rhetorical attacks and—without waiting for the development of "nonpartisan" Democratic criticism—began a series of political assaults.[48] Yet, while these sentiments were echoed by a few conservative Democrats such as Carter Glass and Harry F. Byrd of Virginia, most conservative Democrats confined themselves to private objections. Direct opposition to the measure in the House also fell to the Republicans, and it was obvious that even some of them felt uneasy about not supporting the plan. One Republican congressman wrote to William Allen White:

> I am enclosing a copy of my remarks on the recovery bill. . . . I think I will have to vote for it. I don't want to be in the attitude of voting against relief. You can see it puts a fellow in a rather tough position.[49]

Still, the measure attracted considerable criticism from the small Republican minority. Representative John Taber of New York attributed the abrupt industrial decline of the previous year to "the terrific spending program of the government over the past five years."[50] Representative Allen Treadway of Massachusetts characterized the then current economic difficulties as the "Franklin D. Roosevelt depression." The failure to produce a lasting recovery was evidence, he felt, that the New Deal was "bankrupt of statesmanship."[51] Representative Charles Gifford, also of

TABLE 9.7

East-West Breakdown of Republican Senate and House Votes: "Pump Priming" Bill of 1938

	SENATE		HOUSE	
	East	West	East	West
Yes	3 (37.5%)	4 (57.1%)	9 (20.4%)	17 (38.6%)
No	5 (62.5%)	3 (42.9%)	35 (79.6%)	27 (61.4%)

Massachusetts, chided the majority for being unaware of the dangers of continual "experimentations."[52]

Still, it was apparent that these efforts were not part of a broader, bipartisan response. The bill passed easily in the House by a vote of 329 to 70, although fifty-nine of the eighty-eight Republicans had voted against it.[53] (Three Republicans who were listed "not voting" were nonetheless paired as voting "no," bringing the total Republican opposition, as calculated in this study, to sixty-two.) Only eleven Democrats voted against the measure.

The conservative bloc in the House, recently so effective against both the labor standards and reorganization measures, had broken down completely on the spending bill. Nor was conservative opposition more successful in the Senate. On June 4, 1938, the pump priming bill passed with ease by a vote of 76 to 14. Seven of the fifteen Republican Senators voted for the measure; only seven of the sixty-seven Senate Democrats present deserted the administration.[54]

The pump priming measure demonstrated the shifting, opportunistic nature of the congressional conservative coalition in 1937. The issue had offered the possibility of immediate political benefits to the powerful electoral coalition assembled in 1936. In the face of renewed recession, many constituencies found tangible benefits to gain through the passage of the pump priming measure. In 1937 the power of the conservative coalition was still limited, and it was virtually powerless on issues where the liberal coalition united.

Nevertheless, the only session of the Seventy-fifth Congress was one of the most surprising and unpredictable in years. Despite the results of the election of 1936, a minuscule number of Republicans had combined with a group of conservative Democrats to deal the administration several severe, debilitating defeats. Reversals of this kind had seemed almost impossible in late 1936. In part, of course, Roosevelt's difficulties with Congress can be attributed to his own extraordinary political success: By 1937 his political appeal had created a Democratic majority of almost unmanageable size and divergent composition. Caught between a powerful new urban coalition and many southern and western congressional Democrats who thought that "the emergency was over," the president often found himself acting as an "arbiter between conflicting pressures."[55] Thus, in the context of the sectional divisions that were coming to occupy the large majority coalition, it is not surprising that significant changes in the character of Republican congressional responses were passing almost unnoticed.

The Republican Congressional Delegation In the Seventy-Fifth Congress

While the controversies of the congressional session had not produced a well-organized, monolithic conservative coalition that could be effective in all areas, it did witness occasional bipartisan conservative alliances that could be effective on particular issues. Central to the effectiveness of this coalition was the achievement of a high degree of voting cohesion among members of the Republican minority. Abruptly, the divergency in voting patterns between the eastern and western wings of the Republican party declined, as the following graphs indicate.

The Unification of the Republican Party Through the Decline of the Progressive Impulse

The newfound unity within Republican ranks was accomplished largely because of a change in sentiment on the part of western Republicans towards the New Deal after 1936. It will be recalled that in the Seventy-fourth Congress of 1934–1935 progressive western Republicans had continued to play a major role in support of the administration. During that period the western Republicans in the Senate had averaged 53.5 percent support for the administration initiatives considered in this study, while their western House counterparts had supported New Deal initiatives 27.6 percent of the time. In the Seventy-fifth Congress, however, Republican western senatorial support averaged only 18.7 percent,

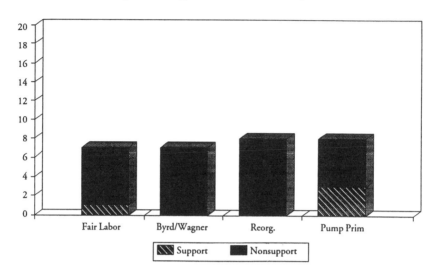

FIGURE 9.1
Seventy-fifth Congress: Eastern Senate Republicans

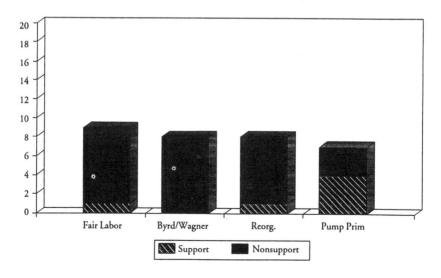

FIGURE 9.2
Seventy-fifth Congress: Western Senate Republicans

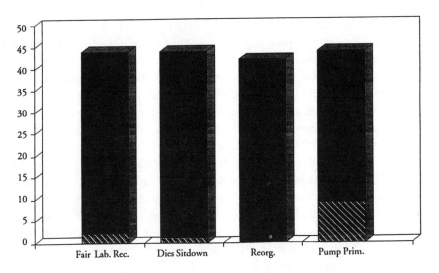

FIGURE 9.3
Seventy-fifth Congress: Eastern House Republicans

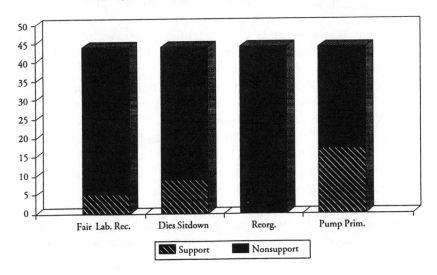

FIGURE 9.4
Sevennty-fiifth Congress: Western House Republicans

while in the House, Republican western support averaged 17.6 percent.[56]

What accounted for this reversal of attitudes on the part of western Republicans in the space of little more than a year? Sundquist has argued that the refashioning of the Democratic party into a "programmatic" liberal party made it attractive to progressive western Republicans and independents who gradually moved into the Democratic party's fold. This movement diminished the influence of the old progressive element within the Republican party, thus making it more solidly conservative.[57] There is considerable merit to this analysis.

The accomplishments of the Progressive National Committee, formed in 1936 to appeal to progressive Republicans and independents on Roosevelt's behalf, are but one indication of the success that the New Deal had in attracting some Republican progressive elements into the Democratic party.[58] Also, it is apparent that the death or resignation of many Republican progressives in the 1940s resulted in their replacement by more conservative western Republicans.[59]

However, our concern in this chapter is not with the long-term trends delineated by Sundquist, but more with the abrupt change in western Republican behavior that was observable between the Seventy-fourth and Seventy-fifth Congresses. In 1936 the Republican western congressional delegation still contained a substantial progressive sentiment, embodied by such individuals as William Borah, Arthur Capper, Lynn Frazier, Hiram Johnson, and Gerald Nye. Yet progressive Republican sentiment towards the New Deal cooled noticeably after 1936.[60] An explanation for this rapid turnabout can be developed through an examination of the way in which progressive Republicans came to view the evolution of the New Deal after 1936.

Much of the 1934 fight over the liberalization of the Republican party undertaken by western progressives obscured the fact that many of these individuals were not modern urban liberals. While progressive Republicans had entered the 1930s with an established reputation as one of the leading reform elements in the American political system, the broader progressive tradition upon which they drew reflected both continuities with and departures from the liberalism of the New Deal.

Both progressivism and the New Deal had shown a continual concern for the socially underprivileged, while promoting efforts to establish a greater balance between the pursuit of private interest and the public good. Otis Graham has pointed out that the concept of an enhanced sense of social justice figured predominantly in both the progressive period and the New Deal.[61] Similarities between Woodrow Wilson's "New Freedom," with its powerful antimonopoly sentiment and its confidence in public action against industrial abuses, could be seen in the regulation of banking during the early New Deal, the attacks on the structure of holding companies, and the efforts to preserve small agricultural enterprise. The influence of Theodore Roosevelt's "New Nationalism" could be seen in the NRA effort to induce large enterprises to coordinate their efforts for a larger public good.[62]

In a general fashion, both reform movements sought an enlargement of the state, while continually clashing with conservative interests during both periods. Accordingly, to progressive Republicans the initial New Deal period suggested strong continuities with the earlier Bull Moose period—with even such former Bull Moosers as Harold Ickes and Henry Stimson actually rendering service to the Democratic administration. Progressive Republicans had given many of the early New Deal efforts clear support, and Roosevelt had made efforts to attract the support of these individuals.[63]

Still, by 1937 many progressive Republicans were deeply concerned with the direction administration policy was taking. While certainly not criticizing the enactment of humanitarian programs in the areas of relief, public works, and social security, these progressive Republicans began to distrust the growth of centralized power in the executive branch. During the Seventy-Fifth Congress, Senator Borah wrote to a constituent:

> It seems almost impossible to stay the march of centralization and of arbitrary power. Unless the people are thoroughly aroused upon this matter, there is little hope of preserving the fundamental principles.[64]

More than fear of executive power now galvanized progressives. Progressivism had sought to limit the debate over simple material advantages in the public arena and replace it with matters of broader moral and general concern.[65] Yet, by 1937 the New Deal was not deploring "special interests"—it was attempting to utilize them in an effort to develop an effective political coalition. To many, if not a majority, of the veterans of the old progressive movement, the relinquishment of political efforts at moral improvement, in favor of open political bartering between organized groups, constituted an abandonment of the former progressive impulse.[66]

Progressive Republicans, while retaining their prior humanitarian concerns for individual farmers, workers, and consumers, viewed the vast expansion of urban political power with deep concern after 1936. At bottom, they were products of the small towns of the agrarian West and distrusted the evolving group pluralism of the late 1930s. Western Republican votes on such issues as the Fair Labor Standards Act and governmental reorganization simply reflected this increasing distrust of urban power and interest group clientalism. The growing ambivalence within progressive Republican ranks to the problems of an urbanized society was reflected in William Allen White's letter to a Republican congressman concerning the Fair Labor Standards Act:

> I don't know what is right. I don't like the bill. . . . On the other hand, something should be done to establish a standard of living in industry below which no one willing to work need fall. . . . You and I are just pumpkin busters from the wide open spaces and we don't know much about industry. . . . I'm not as smart as I used to think I was.[67]

This ambivalence among the progressives had contributed much to the resurrection of overall Republican partisanship that occurred during the Seventy-Fifth Congress. Encouraged by this heightened unity, and heartened by the successes that coalition with conservative Democrats had produced, party strategists renewed their search for a formula that would restore the party to competitive status.

The Republican Electoral Revival of 1937–1938: The Politics of Opportunism and Adjustment

The magnitude of the GOP's 1936 disaster did more than point toward a need for adjustment of electoral appeals—an adjustment political scientists would see as Downsian movement; it also called into question the ongoing utility of the party itself.

Some Republican spokesmen had observed with interest the successes of the bipartisan conservative coalition during the Seventy-fifth Congress.

Still deeply demoralized by the 1936 election, a number of these Republicans began open contemplation of the development of a formal bipartisan anti–New Deal electoral coalition. Herbert Hoover declared that "fusion or coalition of anti–New Deal Dealers was devoutly to be wished. . . ."[68] Senator Arthur Vandenberg actively promoted the idea, even if it meant the abandonment of previous party lines; in the wake of 1936, he felt that was the only way a successful opposition could be developed.[69]

Discussion of a national conservative coalition actually reached the stage of serious talk among influential men in both parties. In May 1937 Alfred Landon met privately with Senator Burton K. Wheeler of Montana and offered support to Democrats who opposed the court plan, if they would run as independents.[70] Frank Knox even suggested that the Republican party consider changing its name in an effort to appeal to southern Democrats; Knox felt that the name "Constitutional Party" might embody a more effective national appeal.[71] These systematic efforts on the part of individuals such as Landon, Vandenberg, and Knox offer ample testimony to the level of Republican discouragement in 1937.

However, as events unfolded, the advocates of coalition began to encounter strong opposition from within the GOP.[72] Encouraged by the rising criticism of some of the president's proposals in several quarters, noncoalitionist Republicans began to urge that primary attention be given to efforts to revive the Republican party. John D. M. Hamilton, for example, was concerned that coalition efforts would be disruptive to local party organizations.[73] By mid-1937, the national chairman felt that Republican sentiment was reviving and that the party was successfully rebuilding local organizations for the 1938 congressional elections.[74]

In late 1937 a group led by Hoover, Hamilton, and other party officials concluded that the Republicans should undertake a more visible rehabilitation effort. Central to these endeavors would be the convening of a national meeting to, in Hoover's words, "promulgate a fundamental Republican creed."[75] Other party leaders disagreed sharply and questioned the utility of such a national meeting. Landon wrote to former National Chairman Henry Fletcher:

With the Democratic Party splitting wider all the time . . . wouldn't we be a bunch of dummies if we were meeting in a national official party convention in the next four months to attempt to write a party platform. Every week since the Supreme Court bill was proposed a year ago has seen an increasing confusion and doubt in the Democratic ranks.[76]

Senate Minority Leader McNary and Senator Borah also publicly opposed the idea in brief statements.[77]

Opposition to the proposal thus coalesced around Landon, Knox, and a majority of the party's congressional leaders. It became apparent that most elected representatives were pleased with the results obtained by the party's "low key approach" to the political controversies during the Seventy-fifth Congress, and there seemed to be little interest in holding a conference that might call attention to intraparty divisions.

Fearful of any action that might result in another party split, the National Committee compromised and voted to establish a "program committee" to identify a "party position" on major issues. The proposed committee would simply issue a series of reports to the National Committee. The Republicans thus succeeded in maintaining an outward display of party harmony. By side-stepping the midterm convention idea, the Republicans continued to rely upon bipartisan cooperation in their effort to exploit divisions within the Democratic majority. Thus, this strategy continued to be the dominant one for the time being among the small Republican contingent in the Congress.

The Congressional Elections of 1938

Ongoing disagreements among party leaders over tactics aside, polls taken in early 1938 suggested increases in GOP strength. In March the AIPO (Gallup) poll reported that Republican congressional prospects had shown sharp improvement in ten major states, including New York, Pennsylvania, New Jersey, Ohio, and Michigan. The poll went on to suggest that the party could gain eighty-five congressional seats if the elections were held at that time. The survey also found that the overall decline in business conditions had vastly improved the party's prospects.[78]

Other polls indicated that the decline in the administration's popularity was nationwide. The Gallup poll reproduced in table 9.8, taken in June 1938, on voter preferences in congressional races that year suggested improved chances for the GOP.

TABLE 9.8

Potential GOP Support in the 1938 Congressional Campaign

SECTION OF COUNTRY	REPUBLICAN	DEMOCRATIC
New England	55%	45%
Middle Atlantic	52%	48%
East Central	52%	48%
West Central	48%	52%
Far West	41%	59%

SOURCE: Cantril and Strunk, *Public Opinion*, p. 933.

Still, major questions persisted. What would be the nature of Republican electoral strategy that year? Would the polarized business and industrial groups so critical to the formulation of GOP appeals in 1936 renew their assault on the political economy of the New Deal? What would become of the efforts of some party leaders to formulate electoral alliances with antiadministration Democrats? Could a national "conservative coalition" of antiadministration forces actually be developed?

The campaign that developed in 1938 illustrated a number of lasting changes in the nature of Republican electoral appeals, while illuminating the difficulties that confront efforts to establish bipartisan electoral coalitions in the American political system.

The Emergence of Positive Business Response, to Government Macroeconomic Management After 1936

The Republican party's efforts at electoral adjustment were aided by an intellectual transformation occuring within the business community. As pointed out earlier, by 1935 much of American heavy industry had a strong negative reaction to the increased role of government in macroeconomic management. This had dramatically affected the ability of the Republican party to alter electoral appeals. But with the introduction after 1936 of Keynesian principles of economic management, important segments of the business community came to strongly support an activist fiscal and monetary policy. The gradual adoption of these attitudes by a number of business elites presaged a substantial modification of the polarized political debates over the political economy characteristic of the early 1930s and the 1936 election.

April 1938 was an important turning point in the development of American political economy. Robert M. Collins, in his *Business Response to Keynes,* notes that that month marked Roosevelt's decision to use fiscal policy as a mechanism for economic stabilization.[79] Roosevelt's acceptance of that notion was hastened by the publication of John Maynard Keynes's *General Theory of Employment, Interest and Money* in 1936.

While Keynes's analysis could be appreciated on several levels, it specifically called for the use of deficit spending as a macroeconomic tool central to the recovery process. This use of monetary policy in a positive, expansionist fashion was an indication of the major changes in the direction of post-Depression American political economics that were to come—changes that would profoundly affect the American business community and, consequently, the Republican electoral coalition.

Keynes's recommendation for increased government spending during periods of inadequate private investment was not incompatible with the interests of private corporations. The policy did not trigger the fears of direct governmental control over corporate decisions that had been so vexing during the NRA period. The movement away from efforts to engage in overt national planning enabled a wide variety of individuals to the right of center to reconsider the nature of business-government relations.[80]

By the post–World War II period a "commercial Keynesianism" that stressed an activist monetary policy, reductions in taxation, and acceptance of a level of unemployment—in lieu of a continual high level of inflation—would be the most widely accepted approach in the United States to problems of political economy.[81]

The introduction of Keynesian analysis in the United States after 1936 coincided with a widespread recognition on the part of business organizations that, because of their 1935–1936 behavior, they now exercised little influence over administration policy.[82] Their almost completely negative stance during that period left them little to offer beyond further demands to "roll back" the entire New Deal.

After 1936, however, new efforts to reestablish a government-business alliance were undertaken in the context of Keynesian analysis. These patterns of positive response again suggest the impact of attitudinal changes by political elites on the formulation of mass political appeals. In 1939 *Fortune's* "Round Table" surveys of executive opinion found that stagnation and chronic unemployment were regarded as the greatest dangers facing the economy.[83]

Organizations such as the Business Advisory Council (BAC), which operated in an advisory capacity within the government, facilitated the reemergence of government-business ties. By 1938 the University of Chicago was regularly sponsoring round table discussions between high-level business executives and the academic community.[84] This forum enabled industry and trade association leaders became aware of the impact Keynesian analysis was having within academia. While the process of adjustment on the part of the business community was by no means complete by 1938 (throughout the year the Chamber of Commerce and the NAM both condemned continued deficit spending), a new pattern of response had begun among business groups that would eventually lead to both the acceptance of governmental macroeconomic management and the emergence of the modern welfare state after the conclusion of the Second World War.

Wearing Many Hats: The Onset of Rationalized Downsian Behavior in the GOP

Despite the fact that Republican rehabilitation efforts continued to be plagued by internal conflicts throughout 1937 and 1938, several long-term trends were evident. The political awakening of a powerful new urban coalition, as evidenced by the 1936 election, finally convinced eastern Republicans of the need to refashion the party's appeals, and the "perceptual problems" of 1932–1936 rapidly disappeared. William S. Murray, chairman of the New York State Republican Committee, told the state convention that the party "must adopt a humane program of its own, rather than be contented with taking advantage of the mistakes of the New Deal."[85] Governor George Aiken of Vermont called upon the Republican National Committee to "purge" itself of militantly conservative spokesmen, and Governor Francis Murphy of New Hampshire urged a similar course.[86]

Changes in the composition of the committee membership that represented the eastern United States also affected Republican electoral appeals in that area. In 1937 the prominent old guard leader of New York, Charles Hilles, resigned from the committee.[87] His Connecticut counterpart, William Rorabach, committed suicide that same year. Both were replaced by new, more liberal leaders.

The changes now manifest in eastern Republican circles are perhaps best illustrated by the nearly successful gubernatorial campaign of New York's Thomas Dewey. Overcoming upstate conservative opposition to his candidacy in 1938, Dewey ran a forceful, liberal race. Instead of directly attacking the New Deal, Dewey stressed state issues and the importance of efficient administration of existing relief programs. In addition, he refrained from direct attacks on the concepts of unemployment relief, social security, and other forms of social assistance.[88]

The New York senatorial contest that year also delineated the changed character of eastern Republican electoral appeals, with Republican candidate John L. O'Brian stressing unemployment as the single most important issue.[89] Similar trends were evident throughout Massachusetts, Rhode Island, and Connecticut where the party nominated young gubernatorial candidates who refrained from systematic attacks on the New Deal. In Massachusetts, for example, Leverett E. Saltonstall endorsed the principles of old-age pensions and expanded workers' compensation.[90]

Races for national offices in the East exhibited a similar pattern. Former New Jeresey senator Warren Barbour, attempting to recapture his seat, emphasized those elements of the Roosevelt program that he had supported. Barbour pointed out that he had voted for both the Wagner Act and the Social Security Act and added, "I am proud of the part I took in bringing these things to pass."[91] Republicans in Pennsylvania were aided by intra-party conflicts among Democratic candidates during the primary contests, but confined much of their criticism to charges of corruption in state government. Capitalizing on current economic discontent, these candidates emphasized the high unemployment rate in Pennsylvania, and Republican Senator James Davis stressed his own blue-collar origins and recalled his support for public works.[92]

Still, it is important to recognize that the campaigns of eastern Republicans in 1938 also reflected some clear continuity with party appeals of earlier campaigns. Generally, however, party spokesmen avoided the broad indictments of the Democratic program that characterized 1936 and concentrated on more recent issues that had produced changes in public sentiment. Republican candidates continued to criticize the court reform proposal, making the spectre of "one-man government" a recurrent theme. The Republican effort was also aided by the association in the general public's mind of CIO sit-down strikes with the Roosevelt administration.

Above all, Republicans throughout the nation were able to exploit effectively the onset of the recession, utilizing this economic downturn to criticize many of the Democratic administration's recovery measures. In June 1938 Republican congressional leaders McNary and Snell issued a nine-point program designed to produce "sound recovery," stating that New Deal policies "have strangled business and discouraged private investment," while decreasing "opportunities for employment." The document went on to urge the curbing of government regulation of private industry.[93] These fundamental themes were echoed by Republican spokesmen throughout the Northeast.

Despite continuity in many campaign appeals, however, 1938 saw the beginning of basic changes in the character and responses of eastern Republicans. This study contends that systematic conservative opposition to the New Deal before 1936 originated in the eastern United States. By the late 1930s, however, the political power of the new urban coalition in that region was apparent. Accordingly, Republicans in the Northeast now publicly accepted many of the innovations of positive government brought about under the New Deal. Thus, while the political appeals of northeastern Republicans were clearly based on expediency throughout 1938, a real remolding of the character of eastern Republicanism had also begun.

The political vigor of the New Deal urban coalition also altered the nature of western Republicanism. Republican progressivism was rapidly losing influence in the western states where it had thrived for so long. Part of the older insurgent movement had been absorbed by the Democratic party, while most of the remaining Republican insurgents in the Congress viewed the emerging urban agenda of the new Democratic party with suspicion.[94] As the impetus for political innovation in government passed from the country to the city, Republican insurgency continued to decline.

Events in Ohio in 1938 established a pattern that was replicated throughout the western states, with the Ohio campaign exemplifying the rising importance of midwestern conservatism. Indeed, the Republican senatorial candidate there, Robert A. Taft, would later become the national leader of the Republican party's conservative wing. Although a considerable number of Ohioans resided in cities, the state also had a large rural and small-town population: approximately 800,000 Ohioans lived on farms in 1938.[95] Moreover, 1938 polls indicated that over the previous two years low farm prices and "industrial turmoil" in the state had sharply reduced the Roosevelt administration's popularity in rural areas.[96]

Taft's campaign, while not proposing the abolition of programs instituted under the New Deal, was uniformly critical of the administration. Taft maintained that economic recovery required the maintenance of a sound fiscal policy, a reduction of federal regulation, and the abandonment of policies causing the climate of "uncertainty" that surrounded business operations.[97] The contrast between these appeals and those of the older insurgent tradition is striking. The Ohio gubernatorial campaign of John Bricker took on a similar conservative character, with Bricker condemning the discord created in Ohio by sitdown strikes and linking the CIO to the New Deal administration.[98]

In Michigan similar efforts were made to associate incumbent Governor Frank Murphy with organized labor. Republicans argued further that the Democratic governor had shown a complete inability to maintain industrial peace, thereby driving industry from the state.[99] The Illinois campaign also reflected this emerging conservative trend among Republicans in the Midwest and Far West. There the Republican senatorial candidate, Richard Lyons, called for an end to social experimentation and accused President Roosevelt of attempting to neutralize the Supreme Court in preparation for fundamental changes in the American form of government.[100] Republican appeals in the formerly insurgent state of Wisconsin also mirrored these trends. With the Progressive Party now operating as an independent political force, the regular Republican organization nominated candidates strongly critical of the New Deal.[101]

The nomination of Harold Stassen as the gubernatorial candidate in Minnesota was perhaps the only occasion in 1938 where the western Republican party showed evidence of its earlier progressive tendencies. In Minnesota, however, Republicans were eager to gain votes from the Farmer-Labor party, which had gone into rapid decline since the death of its flamboyant leader, Floyd Olson. Thus, it seems that the Republican party's progressive appeals in Minnesota were a response to particular local circumstances.

However, the general direction of Republican efforts in the West had become clear: in 1938 western Republicans were running candidates who demonstrated clear conservative appeals. Having already lost some progressive elements to the Democratic coalition, the conservatives remaining within Republican organizations were simply reacting to the increasingly urban orientation of the New Deal. As a result, the electoral appeals of western Republicans were undergoing lasting modification.

As the 1938 elections approached, many political commentators speculated that a historic party realignment was about to take place. The result of this realignment, it was thought, would be the emergence of a political system reflecting a clearcut liberal-conservative dichotomy.[102] Discussions between Republican leaders and antiadministration Democrats had taken place throughout 1937. Moreover, as these discussions continued the president's anger at a number of conservative Democratic senators exploded into public view. Increasingly combative as a result of the congressional revolts over court reform and governmental reorganization, Roosevelt now planned direct intervention in a series of upcoming Democratic primaries. Here, at last, was an opportunity to see whether antiadministration forces would cast partisanship aside in favor of a common effort.

Simply put, this bipartisan electoral coalition never materialized. While Republicans had shown clear interest in bipartisan efforts in the aftershock of the results of the 1936 election, they now felt that declines in Roosevelt's prestige would enable the Republican party to recapture, on its own, congressional seats in November, and that endorsement of conservative Democrats would weaken Republican tickets on both the state and local levels.[103] Practical considerations of partisanship were rapidly exposing the formidable problems of coalition politics. While continuing to offer rhetorical support to the idea of coalition efforts, Republican strategists contributed to these efforts only in the South, where such support was largely costless.[104]

In any event, it became clear that antiadministration Democrats wanted little help from the Republican party in the South in 1938. Even Senator Carter Glass of Virginia, an original advocate of bipartisan efforts in Congress, wrote that "Republicans showed themselves more interested in Republican political advantage than in fighting, as well as speaking for, Jeffersonian principles."[105]

Efforts to establish a bipartisan electoral coalition had deteriorated because of the enduring importance of partisanship in American electoral politics. Contemplating the possibility of electoral gains that could be achieved on their own, the Republicans became progressively less inter-

ested in coalition politics. Also, the existing party structures were reinforced by primary laws, ballot laws, concerns over political patronage,
and by the interest Democratic incumbents had in maintaining seniority
within Congress's committee structure. Above all, both major parties
were composed of large numbers of voters who had formed the habit of
consistently taking one side in the ongoing political conflicts. By 1938
Republicans were becoming increasingly confident that their appeals
could be made through the vehicle of their own party.

The 1938 Elections

For the first time since 1928 the Republican party gained seats in the
congressional elections of 1938. The party, apparently moribund in
1937, scored remarkable gains throughout the nation the following year.
In senatorial races the GOP won 11 of 27 contests for a net gain of 8
seats. The minority contingent in the Senate increased from 15 to 23, and
6 of the 8 new Republican Senators displaced reliable liberal supporters of
the administration.[106] Among the most notable victories were Senator
James Davis's reelection in Pennsylvania, Warren Barbour's return to the
Senate in New Jersey, and Robert Taft's election in Ohio.

The Republicans also registered substantial gains in the House of
Representatives, where they almost doubled their strength, increasing
their numbers from 89 to 169.[107] Of the 80 new Republican seats, 45
were won in the Midwest, while 27 had been gained in the Northeast. In
recording these victories Republicans left untouched conservative southern Democrats, while weakening the new liberal base of the Democratic
party. Many of the defeated Democrats had come from the industrial
sections of the East and Midwest, and many were recently elected congressmen who had been swept into office by the 1932, 1934, and 1936
Democratic landslides.

In Pennsylvania the Republicans defeated 12 incumbent Democratic
representatives, while in Ohio they had gained 11 seats.[108] Republican
gains increased the eastern membership of its House of Representatives
contingent from forty-five to seventy-two. Included in this group were
eastern rural veterans—such as James Wadsworth, John Taber, and
Joseph Martin—who had survived throughout the early New Deal. The
western wing of the party also increased its numbers from forty-two to
ninety-five.

TABLE 9.9

Incumbency Patterns of Congressional Seats Recaptured by the
Republican Party in 1938

NUMBER OF SEATS	YEAR SEAT WENT DEMOCRATIC
6	1930
28	1932
19	1934
27	1936
Total 80	

SOURCE: Author's calculations.

In addition, the party recovered some of its influence on the state level. Of the twenty-seven gubernatorial contests outside the South, Republicans won 18. Notable among the new Republican governors were Leverett E. Saltonstall of Massachusetts, Raymond Baldwin of Connecticut, and Harold Stassen of Minnesota. Republicans also recaptured the governorships of such large states as Pennsylvania, Ohio, and Michigan, while in New York Thomas Dewey came extremely close to defeating Governor Herbert Lehman.

Abruptly, then, the Republican party had been restored to a fair degree of competitiveness on the national scene. Clearly, many of the Republicans elected in 1938 accepted the broad outlines of the New Deal. But Republican leaders, greatly encouraged by their party's showing at the polls, were quick to express confidence that, by combining with conservative Democrats who were critical of some administration policies, they could block the president if he persisted in a "leftward" direction. Representative John Taber of New York warned that if the president insisted on following an unaltered course with the new Congress, he would be quickly stalemated.[109]

At the same time, the reconstituted minority saw little prospect of undoing any major New Deal legislation already enacted, because of the prospect of a presidential veto (and the virtual impossibility of mustering a two-thirds majority to override the still immensely popular president).[110] Nonetheless, the Republican restoration had greatly enhanced the prospects for cooperation with conservative Democrats, while establishing a pattern of deadlock that would increasingly become the norm in American political life.

The Renewal of Republican Partisanship and the Limits of Domestic Reform

Despite its descent to minority status after 1932, the Republican party had retained its historical connection to political power while invoking its symbolic identification with national values and belief systems that were meaningful to millions of voters. The abrupt succession of Republican electoral defeats had concealed the extent to which the party still reflected general attitudes of a somewhat wider nature. While the fear evoked by economic crisis had produced a call for government assistance, even from conservative groups, the abatement of this sense emergency by 1937 demonstrated the persistence of previous ideological patterns. Attitudes have remarkable staying power, and even the disastrous dislocations of the 1930s did not dispell decades of support for the idea of limited government activity. The notions of individualism, self-help, and the general legitimacy of entrepreneurial activity remained important components of the American belief system.[111] A Gallup poll conducted in November after the 1936 election was revealing on this score. In response to the question: "Should President Roosevelt's second administration be more liberal, more conservative, or about the same as his first?" Fifty percent of the electorate preferred a more conservative course, with 35 percent preferring that it be about the same; only 15 percent of the respondents sought a more liberal administration.[112]

Given the persistence of these belief patterns, any voter reaction against the administration after 1936 had the potential of resulting in GOP electoral gains. The rise of a candidly urban liberalism after 1936 had finally enabled Republicans to minimize their own internal divisions and to develop cohesive party responses to efforts to expand the New Deal. Simultaneously, a downward trend in the business cycle, increased divisiveness within the enlarged Democratic party, and a general unease with the continued exercise of larger-than-life efforts by Roosevelt presented the Republicans with opportunities not of their own making. Thus, the events of 1937–1938 had done more than reawaken submerged feelings of congressional independence; they had given renewed intensity to expressions of partisanship on the part of the minority party. After the success achieved in the 1938 elections, the Republican congressional delegation remained cohesive, providing some three-quarters of the anti-administration votes on most major controversial measures by 1939.[113]

Revived Republican partisanship had become the indispensable component of the modern conservative congressional coalition. The party's return to competitive status also suggested that there were clearly limitations to the reform impulse that flourished in the Congress and the nation from 1932 through 1937.

By 1938 the renewal of Republican partisanship, the inability of the president to dominate state Democratic organizations, and the economic crisis of 1937 had transformed the New Deal. The "Thermidor," or final stage, of the domestic New Deal had arrived, and it increasingly became the norm in American reform politics. While Roosevelt's personal popularity remained intact, he nevertheless faced a conservative coalition in Congress that was increasingly willing to undertake responsibility for negotiating local and regional adjustments to the national policies advocated by the president. The successful development of the congressional conservative coalition after 1937 thus established a model of policy making that became standard in American political life for decades to come.

CONCLUSION

Minority Party Dynamics During
Political Realignment

•

State-building, Party Theory, and the GOP in the 1930s

During the 1980s a large body of scholarship concerned itself with "structural constraints" imposed on the domestic New Deal due to the limited development of American governmental and bureaucratic institutions as of the 1930s.[1] A case was made for considering the organization and actions of governmental institutions and administrative groupings as central to the development of policy during the New Deal period. As a result, in these works the state became an important independent focus of the study of policy development.

However, if, as state theorists have suggested, the autonomous decisions of state administrators are important factors in policy development, so to are the decisions made by party elites. But the activities of political parties are often treated simply as by-products of changes in mass voting behavior, with little consideration given to party strategies, elite perceptions, and the ability of party leaders to shape and influence political conflict. Consequently, the independent actions that can emerge from these groups have often been overlooked.

Yet important autonomous actions were undertaken by elites within the minority Republican party that helped shape the political results of the early 1930s. For example, evaluations of political conditions that

increased the "issue space" between the majority and minority parties
were particularly important during the 1934–1935 period.

Everett Carll Ladd has effectively summarized the prevailing outlook
toward minority parties:

> Calling the minority the "moon" suggests not only that it has
> gleamed less brightly than the majority sun, but that it has been
> bound in some fixed way to the majority and that it has been forced
> to follow a course determined by the majority.[2]

Yet the Republican party was not initially a pale reflection of the
political and social appeals utilized with such effectiveness by the Democratic party during the 1930s. Its reactions to the majority's innovations
went through several stages and were a critical element of the political
realignment that occurred during the period. After a time of hesitation
and paralysis induced by the incorporation of conservative elements into
early New Deal recovery efforts, most Republican party leaders by 1935
came to see direct ideological criticism of the New Deal as the party's
most advantageous electoral course.

Nowhere has the relative autonomy and importance of party elites
been better demonstrated than in 1935 and 1936. It was only after the
1936 election that the GOP could begin to travel a more clearly marked
road of reevaluation and reassessment. The effect of this initial polarization was to minimize electoral appeal and doom the party to a minority
status that still has not been wholly overcome. Given the dimensions of
Democratic majority party success from 1930 through 1934, its minority
party behavior after 1934 seemed contrary to the predictions of models of
rational party behavior. Yet, before the advent of modern polling, minority parties at the start of realignments have acted contrary to the predictions of such models in several cases.[3]

The emphasis of many political scientists on majority party dynamics
often obscures the important role that minority parties play in framing
the nature of policy debates during these periods. The key to the successful consummation of political realignment lies in the reaction of the
minority party to majority party policy innovations. While it has long
been recognized that party activists or programmatic constituencies can
be important within party coalitions, they are particularly influential in
minority parties. With the size of the party's electoral coalition reduced

and the level of its direct influence on events weakened, such diehard constituencies come to exercise disproportionate influence. This problem is particularly acute when political conditions are uncertain or subject to a wide variety of interpretations, as is the case at the beginning of partisan realignment. Perceptual problems constitute the most underappreciated aspect of historic party behavior during political realignment, and these problems were particularly acute before the legitimization of modern polling techniques which occurred after 1936. Much historical party behavior is understandable only in this context.

Minority Party Dynamics During Political Realignment

Efforts to formulate explanations for party behavior have always drawn heavily from the framework of political economy. A central assumption is that parties are rational actors, designing electoral strategies to maximize electoral gains. As both majority and minority parties ultimately face an identical distribution of voters, the minority party's "moon" should readily come to orbit around the majority party's "sun."

However, the historical evidence considered here suggests limitations to this view. Realignments are often consolidated by minority party movement toward a position of polar opposition to the innovations of the majority party. Thus Franklin Roosevelt abandoned his initial efforts to maintain an "all-class" coalition in support of New Deal recovery efforts only as it became apparent that the business community and Republican leaders sought to limit sharply or dismantle most of the New Deal recovery structure by 1935. At the same time, the Republican party began stridently criticizing administration recovery measures in a fashion that defied the electoral results of 1930, 1932, and 1934. The result was a rapid polarization of party appeals.

Additional examples suggest themselves from other electoral periods. For instance, due to economic conditions, the Democratic party would have suffered severe setbacks in 1894 under any circumstances. Nevertheless, it was the party's embrace of William Jennings Bryan and the 16–1 monetary standard two years later that polarized party appeals and brought about in the realignment of 1896. This change of course was undertaken despite the success the Democratic party had enjoyed since 1876 utilizing vastly different conservative appeals.

Substantial modification of electoral appeals by a minority party was also important to the electoral realignment of 1852–1860. Despite their minority status the Whigs had enjoyed a substantial measure of electoral and political success during the period from 1832 through 1848 by the utilization of nonsectional appeals. Yet the movement of "conscience Whigs" toward the abolitionist position gradually limited the party's ability to moderate internal disputes and compete electorally on a national basis. The result was the collapse of the Whig party and the "second party system."

These examples again suggest limitations on models based on political economy. Polar movement, coupled with often sharp breaks from previous political appeals, has long been recognized as a key element of the realignment process. But why does departure from the principles of political economy or vote maximization occur during these periods? Part of the answer lies in the intense nature of the social and political conflicts that are characteristic of such periods of political realignment. Samuel Huntington's study of the periods of "creedal passion" in American history notes a sharp and persistent distinction between the politics of group bargaining and compromise normally characteristic of American politics and the heightened level of moral passion embodied by periods of creedal passion. While Huntington focuses his analysis of creedal passion on four periods in American history (the Revolutionary period, the Jacksonian era, the Progressive era, and the late 1960s), he also points out that such sentiments were not confined to such periods. Both the American abolitionist movement and the conservative opposition to the New Deal were characterized by a moral indignation similar to that of periods of creedal passion.[4]

Thus a number of parallels to earlier realignments suggest themselves. The politics of "creedal passion" have seized the Democratic party since 1968, and the result has been clear changes in both the party's nomination process and its electoral appeals. The rapid expansion of primary elections and grassroots caucuses since 1972 has resulted in greatly increased influence for party activists, usually at the expense of the party's more conservative rank and file. Moreover, as was the case in the previous examples, party activists have hardly led the party in the direction of vote maximization. All Democratic presidents from Woodrow Wilson through John F. Kennedy had, at least on a presidential level, recognized the importance of the South to the Democratic presidential coalition. However, with the exception of the 1976 Carter campaign and the most recent Clinton-Gore effort, the party's ideological appeals and candidates have not been designed to appeal to the South's conservative sensibilities. Thus while the Democratic party retains its vitality on a congressional level, it is fair to say that party activists swayed by creedal passion may have severely limited the party's presidential opportunities at times.

The importance of groupings within party coalitions that are motivated by overly intense or disproportionate interests has long been recognized in historical accounts, but is seldom considered in a systematic fashion by those positing models of rationalized political behavior. Yet political change in the United States is often associated with the rise of new social groupings within the existing two major parties rather than with the rise of new parties, and this can have an immediate effect on the nature of electoral appeals. The expansion of the franchise, coupled with the development of mass party organization, allowed most deep-seated social conflicts in the United States to be played out within the party system. Simply put, social conflict of any kind rapidly became political conflict.

Minority parties, in constant search of additional support (along with strategies that will enable them to unseat the party in power) are often deeply affected by polar groupings. Such parties—enjoying fewer of the fruits of political power, functioning under less pressure to enunciate consistent appeals, and often reflecting weakened political coalitions— become easily influenced by polar social forces. Groups such as the Abolitionists, the Populists, and the conservative opposition to the New Deal—all central to an understanding of the politics of creedal passion— also must be factored in if one is comprehend polar movements by minority parties.

The behavior of minority parties thus remains the most underappreciated component of the realignment process. The movement of the minority party to a position of polar opposition to majority party policy usually results from the deep disaffection substantial elements of the minority coalition come to feel toward national policy. While the methodological and conceptual problems that surround questions of "elite" and "mass" control of political parties go back at least to the succinct analysis offered by E. E. Schattschneider in *Party Government,* historical analysis clearly suggests the continual importance to political parties of activists within party coalitions. The effect that individuals with disproportionate interests can have on weakened minority coalitions during periods of heightened political conflict remains one of the unappreciated components of the realignment process. The realignment paradigm needs to move beyond the consideration of mass electoral behavior to an understanding of the role activists and elites can play in party coalitions.

Could this analysis of historic party behavior be applied to contemporary American politics? Clearly the entire concept of political realignment has been circumscribed by the increasing insulation of congressional and statewide officeholders from results on a presidential level: the ability of the Democratic congressional party to actually gain seats in the 1988 presidential election offers compelling evidence of this fact.

Previous political realignments featured aggregation of presidential and congressional results; this made change on the part of the losing party a rather compelling strategy. The diminution of such simultaneous congressional reversals can only serve to limit the rate of change within a declining electoral coalition. In addition, the perceptual problems that plagued Republican officeholders and strategists in the 1930s are now clearly a thing of the past now that sophisticated polling techniques serve to preclude any widespread misreading of the direction of public opinion on major issues. Adjustment to the mid-range of public opinion thus becomes a fairly easy matter, and hence deep-seated divisions between the parties could become a matter solely of historical interest.

Still, the dilemmas of party and electoral adjustment cannot be resolved simply by using polling data. There is something curiously familiar about the Republican debates of the 1930s—something that anyone aware of the Democrats' dilemma today will recognize. How does a political party undertake a process of electoral rehabilitation in the wake of political setback? Can such a process be easily reconciled with the preferences of activist groupings? Can cherished values be endlessly sacrificed to achieve vote maximization? Should they be? To what extent has mass opinion actually shifted during the period of electoral reversals? There was a high degree of validity to the assertion made by both the Republican old guard of the 1930s and the Democratic party activists of the 1980s that mass public opinion had not changed very much in those respective periods. In both instances, moreover, party renewal occurred largely as a result of opportunities not of the party's making.

Finally, does a process of party rehabilitation really make much difference anyway? Ultimately the GOP achieved a mild renewal in 1938 only by the time-honored tactic of blaming the "in party" for worsening economic conditions that year. The similarities to Democratic party strategy in the 1992 election need hardly be elaborated. The rehabilitation process, so much the concern of both the GOP in the 1930s and the Democrats in the 1980s, yielded few final decisions as to the direction the party should take. While the Republican party had gradually accepted many New Deal innovations, it remained far from the center of public opinion on a variety of issues. In both cases, however, politics and party positions had come to rest on more than strictly utiliarian concerns, as the hopes and promises of American life often outstrip considerations of partisan advantage.

A P P E N D I X   A

Republican Congressional

Delegations, 1933–1938

•

Throughout this study, the following roll calls were used to establish the degree of opposition or support that existed within the Republican minority for New Deal innovations during the Seventy-third, Seventy-fourth and Seventy-fifth Congresses:

Seventy-third Congress (1933–34): Glass-Steagall Banking Act; Economy Act of 1933; Federal Emergency Relief Act (FERA); Agricultural Adjustment Act (AAA); National Industrial Recovery Act (NRA); Tennessee Valley Authority (TVA); Gold Recovery Act; and Securities and Exchange Act.

Seventy-fourth Congress (1935–36): Public Utility Holding Company Act; Wagner Act; Social Security Act (Hastings Amendment in the Senate and the Motion to Recommit in the House); Wealth Tax; and Soil Conservation and Domestic Allotment Act.

Seventy-fifth Congress (1937–38): Fair Labor Standards Act; Byrd Amendment to Wagner Housing Act (Senate only); Dies Sitdown Resolution (House only); Executive Reorganization; and Pump Priming.

By totaling the positive (proadministration) votes produced by individual Republican congressmen and senators as a percentage of overall roll call responses on these measures, it is possible to provide some statistical evidence for generalizations made in the text. For example,

House Minority Leader Bertrand Snell, who served throughout the period from 1933 through 1938, supported the administration on only one of the fifteen roll call votes considered here. Thus, his level of support for administration initiatives averages only 6.7 percent. In contrast, Congressman William Lemke of North Dakota (the Union Party presidential candidate of 1936) served during the same congressional sessions, but supported administration initiatives on eleven of the fifteen roll call votes presented here (73 percent). The contrast between the levels of support provided to the administration by these two Republican congressmen thus serves as one example of the divergent attitudes that came to exist within the Republican congressional delegation as it responded to the New Deal. Tables A.1 and A.2 present individual data for each member of the Republican congressional delegation who served from 1933 through 1938 and are organized by percentage of administration support in descending order.

TABLE A. 1
House Republicans: Individual Data

NAME	STATE	CONGRESSES	PERCENTAGE OF SUPPORT
Boileau, Gerald J.	WI	73	85.7 (6/7)
Frear, James A.	WI	73	85.7 (6/7)
James, W. Frank	MI	73	85.7 (6/7)
Peavey, Hubert H.	WI	73	85.7 (6/7)
Sinclair, James H.	ND	73	85.7 (6/7)
Welch, Richard J.	CA	73, 74, 75	80 (12/15)
Lemke, William	ND	73, 74, 75	73 (11/15)
Traeger, William	CA	73	71.4 (5/7)
Evans, William E.	CA	73	66.7 (4/6)
Gilchrist, Fred C.	IA	73, 74, 75	66.7 (10/15)
Christianson, Th.	MN	73, 74	63.7 (7/11)
Dowell, Cassius C.	IA	73, 75	63.7 (7/11)
Gibson, Ernest W.	VT	73	60 (3/5)
Mott, James W.	OR	73, 74, 75	60 (9/15)
Withrow, Gardner R.	WI	73, 74, 75	60 (9/15)
Blanchard, George W.	WI	73	57.1 (4/7)
Carter, Vincent M.	WY	73	57.1 (4/7)
Chase, Ray P.	MN	73	57.1 (4.7)
Foss, Frank H.	MA	73	57.1 (4/7)
Kelly, M. Clyde	PA	73	57.1 (4/7)
McGugin, Harold C.	KS	73	57.1 (4/7)
Muldowney, Michael	PA	73	57.1 (4/7)
Strong, Nathan L.	PA	73	57.1 (4/7)
Wolverton, Charles	NJ	73, 74, 75	57.1 (8/14)
Thurston, Lloyd	IA	73, 74, 75	53.4 (8/15)
Hope, Clifford R.	KS	73, 74, 75	53.4 (8/15)
Marshall, L. T.	OH	73, 74	54.5 (6/11)
Marcantonio, Vito	NY	74	50 (2/4)
Stefan, Karl	NE	74, 75	50 (4.8)
Taylor, J. Willis	TN	73, 74, 75	50 (7/14)
Reece, B. Carroll	TN	73, 74, 75	46.7 (7/15)
Tobey, Charles W.	NH	73, 74, 75	46.7 (7/15)
Woodruff, Roy O.	MI	73, 74, 75	46.7 (7/15)
Collins, Samuel L.	CA	73, 74	45.5 (5/11)

TABLE A.1 *(Continued)*

NAME	STATE	CONGRESSES	PERCENTAGE OF SUPPORT
Cooper, John G.	OH	73, 74	46.5 (5/11)
Doutrich, Isaac H.	PA	73, 74	45.5 (5/11)
Focht, Benjamin K.	PA	73, 74	45.5 (5/11)
Beedy, Carroll L.	ME	73	42.9 (3/7)
Britten, Fred A.	IL	73	42.9 (3/7)
Cochrane, Thomas C.	PA	73	42.9 (3/7)
Connolly, James J.	PA	73	42.9 (3/7)
Edmonds, George W.	PA	73	42.9 (3/7)
Goss, Edward W.	CT	73	42.9 (3/7)
Buckbee, John T.	IL	73, 74	40 (4/10)
Culkin, Francis D.	NY	73, 74, 75	40 (6/15)
Dirksen, Everett M.	IL	73, 74, 75	40 (6/15)
Guyer, Ulysses S.	KS	73, 74, 75	40 (6/15)
Brewster, Ralph O.	ME	74, 75	37.5 (3/8)
Burdick, Usher L.	ND	74, 75	37.5 (3/8)
Carlson, Frank	KS	74, 75	37.5 (3/8)
Gwynne, John W.	IA	74, 75	37.5 (3/8)
Carter, Albert E.	CA	73, 74, 75	33.3 (5/15)
Eltse, Ralph R.	CA	73	33.3 (2/6)
Hooper, Joseph L.	MI	73	33.3 (2/6)
Jenkins, Thomas A.	OH	73, 74, 75	33.3 (5/15)
Kinzer, J. Roland	PA	73, 74, 75	33.3 (5/15)
Knutson, Harold	MN	73, 74, 75	33.3 (5/15)
Mapes, Carl E.	MI	73, 74, 75	33.3 (5/15)
Clarke, John D.	NY	73	28.6 (2/7)
Kurtz, J. Banks	PA	73	28.6 (2/7)
Moynihan, P. H.	IL	73	28.6 (2/7)
Simpson, James	IL	73	28.6 (2/7)
Whitley, James L.	NY	73	28.6 (2/7)
Bacharach, Isaac	NJ	73, 74	27.3 (3/11)
Burnham, George	CA	73, 74	27.3 (3/11)
Cavicchia, Peter A.	NJ	73, 74	27.3 (3/11)
Hess, William E.	OH	73, 74	27.3 (3/11)
Higgins, William L.	CT	73, 74	27.3 (3/11)

NAME	STATE	CONGRESSES	PERCENTAGE OF SUPPORT
Kahn, Florence P.	CA	73, 74	27.3 (3/11)
Lehlbach, Frederick	NJ	73, 74	27.3 (3/11)
Perkins, Randolph	NJ	73, 74	27.3 (3/11)
Turpin, C. Murray	PA	73, 74	27.3 (3/11)
Allen, Leo E.	IL	73, 74, 75	26.7 (4/15)
Crowther, Frank	NY	73, 74, 75	26.7 (4/15)
Dondero, George A.	MI	73, 74, 75	26.7 (4/15)
Hartley, Fred A.	NJ	73, 74, 75	26.7 (4/15)
Holmes, Pehr G.	MA	73, 74, 75	26.7 (4/15)
Lambertson, William	KS	73, 74, 75	26.7 (4/15)
Powers, D. Lane	NJ	73, 74, 75	26.7 (4/15)
Seger, George N.	NJ	73, 74, 75	26.7 (4/15)
Andresen, August H.	MN	74, 75	25 (2/8)
Case, Francis H.	SD	75	25 (1/4)
Douglas, Fred J.	NY	75	25 (1/4)
Ekwall, William A.	OR	74	25 (1/4)
Engel, Albert J.	MI	74, 75	25 (2/8)
Gearhart, Bertrend	CA	74, 75	25 (2/8)
Robsion, John M.	KY	74, 75	25 (2/8)
Oliver, James C.	ME	75	25 (1/4)
Parker, James S.	NY	73	25 (1/4)
Pittenger, William	MN	74	25 (1/4)
Rees, Edward H.	KS	75	25 (1/4)
Smith, Clyde H.	ME	75	25 (1/4)
Eaton, Charles A.	NJ	73, 74, 75	21.4 (3/14)
Gifford, Charles L.	MA	73, 74, 75	21.4 (3/14)
Andrews, Walter G.	NY	73, 74, 75	20 (3/15)
Englebright, Harry	CA	73, 74, 75	20 (3/15)
Fish, Hamilton, Jr.	NY	73, 74, 75	20 (3/15)
McLean, Donald H.	NJ	73, 74, 75	20 (3/15)
de Priest, Oscar	IL	73	20 (1/5)
Wolcott, Jesse P.	MI	73, 74, 75	30 (3/15)
Darrow, George P.	PA	73, 74	18.2 (2/11)
McLeod, Clarence	MI	73, 74	18.2 (2/11)
Millard, Charles D.	NY	73, 74	18.2 (2/11)
Ransley, Harry C.	PA	73, 74	18.2 (2/11)

TABLE A.1 (*Continued*)

NAME	STATE	CONGRESSES	PERCENTAGE OF SUPPORT
Bakewell, Charles M.	CT	73	14.3 (1/7)
Brumm, George F.	PA	73	14.3 (1/7)
McFadden, Louis T.	PA	73	14.3 (1/7)
Stalker, Dale H.	NY	73	14.3 (1/7)
Stokes, Edward L.	PA	73	14.3 (1/7)
Swick, J. Howard	PA	73	14.3 (1.7)
Waldron, Alfred M.	PA	73	14.3 (1/7)
Martin, Joseph	MA	73, 74, 75	13.3 (2/15)
Rich, Robert F.	PA	73, 74, 75	13.3 (2/15)
Wolfenden, James	PA	73, 74, 75	13.3 (2/15)
Arends, Leslie C.	IL	74, 75	12.5 (1/8)
Church, Ralph E.	IL	74, 75	12.5 (1/8)
Cole, William S.	NY	74, 75	12.5 (1/8)
Crawford, Fred L.	MI	74, 75	12.5 (1/8)
Plumley, Charles A.	VT	74, 75	12.5 (1/8)
Reed, Chauncey W.	IL	74, 75	12.5 (1/8)
Andrew, A. Piatt	MA	73, 74	9.1 (1/11)
Bolton, Chester C.	OH	73, 74	9.1 (1/11)
Goodwin, Philip A.	NY	73, 74	9.1 (1/11)
Hollister, John D.	OH	73, 74	9.1 (1/11)
Luce, Robert	MA	73, 74	9.1 (1/11)
Merritt, Schuyler	CT	73, 74	9.1 (1/11)
Wadsworth, James W.	NY	73, 74, 75	8.3 (1/12)
Bacon, Robert A.	NY	73, 74, 75	6.7 (1/15)
Ditter, J. William	PA	73, 74, 75	6.7 (1/15)
Hancock, Clarence E.	NY	73, 74, 75	6.7 (1/15)
Reed, Daniel A.	NY	73, 74, 75	6.7 (1/15)
Rogers, Edith Nourse	MA	73, 74, 75	6.7 (1/15)
Snell, Bertrand H.	NY	73, 74, 75	6.7 (1/15)
Taber, John	NY	73, 74, 75	6.7 (1/15)
Tinkham, George H.	MA	73, 74, 75	6.7 (1/15)
Treadway, Allen T.	MA	73, 74, 75	6.7 (1/15)
Wigglesworth, R. B.	MA	73, 74, 75	6.7 (1/15)
Bates, George J.	MA	75	0 (0/4)

NAME	STATE	CONGRESSES	PERCENTAGE OF SUPPORT
Beck, James M.	PA	73	0 (0/7)
Blackney, William W.	MI	74	0 (0/4)
Clason, Charles R.	MA	75	0 (0/4)
Cluett, Ernest H.	NY	75	0 (0/4)
Fennerty, Claire G.	PA	74	0 (0/2)
Halleck, Charles A.	IN	74, 75	0 (0/8)
Hoffman, Claire E.	MI	74, 75	0 (0/8)
Jarrett, Benjamin	PA	75	0 (0/4)
Jenks, Arthur B.	NH	75	0 (0/4)
Kimball, Harry M.	MI	74	0 (0/3)
Lord, Bert	NY	74, 75	0 (0/8)
Maas, Melvin J.	MN	74, 75	0 (0/8)
Mason, Noah M.	IL	75	0 (0/4)
Michener, Earl C.	MI	74, 75	0 (0/8)
Rutherford, Albert	PA	75	0 (0/4)
Shafer, Paul W.	MI	75	0 (0/4)
Short, Dewey	MI	74, 75	0 (0/8)
Simpson, Richard M.	PA	75	0 (0/3)
Stewart, John G.	DE	74	0 (0/4)
Thomas, John P.	NJ	75	0 (0/4)
Thomas, William D.	NY	74	0 (0/4)
Watson, Henry W.	PA	73	0 (0/5)
White, Dudley A.	OH	75	0 (0/4)
Wilson, William H.	PA	74	0 (0/4)

TABLE A.2
Senate Republicans: Individual Data

NAME	STATE	CONGRESSES	PERCENTAGE OF SUPPORT
Norris, George W.	NE	73, 74, 75	100 (15/15)
La Follette, Robert	WI	73, 74, 75	93.8 (16/17)
Norbeck, Peter	SD	73, 74	87.5 (7/8)
Cutting, Bronson	NM	73	85.7 (6/7)
Couzens, James	MI	73, 74	80 (8/10)
Capper, Arthur	KS	73, 74, 75	76.5 (13/17)
Johnson, Hiram W.	CA	73, 74, 75	76.5 (13/17)
Frazier, Lynn J.	ND	73, 74, 75	75 (12/16)
Robinson, Arthur R.	IN	73	71.4 (5/7)
Nye, Gerald P.	ND	73, 74, 75	68.6 (11/16)
Borah, William E.	ID	73, 74, 75	57.1 (8/14)
McNary, Charles L.	OR	73, 74, 75	52.9 (9/17)
Lodge, Henry Cabot	MA	75	50 (2/4)
Steiwer, Frederick	OR	73, 74, 75	50 (7/14)
Schall, Thomas D.	MN	73, 74	37.5 (3/8)
Dickinson, Lester J.	IA	73, 74	33.3 (4/12)
Reed, David A.	PA	73	33.3 (2/6)
Davis, James J.	PA	73, 74, 75	30.8 (5/13)
Vandenberg, Arthur	MI	73, 74, 75	29.4 (5/17)
Dale, Porter H.	VT	73	25 (1/4)
Fess, Simeon D.	OH	73	25 (2/8)
Goldsborough, P. L.	MD	73	25 (2/8)
Hébert, Felix	RI	73	25 (2/8)
Kean, Hamilton F.	NJ	73	25 (2/8)
Walcott, Frederick	CT	73	25 (2/8)
Barbour, Warren W.	NJ	73, 74	23.1 (3/13)
Keyes, Henry W.	NH	73, 74	23.1 (3/13)
Hastings, Daniel O.	DE	73, 74	15.4 (2/13)
Townsend, John G.	DE	73, 74, 75	14.3 (2/14)
White, Wallace H.	ME	73, 74, 75	13.3 (2/15)
Austin, Warren R.	VT	73, 74, 75	12.5 (2/16)
Patterson, Roscoe C.	MI	73	12.5 (1/8)
Hale, Frederick	ME	73, 74, 75	11.8 (2/17)
Gibson, Ernest W.	VT	74, 75	11.1 (1/9)

NAME	STATE	CONGRESSES	PERCENTAGE OF SUPPORT
Carey, Robert D.	WY	73, 74	8.3 (1/12)
Metcalf, Jesse H.	RI	73, 74	8.3 (1/12)
Bridges, Styles	NH	75	0 (0/4)
Hatfield, Henry D.	WV	73	0 (0/7)

APPENDIX B

Background of Republican

Congressional Delegations,

1933 – 1938

•

House

While there was no "typical" Republican member of Congress of the 1930s, several patterns are worthy of note. The average age of the eighty-nine Republican representatives in 1937 was fifty-four. The average age of all representatives that same year was fifty-two. Thus the Republican congressional minority was not predominantly composed of "older" men.

The Republican congressman of the 1930s was usually well educated. One hundred sixty-three individuals served in the House minority between 1933 and 1938; 55 percent had completed some graduate work, with the great majority of these individuals having attended law school. The high percentage of Republicans who received postgraduate training during a period characterized by less formal education suggests that these individuals came from families affluent enough to assist their children through graduate education. Table B.1 suggests that these Republicans also proceeded to occupations entirely consistent with middle- and upper-middle-class backgrounds.

TABLE B.1

Career Patterns of Republican Members of Congress, 1933–1938

PRINCIPAL OCCUPATION

Lawyer:	60	(36%)
Businessman:	49	(30%)
Farmer/Rancher:	11	(7%)
Teacher/Educator:	11	(7%)
Publisher:	10	(6%)
Laborer:	3	(2%)
Misc.:	19	(12%)

SOURCE: U. S. Congress, Joint Committee on Printing, *Biographical Directory of the American Congress, 1789–1949*, 81st Cong., House Document No. 807 (Washington D.C.: U.S. Government Printing Office, 1950.)

Senate

The average Republican Senator was fifty-nine years old in 1937, the same as that of the entire Senate. As was true in the House, age appears to have had little to do with voting records.

Like their House counterparts, Republican Senators of the 1933–1938 period had strong educational backgrounds, with 54 percent of the thirty-nine Senators having completed some graduate education. This again suggests the intuitive conclusion that these individuals were the

TABLE B.2

Career Patterns of Republican Senators, 1933–1938

PRINCIPAL OCCUPATION

Lawyer:	15	(38%)
Businessman:	10	(26%)
Farmer/Rancher:	4	(10%)
Teacher/Educator:	1	(2.5%)
Publishers:	5	(13%)
Laborer:	1	(2.5%)
Misc.:	3	(8%)

SOURCE: U. S. Congress, Joint Committee on Printing, *Biographical Directory of the American Congress, 1774–1949*, 81st Cong., 2d Sess., House Document No. 607 (Washington, D.C.: U.S. Congress, Joint Committee on Printing, 1950.)

products of upper-middle class environments. Table B.2 suggests that their occupational patterns were (as would be expected) entirely consistent with such backgrounds.

In one sense, however, these tables reveal little. Most congressmen of both parties were lawyers and most came from middle- or upper-middle-class backgrounds. Yet, while the available occupational evidence is too limited to permit final conclusions, it seems apparent that few Republicans followed educational or occupational patterns that brought them into close, continual association with newly arrived immigrants, labor organizations, or other underprivileged groups that were transforming the political scene between 1933 and 1936.

A P P E N D I X   C

Geographical Mobility of

Republican Members of Congress

•

House

Of the 163 Republicans who served in the House between 1933 and 1938, 120 (74 percent) were raised in the same state that they represented in Congress, while 43 were raised in one state and eventually came to represent a district in another. However, only 18 representatives (11 percent) represented districts that differed in rural/urban character from the environment in which they had been raised; the remaining 145 represented districts similar in urban/rural composition to the areas where they grew up. (See U.S. Congress, Joint Committee on Printing, *Biographical Directory of the American Congress, 1774–1949,* 81st Cong., 2d Sess., House Document No. 607 [Washington, D.C.: U.S. Government Printing Office, 1950].) While it would be a mistake to place too much emphasis on this limited residential data, it does suggest that, despite superior educational backgrounds, most Republican representatives had returned to professional occupations in districts not dissimilar to those in which they had been raised. To some extent, this may help explain the limited understanding of changing political conditions that often characterized party elites during the period.

Senate

Twenty-six of the thirty-nine Senate Republicans grew up in the states that they would ultimately represent. While it is apparent from the biographical data available that virtually all Senate Republicans spent their childhood in predominantly rural or small-town areas, these figures must be approached with caution. Although most conservative Republican Senators came from rural backgrounds, so too did most liberal and progressive senators, as the nation at the time of their childhoods (circa 1880–1890) was still largely rural.

Notes

•

Introduction: Previous Concepts of Party Realignment

1. V. O. Key, Jr., "A Theory of Critical Elections," *Journal of Politics* 17 (February 1955): 3–18.

2. The exception to this rule involves the period after the political realignment of 1860; the period from 1876 through 1892 was one of rough parity between the two major parties. Superior works on the subject of American political realignment include: Walter Dean Burnham, *Critical Elections and the Mainsprings of American Politics*, (New York: Norton, 1969); Everett Carll Ladd, Jr., and Charles D. Hadley, *Transformations of the American Party System: Political Coalitions from the New Deal to the 1970s* (New York: Norton, 1975); Jerome M. Clubb, William H. Flanigan, and Nancy H. Zingale, *Partisan Realignment: Voters, Politics, and Government in American History*, Sage Library of Social Research, vol. 108 (Beverly Hills: Sage, 1980); Everett Carll Ladd, Jr., *American Political Parties: Social Change and Political Response* (New York: Norton, 1970). See Byron E. Shafer, ed., *The End of Realignment: Interpreting American Electoral Eras*, (Madison: University of Wisconsin Press, 1991), for an important statement of the controversies that now surround the realignment concept.

3. James L. Sundquist, *Dynamics of the Party System: Alignment and Realignment of Political Parties in the United States* (Washington, D.C.: The Brookings Institution, 1973); Angus Campbell, Philip E. Converse, Warren E. Miller,

and Donald E. Stokes, *Elections and the Political Order* (New York: Wiley, 1966).

4. Sundquist, *Dynamics of the Party System.*

5. E. E. Schattschneider, *Party Government* (New York: Rinehart, 1942), p. 35.

6. Franklin Roosevelt received 22,825,016 votes to Herbert Hoover's 15,758,397. *Presidential Elections Since 1789,* 2d ed. (Washington, D.C.: Congressional Quarterly, 1979), p. 91.

7. Samuel Lubell, *The Future of American Politics* (New York: Harper, 1955), p. 6. See also, Judith Stein, "The Birth of Liberal Republicanism in New York State," Ph.D. diss., Yale University, 1968, *passim.*

8. William E. Leuchtenburg, *Franklin D. Roosevelt and the New Deal, 1932–1940* (New York: Harper & Row, 1963), p. 84.

9. See Judith Stein's ("The Birth of Liberal Republicanism" chap. 1) for an excellent formulation of Republican dilemmas on a statewide level.

10. Anthony Downs, *An Economic Theory of Democracy* (New York: Harper & Row, 1957).

11. Burnham, *Critical Elections,* p. 7; Sundquist, *Dynamics of the Party System,* p. 290. The subject of non-Downsian behavior on the part of majority party elites has received intriguing treatment in Barry Cooper, Allan Kornberg, and William Mischler, *The Resurgence of Conservatism in Anglo-American Democracies,* (Durham: Duke University Press, 1987) and Ivor Crewe and Donald D. Searing, "Ideological Change in the British Conservative Party," *APSR* 82 (1988): 361–85.

12. Steve Fraser and Gary Gerstle, *The Rise and Fall of the New Deal Order, 1930–1980* (Princeton: Princeton University Press, 1989), pp. ix–x; Gerald M. Pomper, "The Presidential Nominations," in Pomper, ed., *The Elections of 1988: Reports and Interpretations* (Chatham, N.J.: Chatham House, 1989), pp. 33–34.

13. James Q. Wilson, "Realignment and Dealignment at Top and Bottom," in Austin Ranney, ed., *The American Elections of 1984* (Durham: Duke University Press for The American Enterprise Institute, 1985), p. 301; Nelson Polsby and Aaron Wildavsky, *Presidential Elections: Strategies of American Electoral Politics,* 6th ed. (New York; Scribners, 1984), pp. 208–223.

14. Several broad histories consider the regular Republicans of the New Deal period but only in a cursory fashion. See, for example, George H. Mayer, *The Republican Party, 1854–1966,* 2d ed. (New York: Oxford University Press, 1967); Malcolm Moos, *The Republicans* (New York: Random House, 1956). There are also several treatments of the party in the 1940s after the "thermidor" of the domestic New Deal: Richard Norton Smith, *Thomas E. Dewey and His Times* (New York: Simon and Schuster, 1982); Donald Bruce

Johnson, *The Republican Party and Wendell Wilkie* (Urbana: University of Illinois Press, 1960).

15. The results of state legislative races were examined for the period from 1928 through 1938. The GOP was able to remain competitive in such states as New York and Connecticut, but in most cases they were all but swept out of office by 1936. For example, in New Mexico and Idaho the party had all but disappeared on the local level by 1936. Typically, Republicans suffered persistent electoral losses in the four consecutive elections from 1930 through 1936, reducing their local legislative influence to very low levels.

I. The Anatomy of the Republican Party in the 1920s

1. Wesley M. Bagby, *The Road to Normalcy: The Presidential Campaign and Election of 1920,* (Baltimore: Johns Hopkins Press, 1962), pp. 13–24; David B. Burner, "The Breakup of the Wilson Coalition in 1916," in Paul Murphy, ed., *Political Parties in American History* (New York: Putnam, 1974), p. 1059. Historians continue to disagree about the reasons for the decline of the Progressive movement and its fate in the 1920s. The movement had always contained substantial business representation, and many businessmen simply returned to their traditional Republican leanings after 1920. While World War I may not have resulted in the final death of the movement, it unquestionably led to its long-term fragmentation and the reentry of many progressives into the business culture and "welfare capitalism" structure of the 1920s. See Arthur S. Link, "What Happened to the Progressive Movement in the 1920's," *American Historical Review* 64 (1959): 833–51; Herbert F. Margulies, "Recent Opinion on the Decline of the Progressive Movement," *Mid-America* (Oct. 1963): 250–66; Paul W. Glad, "Progressives and the Business Culture of the 1920's," *Journal of American History* (June 1966): 75–89; and Jackson K. Putnam, "The Persistence of Progressivism in the 1920's: The Case of California," *Pacific Historical Review* (Nov. 1966): 395–411.

2. James Holt, *Congressional Insurgents and the Party System,* Harvard Historical Monographs LX (Cambridge: Harvard University Press, 1967), p. 166.

3. Ibid., p. 162; Norman M. Wilensky, *Conservatives in the Progressive Era: The Taft Republicans of 1912,* University of Florida Monographs, Social Sciences, no. 25, Winter 1965 (Gainesville: University of Florida Press, 1965), p. 72.

4. Holt, *Congressional Insurgents,* p. 163.

5. David M. Kennedy, *Over Here: The First World War and American Society* (New York: Oxford University Press, 1980), pp. 247–48; Burl Noogle, *Into the Twenties: The United States from Armistace to Normalcy* (Urbana: University of Illinois Press, 1974), passim.

6. Bagby, *The Road to Normalcy,* p. 23.

7. Ibid., p. 154.

8. Robert K. Murray, *The 103rd Ballot: Democrats and the Disaster in Madison Square Garden* (New York: Harper & Row, 1976), p. 3.

9. Morton Keller, *In Defense of Yesterday: James M. Beck and the Politics of Conservatism, 1861–1936* (New York: Coward-McCann, 1958), p. 149.

10. Ibid., chap. 13.

11. Still, the insurgents would provide many of the key administrators in the later Agricultural Adjustment Administration (AAA), as the careers of George Peek and Chester Davis illustrate. The rural insurgency of the 1920s remained a cause in search of an organizational vehicle which the early New Deal would provide.

12. Holt, *Congressional Insurgents,* p. 164.

13. For an excellent treatment of a rural insurgent within the GOP during the 1920s, see Richard Lowitt, *George W. Norris: The Persistence of a Progressive, 1913–1933* (Urbana: University of Illinois Press, 1971), especially pp. 164–80 for Norris's attitudes on agricultural relief during the 1920s.

14. Robert K. Murray, *The Harding Era* (Minneapolis: University of Minnesota Press, 1969).

15. The term *associationalism* is from Ellis W. Hawley, "Herbert Hoover, the Commerce Secretariat, and the Vision of an 'Associative State,' " *Journal of American History* 61 (1974): 116–140. See also Albert U. Romasco, *The Poverty of Abundance: Hoover, the Nation, and the Great Depression* (New York: Oxford University Press, 1965), p. 43.

16. Kennedy, *Over Here,* p. 133.

17. Ibid., p. 134. Robert Cuff, however, has stressed the complexity of the war mobilization experience during this period. It involved elements of both industrial self-government and coercive central planning, thus defying easy categorization. For a complete evaluation of the mobilization experience see: Robert D. Cuff, *The War Industries Board: Business-Government Relations During World War I* (Baltimore: Johns Hopkins University Press, 1973); and "Herbert Hoover, the Ideology of Volunteerism, and War Organization During the Great War," *Journal of American History* 64 (1977): 358–72.

18. For an intriguing essay crediting Bernard Baruch himself for the creation of the War Industries Board's positive image in the 1920s, see Robert D. Cuff, "Bernard Baruch: Symbol and Myth in Industrial Mobilization," in Edwin J. Perkins, ed., *Men and Organizations: The American Economy in the 20th Century* (New York: Putnam, 1977), pp. 104–19.

19. Hawley, "Herbert Hoover, the Commerce Secretariat . . ."; William E. Leuchtenburg, "The New Deal and the Analogue of War," in John Braeman, Robert H. Bremner, and, Everett Walters, eds., *Change and Continuity in Twentieth-Century America* (New York: Harper & Row, 1966).

20. Romasco, *The Poverty of Abundance,* p. 43.
21. Leuchtenburg, "The New Deal and the Analogue of War," passim.
22. Ellis W. Hawley, *The Great War and the Search for a Modern Order* (New York: St. Martin's Press, 1979), p. 101; and "Secretary Hoover and the Bituminous Coal Problem," *Business History Review* 42 (1968): 249. A vague parallel exists between Herbert Hoover and Jimmy Carter. Both were able to secure their party's presidential nomination without a real political base within the party's regular organization. The party organizations of 1976 were vastly different than the ones of 1928, of course, but the parallel is there. President Coolidge made little active effort on Hoover's behalf in the 1928 campaign.
23. Evan B. Metcalf, "Secretary Hoover and the Emergence of Macroeconomic Management," *Business History Review* 44 (1975): 60–62.
24. Ibid.
25. Ibid., p. 65; Robert H. Ziegler, *Republicans and Labor, 1919–1929* (Lexington: University Press of Kentucky, 1969), p. 89; William J. Barber, *From New Era to New Deal: Herbert Hoover, the Economists, and American Economic Planning, 1921–1933,* Historical Perspectives on Modern Economics (New York: Cambridge University Press, 1985), p. 13.
26. Metcalf, "Secretary Hoover and the Emergence of Macroeconomic Management," pp. 66–67.
27. Craig Lloyd, *Aggressive Introvert: Herbert Hoover and Public Relations Management* (Columbus: Ohio State University Press, 1972), p. 126.
28. Hawley, "Secretary Hoover and the Bituminous Coal Problem," pp. 249–55.
29. Kim McQuaid, "Corporate Liberalism in the American Business Community," *Business Historical Review* 52 (Fall 1978): 342–68; Herman E. Krooss, *Executive Opinion: What Business Leaders Said and Thought on Economic Issues, 1920s–1960s* (Garden City, N.Y.: Doubleday, 1970), pp. 39–45.
30. Hawley, "Herbert Hoover, the Commerce Secretariat . . .," pp. 122, 132; Kim McQuaid, "Young, Swope, and General Electric's 'New Capitalism': A Study in Corporate Liberalism, 1920–1933," *American Journal of Economics and Sociology* 36 (1977): 327.
31. See Lloyd, *Aggressive Introvert,* for the importance of public relations to the Hoover nomination drive. See also Kent Schofield, "The Public Image of Herbert Hoover in the 1928 Campaign," *Mid-America* 51 (October 1969): 278–93.
32. Donald R. McCoy, "To the White House: Herbert Hoover, August 1927–March 1929," in Martin L. Fausold and George T. Mazuzan, eds., *The Hoover Presidency: A Reappraisal* (Albany: State University of New York Press, 1974), p. 39.

33. Campaign of 1928, Presidential Papers, Herbert Hoover Presidential Library, West Branch, Iowa. For a discussion of the 1928 election, see McCoy, "To the White House," pp. 29–49. See also Lawrence H. Fuchs, "Election of 1928," in Arthur Schlesinger and Fred Israel, eds., *History of American Presidential Elections, 1789–1968* (New York: Chelsea House, 1971), vol. 3, pp. 2585–2609.

34. Hawley, "Herbert Hoover, the Commerce Secretariat . . .," p. 139.

35. U.S. Department of Commerce, Bureau of the Census, *Historical Statistics of the United States: Colonial Times to 1970* (Washington, D.C.: U.S. Government Printing Office, 1975), vol. 1, pp. 135, 228.

36. Panics and depressions had occurred throughout the nation's history, and this new depression was not initially viewed by most observers as anything more than the most recent version of an occasional affliction. Classical theory, which continued to exert major influence over several members of the Hoover cabinet, held that depressions were most effectively met by patient forebearance. Thus, while the dislocations produced by the depression were extremely serious, they were best addressed through a process of natural price adjustment. Falling wage and price levels would eventually restore adequate profit levels, at which point entreprenuerial activity would resume normal levels. Precedent for official inaction during periods of economic contraction remained strong; presidents from Martin Van Buren to Woodrow Wilson had refrained from any direct official action.

37. Walter Lippmann, "The Permanent New Deal" (*Yale Review* 24 [June 1935]: 649–67) is a contemporary but persuasive attempt to suggest continuities between the recovery measures of the Hoover and Roosevelt administrations. Albert Romasco ("Herbert Hoover's Policies for Dealing With the Great Depression: The End of the Old Order or the Beginning of the New," in Fausold and Mazuzan, eds., *The Hoover Presidency,* pp. 79–84] suggests continuities between Hoover's efforts and those of past presidents. Peri Arnold ("Herbert Hoover and the Continuity of American Public Policy," *Public Policy* 20 [1972]: 525–44) stresses the overriding importance of volunteerism to Hoover's relief efforts.

38. Ellis W. Hawley, "Herbert Hoover and Economic Stabilization, 1921–1922," in Hawley, ed., *Herbert Hoover as Secretary of Commerce,* p. 45.

39. Herbert Stein, *The Fiscal Revolution in America* (Chicago: University of Chicago Press, 1969), p. 22.

40. Barry D. Karl, "Presidential Planning and Social Science Research: Mr. Hoover's Experts," *Perspectives in American History* 3 (1969): 351.

41. Ibid.

42. Stein, *The Fiscal Revolution,* p. 14. This is a point also made by a number of state theorists. See, for example, Margaret Weir and Theda Skocpol, "State

Structures and the Possibilities for 'Keynesian' Responses to the Great Depression in Sweden, Britain, and the United States," in Peter B. Evans, Dietrich Rusechmeyer, and Theda Skocpol, eds., *Bringing the State Back In* (New York: Cambridge University Press, 1985), pp. 108–63.

43. Barry Karl, *The Uneasy State: The United States from 1915 to 1945* (Chicago: University of Chicago Press, 1983), p. 86.

44. Ibid., p. 75.

45. Karl, "Presidential Planning," p. 351.

46. Karl, *The Uneasy State*, p. 75.

47. Richard Hofstadter, *The Age of Reform: From Bryan to FDR* (New York: Knopf, 1955), p. 119.

48. Karl, *The Uneasy State*, p. 83.

49. Jordan A. Schwarz, *The Interregnum of Despair: Hoover, Congress, and the Depression* (Urbana: University of Illinois Press, 1970), p. 242.

50. For a discussion that treats Republican schisms during the 1932 election almost exclusively in terms of progressive disaffection, see Edgar Eugene Robinson and Vaughn Davis Bornet, *Herbert Hoover: President of the United States*, (Stanford: Hoover Institution Press, 1975), pp. 134–49.

51. Robert R. Himmelberg, *The Origin of the National Recovery Administration: Business, Government, and the Trade Association Issue, 1921–1933* (New York: Fordham University Press), pp. 110–46.

52. Otis L. Graham, *Toward a Planned Society: From Roosevelt to Nixon* (New York: Oxford University Press, 1976), p. 16; Edward Berkowitz and Kim McQuaid, *Creating the Welfare State: The Political Economy of Twentieth-Century Reform* (New York: Praeger, 1980), pp. 78–85.

53. Berkowitz and McQuaid, *Creating the Welfare State*, pp. 82–84.

54. Ibid., p. 84.

55. Himmelberg, *The Origins of the National Recovery Administration*, p. 160.

56. The Republicans lost eight seats in the Senate and control of the House of Representatives. Schwarz, *The Interregnum of Despair*, p. 21.

2. The Fragmentation of the Republican Coalition

1. The Hoover-Smith contest in 1928, by contrast, has produced an abundant literature and remains the subject of ongoing analysis. Some observers have argued that the 1928 election marked the delineation of new electoral patterns that foreshadowed a Democratic majority even without the dislocations of the Great Depression. A second interpretation has maintained that Al Smith's candidacy generated an intense conflict between Catholics and Protestants over noneconomic issues that only marginally affected later patterns of political behavior. An excellent treatment of the controversies surrounding the 1928 elections is Allan J. Lichtman, *Prejudice and the Old*

Politics: The Presidential Election of 1928 (Chapel Hill: University of North Carolina Press, 1979); see especially chapter 9, pp. 199–230.

2. Ronald L. Feinman, *Twilight of Progressivism: The Western Republican Senators and the New Deal* (Baltimore: Johns Hopkins University Press, 1981), p. 33.

3. Ibid.

4. Ibid., p. 37.

5. Ibid., pp. 38–41.

6. Ibid., p. 39.

7. Ibid., p. 40.

8. William E. Borah to Walter Lippmann, November 9, 1932, Walter Lippmann Papers, Yale University Library, New Haven.

9. Harris Gaylord Warren, *Herbert Hoover and the Great Depression* (New York: Oxford University Press, 1959), p. 266.

10. Louise Overacker, "Campaign Funds in a Depression Year," *APSR* 27 (October 1933): 772.

11. Ibid.

12. Ibid., p. 773.

13. W. Phillips Shively, "A Reinterpretation of New Deal Realignment," *Public Opinion Quarterly* 35 (Winter 1971–72): 621.

14. Both Shively (Ibid., pp. 621–23) and Burnham (*Critical Elections,* p. 56) have previously utilized *Literary Digest* polls precisely because of this unrepresentativeness. Curiously, the shifts evident in the 1934–35 polls have been subject to little attention; they will be considered here in chapters four and five. See also Peverill Squire, "Why the 1936 Literary Digest Poll Failed," *Public Opinion Quarterly* 52 (1988): 125–33.

15. *Literary Digest,* January 7, 1933, p. 7; *Presidential Elections Since 1789,* p. 91.

16. *Literary Digest,* November 5, 1932, p. 8.

17. Ibid., November 26, 1932, p. 5.

18. Leuchtenburg, *Franklin D. Roosevelt and the New Deal,* p. 12.

19. Ibid., p. 11.

20. Marriner Eccles, *Beckoning Frontiers* (New York: Knopf, 1951), p. 95.

21. *New York Times,* September 15, 1932, p. 13.

22. Ibid., October 29, 1932, p. 9.

23. Ibid., November 6, 1932, p. 1.

24. Ibid.

25. *Presidential Elections Since 1789,* p. 91.

26. Robinson, *Herbert Hoover,* p. 273.

27. Walter Lippmann to Theodore Roosevelt, Jr., November 22, 1932, Lippmann Papers, Yale University.

3. Efforts at Republican Restoration and the 1934 Congressional Campaign

1. *New York Times,* June 24, 1933, p. 5.
2. Ibid., January 2, 1934, p. 10.
3. Ibid., February 24, 1934, p. 1.
4. John O'Laughlin to Herbert Hoover, December 30, 1933, O'Laughlin MSS, Hoover Presidential Library.
5. *New York Times,* February 13, 1934, p. 1.
6. Ibid., April 29, 1934, p. 1.
7. Walter Lippmann, "The Republicans in Search of an Issue," Today and Tomorrow, *The New York Herald Tribune,* June 1, 1934.
8. *New York Times,* May 24, 1934, p. 1; June 10, 1934, p. 20.
9. Ibid., September 8, 1934, p. 1.
10. Ibid., September 17, 1934, p. 4.
11. Ibid., July 8, 1934, p. 1.
12. Unsigned report to Herbert Hoover, entitled "The 1934 Congressional Elections," n.d., Campaign of 1934, Postpresidential Individual Files, Hoover Presidential Library.
13. *New York Times,* October 28, 1934, p. 27; November 4, 1934, section 4, p. 7.
14. Simeon Fess to Herbert Hoover, December 31, 1934, Postpresidential Individual Files, Hoover Presidential Library.
15. *New York Times,* October 30, 1934, p. 12.
16. Ibid.
17. Ibid., November 4, 1934, p. 7.
18. Felix Hébert to Herbert Hoover, October 10, 1934, Postpresidential Individual Files, Hoover Presidential Library.
19. *New York Times,* October 7, 1934, p. 1.
20. Ibid., September 28, 1934, p. 1.
21. *New York Herald Tribune,* November 5, 1934, p. 1.
22. Ibid., November 2, 1934, p. 1.
23. *New York Times,* November 3, 1934, p. 7; Gerald H. Gamm, (*The Making of New Deal Democrats: Voting Behavior and Realignment in Boston, 1920–1940* [Chicago: University of Chicago Press, 1989], p. 107) in a microlevel study of Massachusetts politics during the New Deal, suggests that the onrush of New Deal electoral success resulted in declining participation on the part of the state's Yankee Brahmin elite.
24. Charles McNary to James Couzens, October 16, 1934, Charles McNary MSS, Manuscript Collection, Library of Congress.
25. *New York Herald Tribune,* September 15, 1934, p. 8.
26. *New York Times,* October 27, 1934, p. 1.
27. Ibid., p. 7.

28. Frank Knox to Annie Knox, August 6, 1934, Frank Knox MSS, Manuscript Collection, Library of Congress.

29. William Allen White to Frank Knox, October 9, 1934, White MSS, Manuscript Collection, Library of Congress.

30. *New York Times,* September 2, 1934, section 4, p. 7.

31. Ibid., October 7, 1934, section 4, p. 1.

32. Ibid.

33. *New York Herald Tribune,* Oct. 22, 1934, p. 1.

34. Ibid., November 4, 1934, p. 1.

35. Ibid., November 5, 1934, p. 1.

36. Maine was, until 1957, the only state in the union to elect its governor and federal representatives on the second Monday in September rather than on the first Tuesday in November. The State Constitutional Convention of 1819 set this date "as being the least busy season between . . . harvest[s]" and a time when road conditions would be best. In 1957 the state constitution was altered by referendum to conform with other states. Correspondence between author and Lynn E. Randall, Deputy Law Librarian, Law and Legislative Library, Augusta, Maine, April 4, 1986.

37. *New York Times,* October 7, 1934, p. 1.

38. Ibid., September 16, 1934, p. 1.

39. Daniel Hastings to Herbert Hoover, October 18, 1934, Postpresidential Individual Files, Hoover Presidential Library.

40. Bertrand Snell to Herbert Hoover, October 17, 1934, Postpresidential Individual Files, Hoover Presidential Library.

41. Henry Fletcher to Herbert Hoover, August 31, 1934, Postpresidential Individual Files, Hoover Presidential Library.

42. Republican National Committee, "Statement of Net Income and Surplus, by Periods and Combined, for the Periods October 19, 1933, to June 16, 1936," Henry Fletcher MSS, Manuscript Collection, Library of Congress.

43. Ibid.

44. *New York Herald Tribune,* October 22, 1934, p. 1.

45. Henry Fletcher to Herbert Hoover, August 31, 1934, Postpresidential Individual Files, Hoover Presidential Library.

46. *The Nation,* November 7, 1934, p. 529.

47. *New York Times,* November 4, 1934, p. 1.

48. Both Michigan and Illinois were the scene of extensive labor organizing efforts in 1934. Republican gains in rural parts of these states were then viewed as reactions to this heightened labor and class conflict.

49. Arthur M. Schlesinger, Jr., *The Age of Roosevelt,* vol. 2, *The Coming of the New Deal* (Boston: Houghton Mifflin, 1958), p. 507.

50. *Literary Digest,* November 17, 1934, p. 5.

51. David Reed to Herbert Hoover, November 24, 1934, Postpresidential Individual Files, Hoover Presidential Library.

52. Simeon Fess to Herbert Hoover, December 31, 1934, Postpresidential Individual Files, Hoover Presidential Library.

53. Arthur Vandenberg to Herbert Hoover, January 13, 1934 (italics in the original), Postpresidential Individual Files, Hoover Presidential Library. Vandenburg wrote in the heat of partisan battle but the changes in intergovernmental relationships in the 1930s would prove real and enduring. The pre-1932 system was dominated by local expenditures with only very small intergovernmental transfers taking place. The New Deal brought about a fundamental shift from local to state and federal level spending with an emphasis on large intergovernmental transfers. See John Joseph Wallis, "The Birth of the Old Federalism: Financing the New Deal, 1932–1940," *Journal of Economic History* 44 (1984): 139–59.

54. Herbert Hoover to Henry Hatfield, November 19, 1934, Postpresidential Individual Files, Hoover Presidential Library.

55. See John Joseph Wallis ("The Political Economy of New Deal Fiscal Federalism," *Economic Inquiry,* 29 [1991]: 510–24) for a good discussion of discretionary administration and corruption in the administration of New Deal recovery measures.

56. *New York Times,* November 9, 1934, section 2, p. 5.

57. Ibid.

58. Ibid.

59. George Norris to Ray Tucker, November 30, 1934, Norris MSS, Manuscript Collection, Library of Congress.

60. William Allen White to Frank Knox, October 9, 1934, White MSS, Manuscript Collection, Library of Congress.

61. It is important, however, to recognize that the insurgents were still couching their demands in terms of the progressive agrarian tradition. They were not Downsians in any meaningful way. After all, they had wanted the party to move in this direction in the 1920s when the Republicans were in the majority.

62. *New York Times,* Dec. 14, 1934, p. 1.

63. Theodore Roosevelt, Jr., speech before the National Republican Club, December 5, 1934, Postpresidential Individual Files, Hoover Presidential Library.

64. *New York Times,* December 5, 1934, p. 1.

65. Feinman, *Twilight of Progressivism,* p. 79.

66. *New York Times,* February 1, 1935, p. 22.

67. Ibid., December 4, 1934, p. 4.

68. Ibid., November 11, 1934, p. 1.

69. *New York Herald Tribune,* December 1, 1934, p. 1.
70. Herbert Hoover to John O'Laughlin, November 17, 1934, O'Laughlin MSS, Hoover Presidential Library.
71. *New York Herald Tribune,* December 9, 1934, p. 1.
72. Ibid., November 8, 1934, p. 4.
73. *New York Times,* December 4, 1934, p. 4.
74. Leuchtenburg, *Franklin D. Roosevelt,* p. 84.
75. Ibid.
76. Ibid., p. 85.
77. Franklin D. Roosevelt to Edward M. House, March 10, 1934, Personal Correspondence, Roosevelt Presidential Papers, Hyde Park, N.Y.
78. Theodore Saloutos and John Hicks, *Agricultural Discontent in the Middle West, 1900–1939* (Madison: University of Wisconsin Press), p. 471.
79. Albert U. Romasco, *The Politics of Recovery: Roosevelt's New Deal* (New York: Oxford University Press, 1983), p. 192; Hawley, *The New Deal Deal and the Problem of Monopoly,* p. 56. The "business community" in this context refers to the U.S. Chamber of Commerce and the National Association of Manufacturers. By focusing on the political pressures for cartelization proposed by these groupings during the 1931–1934 period, some violence is done to the variety of business responses that characterized the period. The American business community was fundamentally divided in terms of capital/labor intensity, organizational structure, international/domestic orientation, levels of profitability, and the like. The Chamber and the NAM focused on aggregating industrial attitudes, however, and they were more reflective of older, established industries with low levels of profit throughout this period. As this study focuses on political pressure brought to bear on the Republican coalition, the major business associations so representative of the Republican "system of '96" retain the primary focus here. For an important treatment of industrial divisions during this period, see Bernstein, *The Great Depression, Delayed Recovery, and Economic Response* ([New York: Cambridge University Press, 1987]) and his review of Romasco's *Politics of Recovery: Roosevelt's New Deal* (*Journal of Economic History* 43 [1983]: 1048–49) for an excellent discussion of the distinctions between profit levels and political positions among corporate elites during the period.
80. Karl, *The Uneasy State,* p. 119; Herbert Stein, *Presidential Economics: Economic Policy from Roosevelt to Reagan and Beyond* (New York: Simon & Schuster, 1984), pp. 31–32; Weir and Skocpol, "State Structures," passim.
81. Ogden Mills to Jerome Barnum, January 24, 1934, Mills MSS, Manuscript Collection, Library of Congress.
82. Simeon Fess to Herbert Hoover, November 28, 1933, Postpresidential Individual Files, Hoover Presidential Library.

83. William Allen White to Mark Sullivan, February 28, 1934, White MSS, Manuscript Collection, Library of Congress.
84. *Literary Digest*, July 7, 1934, p. 4.
85. Ibid., p. 35.
86. Walter Lippmann, "Mr. Mills at Topeka," Today and Tomorrow, *New York Times*, February 1, 1934.

4. 1935: The Breakup of the All-Class Coalition of the Early New Deal

1. Leuchtenburg, *Franklin D. Roosevelt*, p. 91.
 2. Ibid.
 3. George Wolfskill, *The Revolt of the Conservatives: The Evolution of the American Liberty League, 1934–1940* (Boston: Houghton Mifflin, 1962), p. 22; Robert F. Burk, *The Corporate State and the Broker State: The Du Ponts and American National Policy, 1925–1940* (Cambridge: Harvard University Press, 1990), pp. 143–235.
 4. Frederick Rudolph, "The American Liberty League, 1934–1940," *American Historical Review* 56 (October 1950): 20.
 5. Newton Baker to Walter Lippmann, January 27, 1936, Lippmann Papers, Yale University.
 6. John W. Davis to Walter Lippmann, June 25, 1935, Lippmann Papers, Yale University.
 7. Keller, *In Defense of Yesterday*, p. 260.
 8. Ibid., p. 261.
 9. Herbert Hoover to John O'Laughlin, n.d. [1934], O'Laughlin MSS, Hoover Presidential Library.
10. Keller, *In Defense of Yesterday*, p. 261.
11. Report of John O'Laughlin to Herbert Hoover, August 28, 1934, p. 2, O'Laughlin MSS, Hoover Presidential Library.
12. The "all-class" unity of American business had had clear limitations even from the beginning. Michael Bernstein has pointed out the growth of new patterns of consumer spending in the 1920s that had led to the growth of industries such as home appliances, food products, medical care, education, and a number of other service-oriented industries. Though not sufficiently developed to lead the economy out of the depression, these industries continued to expand in the 1930s. Bernstein stresses the importance of levels of profitability to understanding the varied reactions of industries to administration recovery measures during the 1933–1935 period. The "all-class" concept remains useful, however, because the newer industries were generally ineffective in making their case within the trade associations, which were dominated by older, slow-growth firms in heavy industry and basic services. By 1935, despite the complexity of the interests they repre-

sented, the trade associations spoke increasingly with a single shrill voice. See Michael Bernstein, *The Great Depression,* p. 199, and his book review of Romasco, *The Politics of Recovery.* Bernstein also provides an excellent discussion of the distinctions between profit levels and political positions among corporate elites during the period.

13. Berkowitz and McQuaid, *Creating the Welfare State,* p. 90.
14. Ibid.
15. Ibid., p. 88.
16. Romasco, *The Politics of Recovery,* p. 193.
17. Ibid.
18. Ellis W. Hawley, *The New Deal and the Problem of Monopoly: A Study in Economic Ambivalence* (Princeton: Princeton University Press, 1966), p. 114; see Donald R. Brand, *Corporatism and the Rule of Law: A Study of the National Recovery Administration* ([Ithaca: Cornell University Press, 1988], p. 169) for a subtle discussion of the divisions that came to exist within the business community over NRA policy. While recognizing the complex patterns involved, Brand sees smaller, peripheral firms as the core consituency of the NRA. His discussion of conflicts on an industry-by-industry basis is invaluable.
19. Hawley, *The New Deal and the Problem of Monopoly,* pp. 114–18.
20. Ibid., p. 118.
21. Romasco, *The Politics of Recovery,* p. 207.
22. Ibid., p. 208.
23. Leuchtenburg, *Franklin D. Roosevelt,* pp. 95–117; Allan Brinkley, *Voices of Protest: Huey Long, Father Coughlin, and the Great Depression* (New York: Knopf, 1982), pp. 155–61.
24. Leuchtenburg, *Franklin D. Roosevelt,* p. 150.
25. Controversies surrounding the existence of a "First" and a "Second" New Deal have continued unabated since the 1930s. For an excellent summary of the early controversies surrounding these distinctions see Richard S. Kirkendall, "The New Deal as Watershed: The Recent Literature," *Journal of American History* 54 (March 1968): 839–52.
26. Walter Lippmann to Arthur Holcombe, January 27, 1936, Lippmann Papers, Yale University.
27. Harry W. Morris, "The Republicans in a Minority Role, 1933–1938," Ph.D. diss., University of Iowa, 1960, p. 121.
28. *New York Times,* November 17, 1935, section 4, p. 3.
29. Ibid., November 21, 1935, p. 4.
30. Ibid., November 26, 1935, p. 9.
31. Ibid.
32. Ibid., December 2, 1935, p. 1.

33. Ibid., December 5, 1935, p. 1.
34. Ibid., September 10, 1935, p. 4.
35. Ibid.
36. Ibid., November 21, 1935, p. 1.
37. Ibid.
38. Ibid.
39. Ibid., February 4, 1934, p. 22.
40. Ibid., March 24, 1934, p. 22.
41. Ibid., May 9, 1935, p. 3.
42. Ibid., March 24, 1935, p. 1.
43. Ibid.
44. Ibid., March 17, 1935, p. 2.
45. Ibid.
46. Ibid., March 31, 1935, section 4, p. 6.
47. Ibid., April 19, 1935, p. 3.
48. Ibid., April 20, 1935, p. 17.
49. Ibid., May 1, 1935, p. 1; *New York Herald Tribune,* May 1, 1935, p. 1.
50. *New York Times,* June 9, 1935, section 4, p. 6.
51. Ibid., p. 1.
52. Ibid., June 13, 1935, p. 1.
53. Ibid., June 11, 1935, p. 1.
54. Ibid., June 12, 1935, p. 12.
55. Ibid., June 12, 1935, p. 1.
56. Ibid., p. 16.
57. *Literary Digest,* May 11, 1935, p. 15.
58. *New York Times,* June 16, 1935, p. 1.
59. Ibid., November 10, 1935, p. 1.
60. Ibid., October 21, 1935, p. 1.
61. Ibid., September 29, 1935, section 4, p. 10.

5. The Breakdown of Republican Electoral Evaluations, 1935-1936

1. Ogden Mills to Hamilton Corbett, August 27, 1935, Mills MSS, Manuscript Collection, Library of Congress.
2. Walter Lippmann to Newton Baker, January 22, 1936, Lippmann Papers, Yale University.
3. Attempts to reconstruct contemporary evaluations of political conditions are seldom undertaken in political science. For exceptions to this, see John Neustadt and Ernest May's concept of "placement" in *Thinking in Time: The Uses of History for Decision Makers* (New York: The Free Press, 1988). See also John Geer's "Critical Realignments and the Public Opinion Poll"

(*Journal of Politics* 53 [May 1991]: 435–51) for an attempt to explore this neglected aspect of party behavior.

4. For example, the gifts of the du Pont family alone to the Republican party in 1936 totaled close to $1 million. (Louise Overacker, "Campaign Funds in the Presidential Election of 1936" *APSR* 31 [June 1937]: 492). This excludes the fact that the family was also the principal financial supporter of the Liberty League.

5. Ibid., p. 486.

6. Ibid., p. 490.

7. Ibid., p. 494.

8. Wolfskill, *The Revolt of the Conservatives,* pp. 104–141.

9. Herbert Hoover to Bertrand Snell, November 9, 1934, Postpresidential Individual Files, Hoover Presidential Library.

10. James Beck to Herbert Hoover, March 8, 1935, Postpresidential Individual Files, Hoover Presidential Library.

11. Herbert Bayard Swope to Walter Lippmann, February 14, 1936, Lippmann Papers, Yale University.

12. John O'Laughlin to Herbert Hoover, June 1, 1935, O'Laughlin MSS, Hoover Presidential Library.

13. Still, the 1935 Democratic National Committee poll found that Long was polling only 10.9 percent of the vote nationally in a direct contest with Roosevelt and an unnamed Republican candidate. Conducted in the spring of 1935, the poll is reproduced in Brinkley, *Voices of Protest,* pp. 234–36.

14. Donald R. McCoy, *Angry Voices: Left-of-Center Politics in the New Deal Era* (Lawrence: University of Kansas Press, 1958), chaps. 3 and 4.

15. Sundquist, *Dynamics of the Party System,* p. 209.

16. Arthur N. Holcombe to Walter Lippmann, January 31, 1936, Lippmann Papers, Yale University.

17. *Literary Digest,* January 18, 1936, pp. 10–11.

18. Ibid., p. 11.

19. "National Inquirer Poll," November 1935 and January 1936, Emil Hurja Manuscripts, Election of 1936, Roosevelt Presidential Papers. (The National Inquirer was Hurja's own polling organization.)

20. See Courtney Brown, "Mass Dynamics of U.S. Presidential Competition," *APSR* 82 (1988): 1153–81, for an effort to distinguish between the changes characteristic of the 1932 election and those that followed. Brown sees conversion of former Repbulicans as the key to the 1932 results, while the 1936 election is best explained by the mobilization of previous nonvoters. His interpretation is consistent with the Hurja data that depicts erosion within the 1932 coalition that elected Roosevelt.

21. Robert E. Lane, *The Regulation of Businessmen: Social Conditions of Government*

Economic Control, Yale Studies in Political Science, vol. 1 (New Haven: Yale University Press, 1954).

22. Ibid., p. 50.

23. Ibid., pp. 1–35.

24. Ibid., p. 20.

25. Richard Hofstadter, *The Age of Reform: From Bryan to FDR* (New York: Knopf, 1955), p. 315; Samuel Huntington, *American Politics: The Promise of Disharmony* (Cambridge: Belknap Press, Harvard University Press, 1981), pp. 61–166.

26. Hofstadter, *The Age of Reform,* p. 316.

27. Arthur M. Schlesinger, Jr., "Sources of the New Deal: Reflections on the Temper of the Time," in Graham, ed., *The New Deal: The Critical Issues,* pp. 108–21.

28. Unpublished "(Tentative) Draft of Declaration of Principles," n.d., Lippmann Papers, Yale University.

29. See for example, F. J. Turner, *The Significance of Sections in American History* (New York: Holt, 1932); Arthur Holcombe, *The Political Parties of Today: A Study in Republican and Democratic Politics* (New York: Harper, 1924); Louis Bean, *How to Predict Elections* (New York: Knopf, 1948); Eugene Edgar Robinson, *The Presidential Vote: 1896–1932* (Stanford: Stanford University Press, 1934); A. M. Ewing, *Presidential Elections: From Abraham Lincoln to Franklin D. Roosevelt* (Norman: University of Oklahoma Press, 1940); Samuel J. Eldersveld, "The Influence of Metropolitan Party Pluralities in Presidential Elections Since 1920: A Study of Twelve Key Cities," *APSR* 43 (1948): 1189–1206.

30. Holcombe, *The Political Parties of Today,* pp. 39–81; *The Middle Classes in American Politics* (New York: Russell & Russell, 1965), pp. 65–123.

31. Holcombe, *The Political Parties of Today,* pp. 82–129.

32. Eldersveld, "The Influence of Metropolitan Party Pluralities," passim.

33. This was, of course, reflected in strongly Republican newspapers such as the *New York Herald Tribune* but was also presented in great detail in the following articles composed by *New York Times* correspondents: Arthur Krock, "Rhode Island Flares as New Deal Portent," *New York Times,* August 11, 1935, section 4, p. 3; Arthur Krock, "Roosevelt's Men Rely on West-South Unity," *New York Times,* August 4, 1935, section 4, p. 3; R. L. Duffus, "Urban States Hold a Lead over Rural," *New York Times,* September 15, 1935, Section 4, p. 7.

6. The Politics of Expediency v. "Saving the Constitution"

1. *New York Times,* July 7, 1935, section 4, p. 7.

2. Ibid., November 10, 1935, p. 11.

3. Ibid., March 28, 1935, p. 20.

4. William Allen White to David Lawrence, September 14, 1935, White MSS, Manuscript Collection, Library of Congress.

5. John D. M. Hamilton to William Allen White, July 30, 1935, White MSS, Manuscript Collection, Library of Congress.

6. William Allen White to Alfred Landon, April 21, 1936, White MSS, Manuscript Collection, Library of Congress.

7. *New York Times,* November 7, 1935, p. 1.

8. Ibid., December 8, 1935, p. 47.

9. Ibid., November 10, 1935, p. 1; July 7, 1935, p. 7.

10. Ibid., May 9, 1935, p. 1.

11. Ibid., September 25, 1935, p. 1. Privately, some Republican candidates discounted Hoover's disavowal of efforts to obtain the 1936 nomination. See especially Frank Knox to Annie Knox, November 25, 1935, Knox MSS, Manuscript Collection, Library of Congress.

12. The increased number of reports on political conditions within the Republican party provided by John O'Laughlin during the period reflect Hoover's continued interest in party affairs. See O'Laughlin MSS, Hoover Presidential Library.

13. *New York Times,* November 10, 1935, p. 11.

14. Ibid., November 10, 1935, p. 1; October 17, 1935, p. 15.

15. Frank Knox to Annie Knox, November 23, 1935, Knox MSS, Manuscript Collection, Library of Congress.

16. *New York Times,* October 17, 1935, p. 17.

17. Morris, "The Republicans in a Minority Role," p. 153.

18. *New York Times,* November 10, 1935, section 4, p. 3.

19. Ibid., November 7, 1935, p. 1.

20. Ibid., November 10, 1935, section 4, p. 3.

21. Ibid., November 7, 1935, p. 1.

22. Ibid., March 11, 1936, p. 1.

23. William Allen White to Alfred Landon, April 21, 1936, White MSS, Manuscript Collection, Library of Congress.

24. *New York Times,* February 5, 1936, p. 18.

25. Ibid., January 30, 1936, p. 6.

26. Ibid., March 9, 1936, p. 6.

27. Ibid., March 24, 1936, p. 2.

28. Ibid., March 1, 1936, p. 1.

29. Donald R. McCoy, *Landon of Kansas* (Lincoln: University of Nebraska Press, 1966), p. 244.

30. *Presidential Elections Since 1789,* p. 144.

31. William Allen White to Amos Pinchot, April 9, 1936, White MSS, Manuscript Collection, Library of Congress.

32. *New York Times,* April 5, 1936, p. 1.
33. *Presidential Elections Since 1789,* p. 144.
34. *New York Times,* May 29, 1936, p. 1.
35. Alfred Landon to William Allen White, December 11, 1936, White MSS, Manuscript Collection, Library of Congress.
36. *New York Times,* June 6, 1936, p. 1.
37. Ibid., June 5, 1936, p. 1.
38. William Allen White to Clyde Reed, July 8, 1936, White MSS, Manuscript Collection, Library of Congress.
39. *New York Herald Tribune,* June 4, 1936, p. 1.
40. *New York Times,* June 6, 1936, p. 12.
41. Walter Lippmann, "The Condition of the Republican Party," Today and Tomorrow, *New York Herald Tribune,* June 9, 1936.
42. Arthur Schlesinger, Jr., *The Age of Roosevelt,* vol. 3, *The Politics of Upheaval* (Boston: Houghton Mifflin, 1960), p. 545.
43. Walter Lippmann, "Putting Last Things First," Today and Tomorrow, *New York Herald Tribune,* June 12, 1936.
44. Walter Lippmann to Herbert Hoover, June 26, 1936, Lippmann Papers, Yale University.
45. William Allen White to Clyde Reed, July 8, 1936, White MSS, Manuscript Collection, Library of Congress.
46. *New York Times,* June 12, 1936, p. 1.
47. Ibid.
48. Ibid., July 3, 1936, p. 1.
49. McCoy, *Landon of Kansas,* p. 265.
50. *New York Times,* June 17, 1936, p. 1.
51. Ibid.
52. Henry O. Evgen, "The Republican Strategy in the Presidential Campaigns of 1936 and 1940," Ph.D. diss., Case Western Reserve University, 1950, pp. 71–73.
53. *New York Times,* July 5, 1936, p. 19.
54. Ibid., July 19, 1936, p. 21.
55. *Washington Post,* June 23, 1936, p. 1.
56. Schlesinger, *The Politics of Upheaval,* p. 603.
57. Alfred Landon to William Borah, August 3, 1936, Borah MSS, Manuscript Collection, Library of Congress.
58. *New York Times,* July 24, 1936, p. 1.
59. Walter Lippmann to Lewis Douglas, July 30, 1936, Lippmann Papers, Yale University.
60. *New York Times,* July 31, 1936, p. 9.
61. Chester H. Rowell to William Allen White, August 7, 1936, White MSS, Manuscript Collection, Library of Congress.

62. *New York Times,* August 16, 1936, p. 28.
63. Walter Lippmann to William Allen White, August 11, 1936, Lippmann Papers, Yale University.
64. Chester H. Rowell to William Allen White, August 7, 1936, White MSS, Manuscript Collection, Library of Congress.
65. *New York Times,* August 19, 1936, p. 1.
66. Alfred Landon to William Allen White, August 7, 1936, White MSS, Manuscript Collection, Library of Congress.
67. *New York Times,* August 23, 1936, p. 1.
68. Ibid., August 25, 1936, p. 1.
69. Ibid., August 27, 1936, p. 1.
70. Karl, *The Uneasy State,* p. 146.
71. *The New Republic,* September 9, 1936, p. 21.
72. Hadley Cantril and Mildred Strunk, eds., *Public Opinion, 1935–1946* (Princeton: Princeton University Press, 1951), p. 597.
73. Reported in *The New Republic,* July 22, 1936, p. 308.
74. Alfred Landon to William Allen White, July 18, 1936, White MSS, Manuscript Collection, Library of Congress.
75. John D. M. Hamilton to Ogden Mills, July 6, 1936, Mills MSS, Manuscript Collection, Library of Congress.
76. Ogden Mills to William O'Neil, June 18, 1936, Mills MSS, Manuscript Collection, Library of Congress.
77. Arthur Capper to William Allen White, July 2, 1936, White MSS, Manuscript Collection, Library of Congress.
78. John O'Laughlin to Herbert Hoover, October 31, 1936, O'Laughlin MSS, Hoover Presidential Library.
79. *New York Times,* June 21, 1936, section 4, p. 3; January 5, 1936, p. 11.
80. Ibid., July 25, 1936, p. 2.
81. Ibid.
82. See, for example, the analysis of congressional races presented, *New York Times,* August 9, 1936, section 3, p. 3.
83. Ibid., September 4, 1936, p. 18.
84. Ibid., September 13, 1936, p. 1.
85. Ibid., September 20, 1936, section 4, p. 3.
86. Ibid., September 17, 1936, p. 22.
87. Ibid., September 20, 1936, section 4, p. 3.
88. *New York Herald Tribune,* September 5, 1936, p. 1.
89. *New York Times,* September 27, 1936, p. 1.
90. Ibid.
91. Cantril and Strunk, *Public Opinion,* p. 597.
92. Clyde Reed to William Allen White, September 6, 1936, White MSS, Manuscript Collection, Library of Congress.

93. McCoy, *Landon of Kansas*, p. 310.
94. *New York Times*, September 12, 1936, p. 1.
95. Dorothy Thompson to William Allen White, September 29, 1936, White MSS, Manuscript Collection, Library of Congress.
96. *New York Times*, October 8, 1936, p. 22.
97. Ibid., October 11, 1936, p. 1.
98. Ibid., October 15, 1936, p. 23.
99. Ibid., October 25, 1936, section 4, p. 3.
100. Final report to James Farley, October 1936, Hurja MSS, Election of 1936, Roosevelt Presidential Library, Hyde Park, N.Y.
101. Ibid. It is clear from the Hurja papers that he was dissatisfied with the *Literary Digest*'s 1936 poll even before the poll's famous discreditation. Hurja adjusted the poll's figures throughout the summer and fall of 1936.
102. Hurja's final personal commentary predicted Landon would carry twelve to fourteen states with 125 to 142 electoral votes.
103. *New York Times*, October 24, 1936, p. 1.
104. Ibid., October 17, 1936, p. 1.
105. William Allen White to Alfred Landon, November 5, 1936, White MSS, Manuscript Collection, Library of Congress.
106. *New York Times*, October 21, 1936, p. 1.
107. Ibid., October 22, 1936, p. 1.
108. Ibid., November 1, 1936, section 4, p. 1.
109. Ibid., p. 1.
110. *Presidential Elections Since 1789*, p. 92.
111. Ibid.
112. Eldersveld, "The Influence of Metropolitan Party Pluralities," p. 1196; Courtney Brown, "Mass Dynamics of U.S. Presidential Competitions, 1928–1936," *APSR* 82 (1988): 1153–1181. Brown stresses the importance of electoral conversion to the 1932 election results while emphasizing the importance of new voters and mobilization to the 1936 results.
113. Odgen Mills to Herbert Hoover, November 16, 1936, Postpresidential Individual Files, Hoover Presidential Library.
114. William Allen White to Joseph Bristol, December 8, 1936, White MSS, Manuscript Collection, Library of Congress.
115. Herbert Hoover to William Allen White, June 9, 1937, Postpresidential Individual Files, Hoover Presidential Library.
116. Alfred Landon to Walter Lippmann, April 20, 1939, Lippmann Papers, Yale University. Landon's Minneapolis speech was considered a particularly vitriolic attack on New Deal programs, as well as a powerful defense of a high tariff.
117. *New York Times*, November 10, 1936, p. 1.

118. Ibid., December 20, 1936, section 4, p. 10.
119. Ogden Mills to Herbert Hoover, November 16, 1936, Postpresidential Individual Files, Hoover Presidential Library.
120. *New York Times,* December 20, 1936, section 4, p. 10.
121. Ibid., November 8, 1936, p. 3.

7. The Old Signs and Portents Have Disappeared

1. See Harry W. Morris, "The Republicans in a Minority Role," for a study that analyzes the Republican divisions of the period primarily in terms of this eastern-western sectional division.
2. For the purposes of this study, the country has been divided into two regions, consisting of the following states: 1) East—Connecticut, Delaware, Maine, Maryland, Massachusetts, New Hampshire, New Jersey, New York, Pennsylvania, Rhode Island, Vermont, and West Virginia; 2) West—Arizona, California, Colorado, Idaho, Illinois, Indiana, Iowa, Kansas, Kentucky, Michigan, Minnesota, Missouri, Montana, Nebraska, Nevada, New Mexico, North Dakota, Ohio, Oregon, South Dakota, Tennessee, Utah, Washington, Wisconsin, and Wyoming. The other eleven states had no Republican senators or representatives during this period. Clearly this two-region division is something of an oversimplification of the dynamics within the Republican party at that time. For example, the political culture of the upper Midwest/Great Lakes region is clearly different from that of the "progressive" western states and the Pacific Coast states. In the case at hand for example, Senator Simeon Fess of Ohio clearly shared many of the attitudes of the party's eastern delegation despite his midwestern domicile. In spite of these limitations, I have chosen to employ this basic division primarily because it reflects the concerns of contemporary party strategists, a key element in the development of this study's perceptual model.
3. As House minority leader, Bertrand Snell would seem to have been an important figure in the reconstruction of Republican strategy during the Seventy-third, Seventy-fourth, and Seventy-fifth congresses. His papers, however, seem largely concerned with his business interests in western New York and Canada and are probably of little value to researchers. Snell's apparent preoccupation with matters outside Congress is symptomatic of the disorganization characteristic of Republican efforts when they were adapting to minority party status. Present-day analysts should keep in mind that most Republican congressional leaders of the period had been teenagers about the time of the election of 1896 and that their perceptions had been shaped during an era of GOP domination. Before the election of 1932 the Democrats had not enjoyed a landslide victory against united opposition since 1852.

4. *New York Times,* February 7, 1933, p. 3.
5. Lippmann Papers, Yale University.
6. James T. Patterson, *Congressional Conservatism and the New Deal: The Growth of the Conservative Coalition in Congress, 1933–1939* (Lexington: University of Kentucky Press, 1967), p. 12.
7. Walter Lippmann to Felix Frankfurter, March 8, 1933, Lippmann Papers, Yale University.
8. Karl, *The Uneasy State,* p. 112; E. Pendleton Herring, "First Session of the Seventy-third Congress, March 9, 1933, to June 16, 1933," *APSR* 28 (February 1934): 65.
9. Leuchtenburg, *Franklin D. Roosevelt,* p. 43; for a study that stresses the importance of new committee chairmen to the legislative output of the First One Hundred Days period, see David W. Brady, *Critical Elections and Congressional Policymaking* (Stanford: Stanford University Press, 1988), pp. 105–06.
10. *Congressional Record,* 73d Cong., 1st sess., p. 76.
11. Ibid., p. 67.
12. William Borah to Joseph J. Turner, April 3, 1933, William Borah MSS, Manuscript Collection, Library of Congress.
13. Feinman, *Twilight of Progressivism,* p. 58.
14. Leuchtenburg, *Franklin D. Roosevelt,* p. 43.
15. Ibid. Later studies of the origins of the Glass-Steagall Act emphasize the willingness of both the commercial and investment banking communities to eliminate competition over their respective market bases. In view of the public outcry that resulted from often sensational congressional hearings, the Glass-Steagall Act became a very acceptable alternative. George J. Benston, *The Separation of Commercial and Investment Banking: The Glass-Steagall Act Revisited and Reconsidered* (New York: Oxford University Press, 1990), pp. 134–38.
16. Walter Lippmann to Felix Frankfurter, March 14, 1933, Lippmann Papers, Yale University.
17. Herring, "First Session of the Seventy-third Congress," pp. 70–71.
18. Leuchtenburg, *Franklin D. Roosevelt,* p. 45.
19. *Congressional Record,* 73d Cong., 1st sess., p. 217.
20. Ibid., p. 206.
21. Ibid., p. 471.
22. Walter Lippmann to Felix Frankfurter, March 5, 1933, Lippmann Papers, Yale University.
23. Ibid., March 14, 1933.
24. David Reed to Herbert Hoover, March 14, 1933, Postpresidential Individual Files, Hoover Presidential Library.

25. Karl, *The Uneasy State,* p. 114.
26. Albert U. Romasco, *The Politics of Recovery: Roosevelt's New Deal* (New York: Oxford University Press, 1983), p. 190.
27. Karl, *The Uneasy State,* p. 114.
28. *Congressional Record,* 73d Cong., 1st sess., p. 4212.
29. Ibid., p. 4213.
30. Ibid., p. 4226.
31. Ibid., p. 4218.
32. Ibid., p. 4227.
33. Ibid., p. 4328.
34. Romasco, *The Politics of Recovery,* p. 186.
35. Ibid., p. 195. Still, some qualifications remain as discussed in chapters 1 and 2. See also Michael A. Bernstein, review of *The Politics of Recovery,* by Albert U. Romasco, *Journal of Economic History* 43 (1983): 1048–49. For a useful survey of business attitudes at the time of the bill's passage, see "Business Agrees to Regulate Itself," *Nation's Business,* June 1933, p. 13 et seq.
36. Romasco, *The Politics of Recovery,* p. 196.
37. *Congressional Record,* 73d Cong., 1st sess., p. 5238.
38. Ibid., p. 5302.
39. Ibid., p. 5303. Mark Sullivan, political columnist for the *New York Herald Tribune* and a Hoover intimate, also questioned the uses to which licensing provisions could be put. Nevertheless, he accepted the general outlines of the legislation. *New York Herald Tribune,* June 8, 1933, p. 4.
40. *Congressional Record,* 73d Cong., 1st sess., p. 5557.
41. Ibid., p. 5556.
42. Ibid., p. 5837.
43. William Borah to George Record, June 19, 1933, Borah MSS, Manuscript Collection, Library of Congress.
44. *Congressional Record,* 73d Cong., 1st sess., p. 5424.
45. Romasco, *The Politics of Recovery,* p. 198.
46. Ellis W. Hawley, *The New Deal and the Problem of Monopoly: A Study in Economic Ambivalence* (Princeton: Princeton University Press, 1966), pp. 35–36.
47. See John Mark Hansen, "Choosing Sides: The Creation of an Agricultural Policy Network in Congress, 1919–1932", *Studies in American Political Development* 2 (1987): 183–229, and Theda Skocpol and Kenneth Feingold, "State Capacity and Economic Intervention in the Early New Deal," *Political Science Quarterly* 97 (1982): 255–278, for a comparison of the conditions that allowed for expeditious state intervention in agriculture as contrasted to the NRA experience.

48. Saloutos and Hicks, *Agricultural Discontent*, pp. 466–68.
49. *New York Times*, March 20, 1933, p. 1.
50. Ibid., March 21, 1933, p. 3.
51. *Congressional Record*, 73d Cong., 1st sess., p. 682.
52. Ibid., p. 692.
53. Ibid., p. 762.
54. Ibid., p. 754.
55. Ibid., p. 747.
56. Ibid., p. 764.
57. Ibid., p. 684.
58. Ibid., p. 1638.
59. Ibid., p. 1724.
60. Ibid., p. 1731.
61. Ibid., p. 2562.
62. Ibid., p. 1036.
63. Ibid., p. 1034.
64. Ibid., p. 2108.
65. Ibid., p. 1038.
66. Leuchtenburg, *Franklin D. Roosevelt*, p. 54.
67. Ibid., p. 165.
68. *Congressional Record*, 73d Cong., 1st sess., p. 2193.
69. Ibid., p. 2200.
70. Ibid., p. 2678.
71. *New York Herald Tribune*, April 23, 1933, p. 1.
72. Bruce J. Schulman, *From Cotton Belt to Sunbelt: Federal Policy, Economic Development, and the Transformation of the South, 1938–1980* (New York: Oxford University Press, 1991), pp. 91–92.
73. *New York Times*, June 26, 1933, p. 1.
74. Simeon Fess to Herbert Hoover, May 4, 1933, Postpresidential Individual Files, Hoover Presidential Library.
75. Leuchtenburg, *Franklin D. Roosevelt*, p. 61.
76. James Beck to Herbert Hoover, June 13, 1933, Postpresidential Individual Files, Hoover Presidential Library.
77. Simeon Fess to Herbert Hoover, June 9, 1933, Postpresidential Individual Files, Hoover Presidential Library.
78. Ogden Mills to Herbert Hoover, June 13, 1933, Ogden Mills MSS, Manuscript Collection, Library of Congress.
79. Herbert Hoover to Ogden Mills, June 23, 1933, Postpresidential Individual Files, Hoover Presidential Library.
80. Warren Austin to Herbert Hoover, November 28, 1933, Postpresidential Individual Files, Hoover Presidential Library.

81. George Norris to J. J. McCarthy, April 7, 1934, George Norris MSS, Manuscript Collection, Library of Congress.
82. William Allen White to Harold Ickes, May 23, 1933, William Allen White MSS, Manuscript Collection, Library of Congress.
83. *New York Times,* December 19, 1933, p. 1.
84. Ibid., December 28, 1933, p. 3.
85. Robert Allen White to William Allen White, December 20, 1933, White MSS, Manuscript Collection, Library of Congress.
86. *Congressional Record,* 73d Cong., 2d sess., p. 1397.
87. Ibid., p. 957.
88. Ibid., p. 986.
89. "Republican Attack on Inflation," *New York Herald Tribune,* April 22, 1933, p. 1.
90. Ibid., p. 1395.
91. *New York Herald Tribune,* January 27, 1934, p. 1.
92. Leuchtenburg, *Franklin D. Roosevelt and the New Deal,* p. 59.
93. *Congressional Record,* 73d Cong., 2d sess., p. 7711.
94. Ibid., p. 7931.
95. Ibid., p. 7937.
96. Ibid., p. 8024.

8. Defending the American Way of Life

1. "State capacity" literature in this context refers to work by scholars that suggest a role for state administrators and policy-makers independent of class dynamics. The central thrust of this school is well represented in *Bringing the State Back In* (Peter B. Evans, Dietrich Rusechemeyer, and Theda Skocpol [New York: Cambridge University, 1985]). See also Theda Skocpol, *Protecting Soldiers and Mothers: Origins of Social Policy in the United States* (Cambridge: Belknap, Harvard University Press, 1992) for a treatment of the effects of immature state development on the evolution of social policy in the immediate post–Civil War period.
2. Patterson, *Congressional Conservatism,* p. 193.
3. Ibid., p. 38.
4. Ibid., p. 39.
5. Ibid., p. 38; Leuchtenburg, *Franklin D. Roosevelt,* p. 154.
6. *Congressional Record,* 74th Cong., 1st sess., p. 8620.
7. Ibid., p. 8621.
8. Ibid., p. 8772.
9. Ibid., p. 8838. (The *Schechter* decision may be found at 295 U.S. 495 1935.)
10. Ibid., p. 8491.
11. Ibid., p. 8504.

12. Ibid., p. 8620.
13. Ibid., p. 8621.
14. Ibid., p. 10335.
15. Ibid., p. 10357.
16. Ibid., p. 9065.
17. Ibid., p. 10639.
18. David Pltoke, "The Wagner Act Again: Politics and Labor, 1935–37," *Studies in American Political Development* 3 (1989): 109.
19. Richard C. Cortner, *The Wagner Act Cases* (Knoxville: University of Tennessee Press, 1964), p. 77; see the letter and memo from J. Warren Madden, chairman, National Labor Relations Board to Franklin D. Roosevelt, January 28, 1936 (Presidential Papers, Roosevelt Presidential Library), for a contemporary assessment of employer resistance to the act's implementation.
20. *Congressional Record*, 74th Cong., 1st sess., p. 9731.
21. Ibid., p. 7673.
22. Ibid., p. 9727.
23. Walter Lippmann, "Today and Tomorrow," *New York Herald Tribune*, March 28, 1935.
24. *Congressional Record*, June 19, 1935, 74th Cong., 1st sess., p. 7668.
25. Ibid., p. 9688.
26. Ibid., p. 9690.
27. Ibid., p. 9691.
28. Ibid., p. 9688.
29. Ibid., p. 7681.
30. Patterson, *Congressional Conservatism*, p. 59.
31. Leuchtenburg, *Franklin D. Roosevelt*, p. 152.
32. Patterson, *Congressional Conservatism*, p. 50.
33. *Congressional Record*, 74th Cong., 1st sess., p. 13045.
34. Ibid., p. 13048.
35. Ibid., p. 13247.
36. Ibid., p. 12304.
37. *New York Herald Tribune*, July 2, 1925, p. 1.
38. Ibid.
39. *Congressional Record*, 74th Cong., 1st sess., p. 12306.
40. Ibid., p. 12324.
41. *New York Times*, July 13, 1935, p. 1.
42. Patterson, *Congressional Conservatism*, p. 68.
43. *Congressional Record*, 74th Cong., 1st sess., p. 13254.
44. Ibid., p. 12499.
45. Despite this, business opposition was not effectively mobilized against the measure. Few industrial leaders testified at the hearings on the bill, ap-

pearing to have little interest in it. In the legislative and political atmosphere of 1935 the more direct question of business-governmental relations attracted far more attention. For a discussion of the legislative hearings on the bill, see Edwin E. Witte, *The Development of the Social Security Act* (Madison: University of Wisconsin Press, 1968).

46. *Congressional Record,* 74th Cong., 1st sess., p. 9419.
47. Ibid., p. 9243.
48. Daniel Hastings to Ogden Mills, May 4, 1935, Mills MSS, Manuscript Collection, Library of Congress.
49. *Congressional Record,* 74th Cong., 1st sess., p. 9542.
50. Ibid., p. 5531.
51. Ibid., p. 5543.
52. Ibid., p. 6061.
53. *New York Times,* April 7, 1935, p. 29.
54. *Congressional Record,* 74th Cong., 1st sess., June 19, 1935, p. 9648.
55. Ibid., pp. 6069–70; 9650. Both Representatives Knutson and Rich answered "present" but were noted as paired in voting "against" the measure. Not voting in the Senate were Republicans Carey, Couzens, Norbeck, and Nye.
56. *New York Herald Tribune,* April 20, 1935, p. 1.
57. Leuchtenburg, *Franklin D. Roosevelt,* p. 170. (The AAA processing case, *U.S. v. Butler,* may be found at 297 U.S. 1 [1936].)
58. Saloutos and Hicks, *Agricultural Discontent,* pp. 504–5.
59. *Congressional Record,* 74th Cong., 1st sess., p. 2466.
60. Ibid., p. 2465.
61. Ibid., p. 2510.
62. Ibid., p. 2165.
63. Ibid., p. 2578.

9. Republican Policies of Restraint and the Genesis of the Congressional Conservative Coalition: 1937–1938

1. Patterson, *Congressional Conservatism,* p. 101.
2. William Allen White to Gifford Pinchot, March 23, 1937, White MSS, Manuscript Collection, Library of Congress.
3. Patterson, *Congressional Conservatism,* p. 85.
4. Joseph Alsop and Turner Catledge, *The 168 Days* (Garden City, N.Y.: Doubleday, Doran, 1938), pp. 54–55. This narrative, while composed only a few months after the "court-packing" proposal, remains an excellent study of the entire controversy.
5. Ibid.
6. Still the degree of reverence for the court as an institution should not be overstated. See Gregory A. Caldeira ("Public Opinion and the U.S. Supreme

Court: FDR's Court-Packing Plan," *APSR* 81 [1987]: 1139–53) for a careful analysis of Gallup Poll data that emphasizes the considerable fluctuation in mass public opinion that accompanied the controversy.

7. Arthur Capper to William Allen White, February 25, 1937, White MSS, Manuscript Collection, Library of Congress.

8. See Michael Nelson ("The President and the Court: Reinterpreting the Court-Packing Episode of 1937," *Political Science Quarterly* 103 [1988]: 267–93) for a treatment that considers Roosevelt's proposals as an example of nonincremental change sought by a president fresh from an "electoral mandate."

9. Patterson, *Congressional Conservatism*, p. 106.

10. Alsop and Catledge, *The 168 Days*, p. 97.

11. Joseph Alsop and Robert Kintner, "Let Them Do the Talking," *Saturday Evening Post*, September 28, 1940, p. 18. See also Carl Lamb, "The Opposition Party as Secret Agent: Republicans and the Court Fight," *Papers of the Michigan Academy of Arts and Letters* 56 (1961): 539–50.

12. Alsop and Catledge, *The 168 Days*, p. 98.

13. Arthur Capper to William Allen White, May 1, 1937, White MSS, Manuscript Collection, Library of Congress.

14. Patterson, *Congressional Conservatism*, pp. 109–10.

15. William Allen White to Charles McNary, December 17, 1936, White MSS, Manuscript Collection, Library of Congress.

16. See Stein, *Fiscal Revolution in America*, pp. 74–108, for an excellent discussion of a wide variety of viewpoints on the origins of the 1937 recession.

17. Frank Knox to Alfred Landon, November 17, 1937, Knox MSS, Manuscript Collection, Library of Congress.

18. Patterson, *Congressional Conservatism*, p. 1984.

19. Ibid., p. 149; James MacGregor Burns, *Congress on Trial* (New York: Harcourt, 1949), pp. 68–82.

20. *Congressional Record*, 75th Cong., 1st sess., p. 7721.

21. Ibid., p. 7791.

22. Ibid., p. 7954.

23. Patterson, *Congressional Conservatism*, p. 153.

24. James Davis to Joseph Pew, October 14, 1937, James Davis MSS, Manuscript Collection, Library of Congress.

25. Leuchtenburg, *Franklin D. Roosevelt*, p. 271.

26. *Congressional Record*, 75th Cong., 2d sess., p. 1831.

27. Julius Turner (*Party and Constituency: Pressures on Congress*, rev. ed. [Baltimore: Johns Hopkins University Press, 1970], pp. 27, 74–75) emphasizes a significant "metropolitan-rural" division among House Democrats during the Seventy-fifth Congress.

28. *Congressional Record*, 75th Cong., 1st sess., p. 3301.

29. Ibid., p. 7967.
30. Ibid., p. 7968.
31. Ibid., p. 8196.
32. Leuchtenburg, *Franklin D. Roosevelt and the New Deal,* p. 277.
33. Patterson, *Congressional Conservatism,* p. 217.
34. Ibid., p. 219. For an incisive discussion of the limits on the possibility of comprehensive planning during the period, see Barry Karl, *Executive Reorganization and Reform in the New Deal: The Genesis of Administrative Management, 1900–1939* (Cambridge: Harvard University Press, 1962).
35. Patterson, *Congressional Conservatism,* p. 221.
36. *Congressional Record,* 75th Cong., 3d sess., p. 2813.
37. Ibid., p. 3251.
38. Ibid., p. 4194.
39. Ibid.
40. Ibid., p. 4204.
41. Alsop and Kintner, "Let Them Do the Talking," p. 18.
42. Patterson, *Congressional Conservatism,* p. 226.
43. *Congressional Record,* 75th Cong., 3d sess., p. 5123.
44. One Republican congressman had died, another had resigned during the third session, and a third was apparently not present. Ibid.
45. Patterson, *Congressional Conservatism,* p. 229.
46. See Stein, *Fiscal Revolution in America,* pp. 91–130, for a useful discussion of the disagreements within the administration over the proper role of fiscal policy during the period.
47. Patterson, *Congressional Conservatism,* p. 235.
48. *New York Times,* April 15, 1938, p. 1.
49. Edward H. Rees to William Allen White, May 12, 1938, White MSS, Manuscript Collection, Library of Congress.
50. *Congressional Record,* 75th Cong., 3d sess., p. 6580.
51. Ibid., p. 6649.
52. Ibid., p. 6655.
53. Ibid., p. 6836.
54. Ibid., p. 8512.
55. O. R. Altman, "First Session of the Seventy-fifth Congress, 1937," 31 *APSR* (October 1937): 1083.
56. Eastern support of administration initiatives considered in this study from the Seventy-fifth Congress had averaged 13.3 percent in the Senate and 6.9 percent in the House. Thus western Republican responses were becoming increasingly similar to those of their eastern counterparts.
57. Sundquist, *Dynamics of the Party System,* pp. 240–42.
58. See Donald R. McCoy, "The Progressive National Committee of 1936," *Western Political Quarterly* 9 (1956): 454–69.

59. Feinman, *Twilight of Progressivism*, pp. 199–201.

60. Strong confirmation of this is also provided by Feinman. Ibid.; see especially pp. 136–56.

61. Otis Graham, Jr., *An Encore for Reform: The Old Progressives and the New Deal* (New York: Oxford University Press, 1967), pp. 3–23.

62. Ibid., p. 6.

63. Feinman, *Twilight of Progressivism*, p. 204.

64. William Borah to E. D. Schock, March 25, 1938, Borah MSS, Manuscript Collection, Library of Congress.

65. Hofstadter, *The Age of Reform*, pp. 200–1.

66. Graham, *An Encore for Reform*, p. 174. Graham's quantitative study found a majority of the progressive leaders who had been active in the 1912–1916 period as favoring Landon in the 1936 election.

67. William Allen White to Edward H. Rees, August 5, 1937, White MSS, Manuscript Collection, Library of Congress.

68. *New York Times*, January 19, 1937, p. 9.

69. Ibid., September 19, 1937, p. 1.

70. Alfred Landon to Henry Fletcher, June 10, 1938, Fletcher MSS, Manuscript Collection, Library of Congress.

71. Frank Knox to Dr. Neil Carothers, July 16, 1937, Knox MSS, Manuscript Collection, Library of Congress.

72. In a 1963 letter to James Patterson, John D. M. Hamilton minimized the actual prospects for a bipartisan conservative coalition: "Coalition was not formed on the basis of any fixed agreements, written or oral. It was no more than a political gravitation—men having similar viewpoints and ideologies. . . . It was completely fluid in that upon one bill a large Democratic vote could be obtained which would go along with the Republican viewpoint, and on others, while the number of votes from the Democratic side might approximate the same number, the individuals casting these votes might well be and often were quite different from those who voted with the Republicans on some other proposition." John D. M. Hamilton to James Patterson, March 7, 1963, quoted in James T. Patterson, "A Conservative Coalition Forms in Congress, 1933–1939," in Joel H. Silbey, ed., *The United States Congress in a Nation Transformed, 1896–1963* (Brooklyn: Carlson, 1991), p. 628.

73. *New York Times*, May 2, 1937, p. 25.

74. See the account provided by Ronald Bridges ("Republican Program Committee," *Public Opinion Quarterly* [April 1939]: 299–306) for a description of Republican reorganization efforts after the 1936 election.

75. *New York Times*, June 27, 1937, p. 1.

76. Alfred Landon to Henry Fletcher, February 1, 1938, Fletcher MSS, Manuscript Collection, Library of Congress.

77. *New York Times,* August 10, 1937, p. 5.

78. Ibid., March 6, 1938, p. 7.

79. Robert M. Collins, *The Business Response to Keynes, 1929–1964* (New York: Columbia University Press, 1981), p. 6.

80. Ira Katznelson, "Comments on 'The Burden of Urban History' " in Stephen Skowronek and Karen Orren, eds., *Studies in American Political Development* (New Haven: Yale University Press, 1989): 30–51.

81. Ira Katznelson and Bruce Pietrykowski, "Rebuilding the American State: Evidence from the 1940's" in *Studies in American Political Development* 5 (1991): 16–17.

82. Katznelson, "Comments on 'The Urban Burden,' " pp. 43–45.

83. *Fortune,* March 1939, p. 124.

84. Collins, *The Business Response,* p. 61.

85. *New York Times,* August 1, 1937, p. 4.

86. Ibid., December 6, 1937, p. 2; December 8, 1937, p. 2.

87. Ibid., September 23, 1937, p. 1.

88. Richard Norton Smith, *Thomas E. Dewey and His Times* (New York: Simon & Schuster, 1982), pp. 205–266.

89. Ibid., p. 231.

90. *New York Times,* November 8, 1938, p. 25.

91. Ibid., September 28, 1938, p. 7.

92. Ibid., October 16, 1938; September 23, 1938, p. 17.

93. Ibid., June 18, 1938, p. 3.

94. Sundquist, *Dynamics of the Party System,* pp. 219–28.

95. *New York Herald Tribune,* October 28, 1938, p. 21.

96. *New York Times,* November 4, 1938, p. 17.

97. Ibid., October 30, 1938, p. 21.

98. Ibid.

99. Ibid., October 21, 1938, p. 6.

100. Ibid., October 31, 1938, p. 1.

101. Ibid., October 30, 1938, p. 33.

102. Ibid., September 22, 1937, p. 4; September 23, 1937, p. 26; and October 24, 1937, section 4, p. 1.

103. Ibid., April 29, 1938, section 4, p. 6.

104. Patterson, *Congressional Conservatism,* p. 282.

105. *Lynchburg News,* July 6, 1938, p. 6, cited by Patterson, *Congressional Conservatism,* p. 283, n. 98.

106. *Guide to U.S. Elections,* 2d ed. (Washington, D.C.: Congressional Quarterly, 1985), pp. 609–36.

107. Ibid., pp. 786–90.

108. Ibid., p. 789.

109. *New York Times*, November 11, 1938, p. 1.

110. Ibid.

111. The strength of an ideology is, of course, difficult to quantify, but the persistence of older ideological patterns throughout the period reflecting probusiness attitudes and resistence to centralized government are recurrent themes in the following works: Karl, *The Uneasy State;* Patterson, *The New Deal and the States;* Patterson *Congressional Conservatism;* Graham, *An Encore for Reform;* Hawley, *The New Deal and the Problem of Monopoly;* Robert and Helen Lynd, *Middletown in Transition,* (New York: Harcourt & Brace, 1939); and Alfred Winslow Jones, *Life, Liberty, and Property: A Story of Conflict and a Measurement of Conflicting Rights* (New York: Octagon Books, 1964).

112. George Gallup, ed., *The Gallup Poll: Public Opinion, 1935–1971,* vol. 1, 1935–1948 (New York: Random House, 1972), p. 41.

113. Patterson, *Congressional Conservatism,* p. 332.

Conclusion: Minority Party Dynamics During Political Realignment

1. Fred Block, "The Ruling Class Does Not Rule: Notes on the Marxist Theory of the State," *Socialist Revolution* 33 (1977): 6–28; Ann Shola Orloff and Theda Skocpol, "Why Not Equal Protection? Explaining the Politics of Public Social Spending in Britain, 1900–1911, and the United States, 1880s–1920," *American Sociological Review* 49 (1984): 726–50; Jill S. Quadagno, "Welfare Capitalism and the Social Security Act of 1935," *American Sociological Review* 49 (1984): 632–47; Theda Skocpol and John Ikenberry, "The Political Formation of the American Welfare State in Historical and Comparative Perspective," *Comparative Social Research* 6 (1983): 87–148; Theda Skocpol, "Political Response to Capitalist Crisis: Neo-Marxist Theories of the State and the Case of the New Deal," *Politics and Society* 10 (1980): 155–201; Theda Skocpol and Kenneth Finegold, "State Capacity and Economic Intervention in the Early New Deal," *Political Science Quarterly* 97 (1982): 255–78; Michael Useem, "Classwide Rationality in the Politics of Managers and Directors of Large Corporations in the United States and Great Britain," *Administrative Science Quarterly* 27 (1982): 199–226; Margaret Weir and Theda Skocpol, "State Structures and Social Keynesianism," *International Journal of Comparative Sociology* 24 (1983): 4–29.

2. Ladd, *American Political Parties,* p. 6.

3. John G. Geer, "Critical Realignments and the Public Opinion Poll."

4. Huntington, *American Politics: The Promise of Disharmony.*

Bibliography

•

Manuscript Collections

William E. Borah MSS, Library of Congress, Washington, D.C.

James Davis MSS, Library of Congress.

Election of 1928 Files, Herbert Hoover Presidential Library, West Branch, Iowa.

Election of 1932 Files, Herbert Hoover Library.

Henry Fletcher MSS, Library of Congress.

Emil Hurja MSS, Franklin D. Roosevelt Presidential Library, Hyde Park, N.Y.

Frank Knox MSS, Library of Congress.

Walter Lippmann MSS, Yale University, New Haven, Conn.

Charles McNary MSS, Library of Congress.

Ogden Mills MSS, Library of Congress.

George Norris MSS, Library of Congress.

John Callan O'Laughlin MSS, Herbert Hoover Library.

Postpresidential Individual Files, Herbert Hoover Library.

Roosevelt Personal Correspondence, Roosevelt Presidential Library.

Everett Sanders MSS, Library of Congress.

William Allen White MSS, Library of Congress.

Reminiscences, Oral History Research Office, Columbia University

John W. Davis

Arthur Krock

James Wadsworth

Government Documents

Congressional Record, 73d–75th Congresses, 1933–1938.

U.S. Congress, Joint Committee on Printing. *Biographical Directory of the American Congress, 1774–1949.* 81st Cong., House Document no. 607. Washington, D.C.: U.S. Government Printing Office, 1950.

——. *Official Congressional Directory.* 73d Cong., 1st sess.; 75th Cong., 3d sess. Washington, D.C.: U.S. Government Printing Office, 1933–1938.

U.S. Department of Commerce, Bureau of the Census. *Historical Statistics of the United States: Colonial Times to 1970.* 2 vols. Washington, D.C.: U.S. Government Printing Office, 1975.

——. *16th Census of the United States: Population.* Vol. 1, *Number of Inhabitants.* Washington, D.C.: U.S. Government Printing Office, 1942.

Books

Alchon, Guy. *The Invisible Hand of Planning: Capitalism, Social Science, and the State in the 1920s.* Princeton: Princeton University Press, 1985.

Alsop, Joseph and Turner Catledge. *The 168 Days.* Garden City, N.Y.: Doubleday, Doran, 1938.

Anderson, Kristi. *The Creation of a Democratic Majority, 1928–1936.* Chicago: University of Chicago Press, 1979.

Bagby, Wesley. *The Road to Normalcy: The Presidential Campaign and Election of 1920.* Baltimore: Johns Hopkins University Press, 1962.

Baker, Gordon E. *Rural vs. Urban Political Power: The Nature and Consequences of Unbalanced Representation.* New York: Random House, 1955.

Baltzell, E. Digby. *Philadelphia Gentlemen: The Making of a National Upper Class.* New York: Free Press, 1958.

Barber, William J. *From New Era to New Deal: Herbert Hoover, the Economists, and American Economic Policy, 1921–1933.* Historical Perspectives on Modern Economics. New York: Cambridge University Press, 1985.

Bensel, Richard Franklin. *Sectionalism and American Political Development, 1880–1980.* Madison: University of Wisconsin Press, 1984.

Bentson, George J. *The Separation of Commercial and Investment Banking: The*

Glass-Steagall Act Revisted and Reconsidered. New York: Oxford University Press, 1990.

Berkowitz, Edward and Kim McQuaid. *Creating the Welfare State: The Political Economy of Twentieth-Century Reform.* New York: Praeger, 1980.

Bernstein, Michael. *The Great Depression, Delayed Recovery, and Economic Response.* New York: Cambridge University Press, 1987.

Best, Gary Dean. *Herbert Hoover: The Postpresidential Years, 1933–1964.* Vol. 1: 1933–1945. Hoover Press Publication 274. Stanford: Hoover Institution, 1983.

——. *The Politics of Individualism: Herbert Hoover in Transition, 1918–1921.* Westport, Conn.: Greenwood Press, 1975.

Binkley, Wilfred E. *American Political Parties: Their Natural History.* 4th ed. New York: Knopf, 1962.

——. *President and Congress.* 3d rev. ed. New York: Vintage Books, Random House, 1962.

Bone, Hugh A. *Party Committees and National Parties.* Seattle: University of Washington Press, 1958.

Brady, David W. *Critical Elections and Congressional Policy Making.* Stanford: Stanford University Press, 1988.

Braeman, John, Robert H. Bremer, and David Brody, eds. *The New Deal: The National Level.* Columbus: Ohio State University Press, 1975.

——. *The New Deal: The State Level.* Columbus: Ohio State University Press, 1975.

Brand, Donald R. *Corporatism and the Rule of Law: A Study of the National Recovery Administration.* Ithaca: Cornell University Press, 1988.

Brinkley, Allen. *Voices of Protest: Huey Long, Father Coughlin, and the Great Depression.* New York: Knopf, 1982.

Burk, Robert F. *The Corporate State and the Broker State: The DuPonts and American National Politics, 1925–1946.* Cambridge: Harvard University Press, 1991.

Burnham, Walter Dean. *Critical Elections and the Mainsprings of American Politics.* New York: Norton, 1969.

Burns, James MacGregor. *Congress on Trial.* New York: Harcourt, 1949.

——. *Roosevelt: The Lion and the Fox.* New York: Harcourt Brace, & World, 1956.

——. *The Deadlock of Democracy: Four-Party Politics in America.* Englewood Cliffs, N.J.: Prentice-Hall, 1963.

Campbell, Angus, Philip Converse, Warren Miller, and Donald Stokes. *Elections and the Political Order.* New York: Wiley, 1966.

Cantril, Hadley and Mildred Strunk, eds. *Public Opinion, 1935–1946.* Princeton: Princeton University Press, 1951.

Chamberlin, John. *The American Stakes.* New York: Carrick & Evans, 1940.

Chambers, William Nisbet and Walter Dean Burnham, eds. *The American Party System: Stages of Development.* New York: Oxford University Press, 1967.

Chubb, John E. and Peter E. Peterson, eds. *The New Direction in American Politics.* Washington, D.C.: The Brookings Institution, 1985.

Clawson, Marion. *New Deal Planning: The National Resources Planning Board.* Baltimore: Johns Hopkins University Press, 1981.

Clubb, Jerome, William H. Flanigan, and Nancy H. Zingale. *Partisan Realignment: Voters, Parties, and Government in American History.* Sage Library of Social Research no. 108. Beverly Hills: Sage Publications, 1980.

Collins, Robert M. *The Business Response to Keynes, 1929–1964.* New York: Columbia University Press, 1981.

Cooper, Barry, Allan Kornberg, and William Mischler. *The Resurgence of Conservatism in Anglo-American Democracies.* Durham: Duke University Press, 1987.

Cortner, Richard C. *The Wagner Act Cases.* Knoxville: University Tennessee Press, 1964.

Creel, George. *Rebel at Large: Recollections of Fifty Crowded Years.* New York: Putnam, 1947.

Cuff, Robert D. *The War Industries Board: Business-Government Relations During World War I.* Baltimore: Johns Hopkins University Press, 1973.

Dahl, Robert, ed. *Political Oppositions in Western Democracies.* New Haven: Yale University Press, 1966.

David, Paul T., Ralph Goldman, and Richard C. Bain. *The Politics of National Party Conventions.* Washington, D.C.: The Brookings Institution, 1960.

Dorfman, Joseph. *The Economic Mind in American Civilization.* Vols. 4 and 5, 1918–1933. New York: Viking, 1959.

Downs, Anthony. *An Economic Theory of Democracy.* New York: Harper & Row, 1957.

Eccles, Marriner. *Beckoning Frontiers.* New York: Knopf, 1951.

Ewing, Corteze A. M. *Presidential Elections: From Abraham Lincoln to Franklin D. Roosevelt.* Norman: University of Oklahoma Press, 1940.

Farley, James A. *Behind the Ballots: The Personal Story of a Politician.* New York: Harcourt Brace & World, 1938.

Fausold, Martin L. *The Presidency of Herbert Hoover.* Lawrence: University Press of Kansas, 1985.

Fausold, Martin L. and George T. Mazuzan, eds. *The Hoover Presidency: A Reappraisal*. Albany: State University of New York Press, 1974.

Feinman, Ronald L. *Twilight of Progressivism: The Western Republican Senators and the New Deal*. Baltimore: Johns Hopkins University Press, 1981.

Fenton, John H. *Midwest Politics*. New York: Holt, Rinehart & Winston, 1966.

Fraser, Steven and Gary Gerstle, eds. *The Rise and Fall of the New Deal Order*. Princeton: Princeton University Press, 1989.

Galambos, Louis and Joseph Pratt. *The Rise of the Corporate Commonwealth: U.S. Business and Public Policy in the Twentieth Century*. New York: Basic Books, 1988.

Gamm, Gerald H. *The Making of New Deal Democrats: Voting Behavior and Realignment in Boston, 1920–1940*. Chicago: University of Chicago Press, 1989.

Goodman, William. *The Two-Party System in the United States*. 3d ed. New York: Van Nostrand, 1964.

Graham, Otis L., Jr. *An Encore for Reform: The Old Progressives and the New Deal*. New York: Oxford University Press, 1967.

———, ed. *The New Deal: The Critical Issues*. Boston: Little, Brown, 1971.

———. *Toward a Planned Society: From Roosevelt to Nixon*. New York: Oxford University Press, 1976.

Graham, Otis L., Jr., and Meghan Robinson Wander. *Franklin D. Roosevelt: His Life and Times—An Encyclopedic View*. Boston: G. K. Hall, 1985.

Guide to U.S. Elections. 2d ed. Washington, D.C.: Congressional Quarterly, 1985.

Handlin, Oscar. *Al Smith and His America*. Boston: Little, Brown, 1958.

Hatch, Alden. *The Wadsworths of the Genesee*. New York: Coward-McCann, 1959.

Hawley, Ellis W. *The New Deal and the Problem of Monopoly: A Study in Economic Ambivalence*. Princeton: Princeton University Press, 1966.

———. *The Great War and the Search for a Modern Order*. New York: St. Martin's Press, 1979.

———, ed. *Herbert Hoover as Secretary of Commerce: Studies in New Era Thought and Practice*. Herbert Hoover Centennial Seminars, No. 2. Iowa City: University of Iowa Press, 1981.

Hays, Samuel P. *The Response to Industrialism: 1885–1914*. Chicago: University of Chicago Press, 1957.

——. *American Political History as Social Analysis* Knoxville: University of Tennessee Press, 1980.

Hicks, John D. *Republican Ascendancy, 1921–1933.* New York: Harper, 1960.

Himmelberg, Robert R. *The Origins of the National Recovery Administration: Business, Government, and the Trade Association Issue, 1921–1933.* New York: Fordham University Press, 1976.

Hofstadter, Richard. *The Age of Reform: From Bryan to FDR.* New York: Knopf, 1955.

——. *The American Political Tradition and the Men Who Made It.* Reprint ed. New York: Knopf, 1973.

Holcombe, Arthur M. *The Political Parties of Today: A Study in Republican and Democratic Politics.* New York: Harper, 1924.

——. *The New Party Politics.* New York: Norton, 1933.

——. *The Middle Classes in American Politics.* Reprint ed. New York: Russell & Russell, 1965.

Holt, Lawrence James. *Congressional Insurgents and the Party System, 1909–1916.* Cambridge: Harvard University Press, 1967.

Hoover, Herbert C. *The Memoirs of Herbert Hoover.* Vol. 3: *The Great Depression, 1929–1941.* New York: Macmillan, 1952.

Huntington, Samuel P. *American Politics: The Promise of Disharmony.* Cambridge: Belknap, Harvard University Press, 1981.

Huthmacher, Joseph and Warren I. Susman, eds. *Herbert Hoover and the Crisis of American Capitalism.* Cambridge: Schenkman, 1973.

Ickes, Harold L. *The Secret Diary of Harold L. Ickes: The First Thousand Days, 1933–1936.* New York: Simon & Schuster, 1953.

——. *The Secret Diary of Harold L. Ickes: The Inner Struggle.* New York: Simon & Schuster, 1954.

Israel, Jerry, ed. *Building the Organizational Society: Essays on Associational Activities in Modern America.* New York: Free Press, 1972.

Johnson, David Bruce. *The Republican Party and Wendell Wilkie.* Urbana: University of Illinois Press, 1960.

——, comp. *National Party Platforms.* Rev. ed. Vol. 1: 1840–1956. Urbana: University of Illinois Press, 1978.

Johnson, Walter. *William Allen White's America.* New York: Holt, 1947.

——, ed. *The Selected Letters of William Allen White.* New York: Holt, 1947.

Jones, Alfred Winslow. *Life, Liberty, and Property: A Story of Conflicting Rights and a Measurement of Conflicting Rights.* New York: Octagon Books, 1964.

Jones, Charles O. *The Republican Party in American Politics.* New York: Macmillan, 1965.

Joyner, Conrad. *The Republican Dilemma: Conservatism or Progressivism.* Tucson: University of Arizona Press, 1963.

Karl, Barry. *Executive Reorganization and Reform in the New Deal: The Genesis of Administrative Management, 1900–1939.* Cambridge: Harvard University Press, 1963.

———. *The Uneasy State: The United States from 1915 to 1945.* Chicago: University of Chicago Press, 1983.

Keller, Morton. *In Defense of Yesterday: James M. Beck and the Politics of Conservatism, 1861–1936.* New York: Coward-McCann, 1958.

Kennedy, David. *Over Here: The First World War and American Society.* New York: Oxford University Press, 1980.

Key, V. O., Jr. *Southern Politics in State and Nation.* New York: Knopf, 1950.

———. *Politics, Parties, and Pressure Groups.* 4th ed. New York: Crowell, 1958.

———. *The Responsible Electorate.* Cambridge: Belknap, Harvard University Press, 1966.

Kirschner, Don S. *City and Country: Rural Responses to Urbanization in the 1920s.* Westport, Conn.: Greenwood Press, 1970.

Kolko, Gabriel. *The Triumph of Conservatism.* New York: Free Press, 1963.

Kroos, Herman E. *Executive Opinion: What Business leaders Said and Thought on Economic Issues, 1920s–1960s.* Garden City, N.Y.: Doubleday, 1970.

Ladd, Everett Carll, Jr. *American Political Parties: Social Change and Political Response.* New York: Norton, 1970.

Ladd, Everett Carll, Jr., and Charles Hadley. *Transformations of the American Party System: Political Coalitions from the New Deal to the 1970s.* New York: Norton, 1975.

Lane, Robert E. *The Regulation of Businessmen: Social Conditions of Government Economic Control.* New Haven: Yale University, 1954.

Leopold, Richard W. *Elihu Root and the Conservative Tradition.* Boston: Little, Brown, 1954.

Leuchtenberg, William E. *The Perils of Prosperity, 1914–1932.* Chicago: University of Chicago Press, 1958.

———. *Franklin D. Roosevelt and the New Deal, 1932–1940.* New York: Harper & Row, 1963.

Lichtman, Allan J. *Prejudice and the Old Politics: The Presidential Election of 1928.* Chapel Hill: University of North Carolina Press, 1979.

Lippmann, Walter. *Interpretations, 1931–1932.* Allan Nevins, ed. New York: Macmillan, 1932.

———. *Interpretations, 1933–1934.* Allan Nevins, ed. New York: Macmillan, 1935.

Lisio, Donald J. *The President and Protest: Hoover, Conspiracy, and the Bonus Riot.* Columbia: University of Missouri Press, 1974.

———. *Hoover, Blacks, and Lily-Whites: A Study of Southern Strategies.* Chapel Hill: University of North Carolina Press, 1985.

Lloyd, Craig. *Aggressive Introvert: A Study of Herbert Hoover and Public Relations Management, 1912–1932.* Columbus: Ohio State University Press, 1972.

Louchiem, Katie, ed. *The Making of the New Deal: The Insiders Speak.* Cambridge: Harvard University Press, 1983.

Lowitt, Richard. *George W. Norris: The Persistence of a Progressive, 1913–1933.* Urbana: University of Illinois Press, 1971.

———. *George W. Norris: The Triumph of a Progressive, 1933–1944.* Urbana: University of Illinois Press, 1978.

Lubell, Samuel. *The Future of American Politics.* New York: Harper, 1955.

Lustig, R. Jeffrey. *Corporate Liberalism: The Origins of Modern American Political Theory, 1890–1920.* Berkeley: University of California Press, 1982.

Lynd, Robert and Helen Lynd. *Middletown in Transition.* New York: Harcourt & Brace, 1939.

McClymer, John F. *War and Welfare: Social Engineering in America, 1890–1925.* Contributions in American History, No. 84. Westport, Conn.: Greenwood Press, 1980.

McCoy, Donald R. *Angry Voices: Left-of-Center Politics in the New Deal Era.* Lawrence: University Press of Kansas, 1958.

———. *Landon of Kansas.* Lincoln: University of Nebraska Press, 1966.

McQuaid, Kim. *Big Business and Presidential Power: From FDR to Reagan.* New York: Morrow, 1982.

Mayer, George H. *The Republican Party, 1854–1964.* New York: Oxford University Press, 1964.

Mills, Ogden L. *What of Tomorrow?* New York: Macmillan, 1935.

———. *Liberalism Fights On.* New York: Macmillan, 1936.

———. *The Seventeen Million.* New York: Macmillan, 1937.

Moley, Raymond. *After Seven Years*. New York: Harper, 1939.

Moos, Malcolm. *The Republicans: A History of Their Party*. New York: Random House, 1956.

Murray, Robert K. *The Harding Era*. Minneapolis: University of Minnesota Press, 1969.

———. *The 103rd Ballot: Democrats and the Disaster at Madison Square Garden*. New York: Harper & Row, 1976.

Neal, Steve. *Dark Horse: A Biography of Wendell Wilkie*. Garden City, N.Y.: Doubleday, 1984.

Neustadt, Richard E. and Ernest R. May. *Thinking in Time: The Uses of History for Decision-Makers*. New York: Free Press, 1988.

Noggle, Burl. *Into the Twenties: The United States from Armistice to Normalcy*. Urbana: University of Illinois Press, 1974.

Nye, Russell B. *Midwestern Progressive Politics: A Historical Study of Its Origin and Development, 1870–1958*. New York: Harper & Row, 1959.

Olson, James Stuart. *Herbert Hoover and the Reconstruction Finance Corporation, 1931–1933*. Ames: Iowa State University Press, 1977.

Oulahan, Richard. *The Man Who . . . The Story of the 1932 Democratic Convention*. New York: Dial Press, 1971.

Overacker, Louise. *Presidential Campaign Funds*. Boston University, College of Liberal Arts, Gaspar G. Bacon Lectures. Boston: Boston University Press, 1946.

Page, Benjamin I. *Choices and Echoes in Presidential Elections: Rational Man and Electoral Democracy*. Chicago: University of Chicago Press, 1978.

Patterson, James T. *Congressional Conservatism and the New Deal*. Lexington: University of Kentucky Press, 1967.

———. *The New Deal and the States*. Princeton: Princeton University Press, 1969.

———. *Mr. Republican: A Biography of Robert Taft*. Boston: Houghton Mifflin, 1972.

Peel, Roy V. and Thomas C. Donnelly. *The 1928 Campaign: An Analysis*. New York: Richard D. Smith, 1931.

———. *The 1932 Campaign: An Analysis*. New York: Farrar & Rinehart, 1935.

Perkins, Edwin J., ed. *Men and Organizations: The American Economy in the 20th Century*. New York: Putnam, 1977.

Polsby, Nelson and Aaron Wildavsky. *Presidental Elections: Strategies of American Electoral Politics,* 6th ed. New York: Scribners, 1984.

Pomper, Gerald. *Elections in America: Control and Influence in Democratic Politics*. New York: Dodd, Mead, 1971.

Porter, David L. *Congress and the Waning of the New Deal.* Port Washington, N.Y.: Kennikat Press, 1980.

Presidential Elections Since 1789. 2d ed. Washington, D.C.: Congressional Quarterly, 1979.

Robinson, Eugene Edgar. *Herbert Hoover, President of the United States.* Stanford: Hoover Institution Press, 1975.

——. *The Presidential Vote, 1896–1934.* Stanford: Stanford University Press, 1934.

——. *The Presidential Vote, 1936.* Stanford: Stanford University Press, 1940.

——. *They Voted For Roosevelt: The Presidential Vote, 1932–1944.* Stanford: Stanford University Press, 1947.

Romasco, Albert U. *The Politics of Recovery: Roosevelt's New Deal.* New York: Oxford University Press, 1983.

——. *The Poverty of Abundance: Hoover, the Nation, and the Depression.* New York: Oxford University Press, 1965.

Rosen, Elliot A. *Hoover, Roosevelt, and the Brain Trust: From Depression to the New Deal.* New York: Columbia University Press, 1977.

Rossiter, Clinton. *Conservatism in America.* New York: Knopf, 1955.

Rubin, Richard. *Party Dynamics: The Democratic Coalition and the Politics of Change.* New York: Oxford University Press, 1976.

Saloutos, Theodore and John Hicks. *Agricultural Discontent in the Middle West, 1900–1939.* Madison: University of Wisconsin Press, 1971.

Schattschneider, E. E. *Politics, Pressures, and the Tariff: A Study of Free Private Enterprise in Pressure Politics, as shown in the 1929–1930 Revision of the Tariff.* New York: Prentice-Hall, 1935.

——. *Party Government.* New York: Rinehart, 1942.

Schlesinger, Arthur M., Jr. *The Age of Roosevelt.* Vol. 1. *The Crisis of the Old Order.* Boston: Houghton Mifflin, 1957.

——. *The Age of Roosevelt.* Vol. 2. *The Coming of the New Deal.* Boston: Houghton Mifflin, 1959.

——. *The Age of Roosevelt.* Vol. 3. *The Politics of Upheaval.* Boston: Houghton Mifflin, 1960.

——. *History of U.S. Elections.* 4 vols. New York: Chelsea House, 1973.

Schlesinger, Arthur M., Jr., and Fred I. Israel, eds. *History of American Presidential Elections, 1789–1968.* 4 vols. New York: Chelsea House, 1971.

Schwarz, Jordan A. *The Interregnum of Despair: Hoover, Congress, and the Depression.* Urbana: University of Illinois Press, 1970.

Shafer, Byron E., ed. *The End of Realignment: Interpreting American Electoral Eras.* Madison: University of Wisconsin Press, 1991.

Skocpol, Theda. *Protecting Soldiers and Mothers: Political Origins of Social Policy in the United States.* Cambridge: Belknap, Harvard University Press, 1992.

Skowronek, Stephen. *Building a New American State: The Expansion of National Administrative Capacities, 1877–1920.* New York: Cambridge University Press, 1982.

Smith, Richard Norton. *Thomas E. Dewey and His Times.* New York: Simon & Schuster, 1982.

Steel, Ronald. *Walter Lippmann and the American Century.* Boston: Little, Brown, 1980.

Stein, Herbert. *The Fiscal Revolution in America.* Chicago: University of Chicago Press, 1980.

——. *Presidential Economics: Economic Policy from Roosevelt to Reagan and Beyond.* New York: Simon & Schuster, 1984.

Stronberg, Roland N. *Republicanism Reappraised.* Washington, D.C.: Public Affairs Press, 1952.

Sundquist, James L. *Dynamics of the Party System: Alignment and Realignment of Political Parties in the United States.* Washington, D.C.: The Brookings Institution, 1973.

Sutton, Francis X., Seymour E. Harris, Carl Kaysen, and James Tobin. *The American Business Creed.* Cambridge: Harvard University Press, 1956.

Tomkins, C. David. *Senator Arthur H. Vandenberg: The Evolution of a Modern Republican.* East Lansing: Michigan State University Press, 1970.

Tufte, Edward R. *Political Control of the Economy.* Princeton: Princeton University Press, 1978.

Turner, Frederick Jackson. *The Significance of Sectionalism in American History.* New York: Holt, 1932.

Warren, Harris Gaylord. *Herbert Hoover and the Great Depression.* New York: Oxford University Press, 1959.

Wehle, Louis. *Hidden Threads of History: Wilson Through Roosevelt.* New York: Macmillan, 1953.

Weinstein, James. *Corporate Ideal in the Liberal State, 1900–1918.* Boston: Beacon Press, 1968.

Weiss, Nancy J. *Farewell to the Party of Lincoln: Black Politics in the Age of FDR.* Princeton: Princeton University Press, 1983.

Wiebe, Robert H. *The Search for Order: 1877–1920.* New York: Farrar, Straus & Giroux, 1967.

Wilensky, Norman. *Conservatives in the Progressive Era: The Taft Republicans of 1912.* University of Florida Monographs: Social Sciences, No. 25. Gainesville: University of Florida Press, 1965.

Wilson, David E. *The National Planning Idea in U.S. Public Policy: Five Alternative Approaches.* Boulder, Colo.: Westview Press, 1980.

Wilson, Joan Huff. *Herbert Hoover: Forgotten Progressive.* Boston: Little, Brown, 1975.

Wolfskill, George. *The Revolt of the Conservatives: A History of the American Liberty League, 1934–1940.* Boston: Houghton Mifflin, 1962.

Wolfskill, George, and John A. Hudson. *All But the People: Franklin D. Roosevelt and His Critics.* New York: Macmillan, 1969.

Ziegler, Robert H. *Republicans and Labor, 1919–1929.* Lexington: University of Kentucky Press, 1969.

Articles

Aaron, Daniel. "Conservatism, Old and New." *American Quarterly* 6 (Summer 1954): 99–110.

Almond, Gabriel A. "The Political Attitudes of Wealth." *Journal of Politics* 7 (August 1945): 213–55.

Altman, O. R. "Second Session of the Seventy-fourth Congress, January 3, 1936, to June 20, 1936." *APSR* 30 (December 1936): 1086–1107.

——. "Second and Third Sessions of the Seventy-fifth Congress, 1937–1938." *APSR* 32 (December 1938): 1099–1123.

Arnold, Peri Ethan. "Herbert Hoover and the Continuity of American Public Policy." *Public Policy* 20 (1972): 525–544.

Benson, Edward G. and Paul Perry. "Analysis of Democratic-Republican Strength by Population Groups." *Public Opinion Quarterly* 4 (September 1940): 464–73.

Bernstein, Marver H. "Political Ideas of Selected American Business Journals." *Public Opinion Quarterly* 17 (Summer 1953): 258–67.

Bernstein, Michael. Review of *The Politics of Recovery: Roosevelt's New Deal,* by Albert U. Romasco. *Journal of Economic History* 43 (1983): 1048–49.

Berthoff, Bernard. "The American Social Order: A Conservative Hypothesis." *American Historical Review* 45 (1960): 495–514.

Block, Fred. "The Ruling Class Does Not Rule: Notes on the Marxist Theory of the State." *Socialist Revolution* 33 (1977): 6–28.

Brady, David. "A Reevaluation of Realignments in American Politics: Evidence from the House of Representatives." *APSR* 79 (1985): 28–49.

Brady, David and Charles S. Bullock III. "Is There a Conservative Coalition in the House?" *Journal of Politics* 42 (1980): 549–72.

Brady, David and Joseph Stewart, Jr. "Congressional Party Realignment and Transformations of Public Policy in Three Realignment Eras." *American Journal of Political Science* 26 (1982): 333–60.

Brogan, D. W. "The Future of the Republican Party." *Political Quarterly* 8 (April–June 1937): 180–93.

Burner, David B. "The Breakup of the Wilson Coalition in 1916." In Paul Murphy, ed., *Political Parties in American History*. New York: Putnam, 1974.

Burnham, Walter Dean. "The Changing Shape of the American Political Universe." *APSR* 59 (1965): 7–28.

Caldeira, Gregory A. "Public Opinion and the U.S. Supreme Court: FDR's Court-Packing Plan." *APSR* 81 (1987): 1139–53.

Cleveland, Alfred S. "NAM: Spokesman for Industry." *Harvard Business Review* 26 (May 1948): 353–71.

Coleman, James. "Internal Processes Governing Party Positions in Elections." *Public Choice* 11 (1971): 35–60.

Cuff, Robert D. "American Historians and the 'Organizational Factor.' " *Canadian Review of American Studies* 4 (September 1973): 19–31.

——. "Herbert Hoover, The Ideology of Voluntarism, and War Organization During the Great War." *Journal of American History* 64 (1977): 358–72.

Eldersveld, Samuel J. "The Influence of Metropolitan Party Pluralities in Presidential Elections Since 1920: A Study of Twelve Key Cities." *APSR* 43 (1948): 1189–1206.

"Fortune Survey of Public Opinion." *Fortune* (October 1939): 52, 90–98.

Galambos, Louis. "The Emerging Organizational Synthesis in Modern American History." *Business History Review* 64 (Autumn 1970): 279–90.

Geer, John. "Critical Realignments and the Public Opinion Poll." *Journal of Politics* 53 (1991): 435–51.

Glad, Paul W. "Progressives and the Business Culture of the 1920s." *Journal of American History* (1966): 75–89.

Gosnell, Harold F. and William G. Colman. "Political Trends in Industrial America: Pennsylvania as An Example." *Public Opinion Quarterly* 4 (1940): 473–86.

Graham, Otis L., Jr. "Historians and the New Deals: 1944–1960." *The Social Studies* 54 (April 1963): 133–40.

Hansen, John Mark. "Choosing Sides: The Creation of an Agricultural Policy Network in Congress, 1919–1932." *Studies in American Political Development* 2 (1987): 183–229.

Hawley, Ellis W. "Secretary Hoover and the Bituminous Coal Problem." *Business History Review* 52 (1968): 247–70.

———. "Herbert Hoover, the Commerce Secretariat, and the Vision of an 'Associative State,' 1921–1928." *Journal of American History* 61 (1974): 116–40.

———. "The Discovery and Study of a 'Corporate Liberalism.' " *Business History Review* 52 (Fall 1978): 309–20.

Heald, Morrell. "Business Thought in the Twenties: Social Responsibility." *American Quarterly* 13 (Summer 1961): 126–39.

Herring, E. Pendleton. "First Session of the Seventy-third Congress, March 9, 1933, to June 16, 1933." *APSR* 28 (1934): 65–83.

———. "Second Session of the Seventy-third Congress, January 3, 1934, to June 18, 1934." *APSR* 28 (1934): 852–66.

———. "First Session of the Seventy-fourth Congress, January 3, 1935, to August 26, 1935." *APSR* 29 (1935): 985–1005.

Jenkin, Thomas P. "Reactions of Major Groups to Positive Government in the United States, 1930–1940." *University of California Publications in Political Science,* vol. 1 (1943–1945).

Karl, Barry D. "Presidential Planning and Social Science Research: Mr. Hoover's Experts." *Perspectives in American History* 3 (1969): 347–412.

———. "Philanthropy, Policy Planning, and the Bureaucratization of the Democratic Ideal." *Daedelus* (Fall 1976): 129–49.

Katznelson, Ira. "Comments on 'The Burdens of Urban History.' " *Studies in American Political Development.* 3 (1989): 30–51.

Katznelson, Ira and Bruce Pietrykowski. "Rebuilding the American State: Evidence from the 1940's." *Studies in American Political Development* 5 (1991): 301–39.

Key, V. O., Jr. "A Theory of Critical Elections." *Journal of Politics* 17 (February 1955): 3–18.

Kirkendall, Richard S. "The New Deal as Watershed: The Recent Literature." *Journal of American History* 54 (1968): 839–52.

Kramer, Gerald H. "Short-Term Fluctuations in U.S. Voting Behavior, 1896–1964." *APSR* 65 (1971): 131–43.

Krock, Arthur. "President Hoover's Two Years." *Current History and Forum* 34 (July 1931): 488–94.

Lamb, Carl. "The Opposition Party as Secret Agent: Republicans and the Court Fight." *Papers of the Michigan Academy of Arts and Letters* 56 (1961): 539–50.

Leuchtenburg, William E. "The New Deal and the Analogue of War." In John Braeman, Robert Bremmer, and Everett Walters, eds., *Change and Continuity in Twentieth Century America*, vol. 1, pp. 81–143. Columbus: Ohio State University Press, 1964.

Link, Arthur S. "What Happened to the Progressive Movement in the 1920's." *American Historical Review* 64 (1959): 833–51.

Lowi, Theodore. "Towards Functionalism in Political Science: The Case of Innovation in Party Systems." *APSR* 57 (1965): 570–83.

McQuaid, Kim. "Young, Swope, and General Electric's 'New Capitalism': A Study in Corporate Liberalism, 1920–1933." *American Journal of Economics and Sociology* 36 (1977): 323–34.

———. "Corporate Liberalism in the American Business Community, 1920–1940." *Business History Review* 52 (Fall 1978): 342–68.

Margulies, Herbert F. "Recent Opinion on the Decline of the Progressive Movement." *Mid-America* (Oct. 1963): 250–66.

Metcalf, Evan B. "Secretary Hoover and the Emergence of Macroeconomic Management." *Business History Review* 49 (1975): 60–80.

Nelson, Michael. "The President and the Court: Reinterpreting the Court-Packing Episode of 1937." *Political Science Quarterly* 103: 267–93.

Noyes, C. Reinold. "The Restoration of the Republican Party." *North American Review* 221 (March 1925): 417–30.

Ogburn, William F. and Lolagene C. Coombs. "The Economic Factor in the Roosevelt Elections." *APSR* 34 (1940): 719–27.

Orloff, Ann Shola and Skocpol, Theda. "Why Not Equal Protection? Explaining the Politics of Public Social Spending in Britain, 1900–1911, and the United States, 1880s–1920." *American Sociological Review* 49 (1984): 726–50.

Overacker, Louise. "Campaign Funds in a Depression Year." *APSR* 27 (1933): 769–83.

———. "Campaign Funds in the Presidential Election of 1936." *APSR* 31 (1937): 473–98.

———. "Campaign Finance in the Presidential Election of 1940." *APSR* 35 (1941): 701–27.

Patterson, James T. "A Conservative Coalition Forms in Congress, 1933–1939." In Joel H. Silbey, ed., *The United States Congress in a Nation Transformed, 1896–1963,* vol. 2, pp. 613–28. Brooklyn, N.Y.: Carlson, 1991.

Plesur, Milton. "The Republican Congressional Comeback of 1938." *Review of Politics* 24 (1962): 525–59.

Pltoke, David. "The Wagner Act Again: Politics and Labor, 1935–37." *Studies in American Political Development* 3 (1989): 105–56.

Polsby, Nelson. "The Institutionalization of the U.S. House of Representatives." *APSR* 62 (1968): 144–68.

Polsby, Nelson, Miriam Gallaher, and Barry Spencer Rundquist. "The Growth of the Seniority System in the U.S. House of Representatives." *APSR* 63 (1969): 787–807.

Pomper, Gerald M. "The Presidential Nominations." In Gerald M. Pomper, ed., *The Elections of 1988: Reports and Interpretations.* Chatham, N.J.: Chatham House, 1989.

Putnam, Jackson K. "The Persistence of Progressivism in the 1920's: The Case of California." *Pacific Historical Review* (November 1966): 395–411.

Quadagno, Jill S. "Welfare Capitalism and the Social Security." *American Sociological Review* 49 (1984): 632–47.

Reed, Thomas H. and Doris D. Reed. "The Republican Opposition." *Survey Graphics* 29 (May 1940): 286–88, 311–15.

"The Republican Party: Up from the Grave." *Fortune* (August 1939): 33–35, 99–103.

Rowell, Chester H. "The Resources of the Republican Party." *Yale Review* 27 (March 1938): 433–49.

Rudolph, Frederick. "The American Liberty League, 1934–1940." *American Historical Review* 56 (October 1950): 19–33.

Schofield, Kent. "The Public Image of Herbert Hoover in the 1928 Election." *Mid-America* 51 (1969): 278–93.

Searing, Donald D. "Ideological Change in the British Conservative Party," *APSR* 82 (1988): 361–85.

Shively, W. Phillips. "A Reinterpretation of the New Deal Realignment." *Public Opinion Quarterly* 35 (1971–72): 621–24.

Sinclair, Barbara Deckard. "Party Realignment and the Transformation of the Political Agenda: The House of Representatives, 1925–1938." *APSR* 71 (1977): 940–53.

Skocpol, Theda. "Political Response to Capitalist Crisis: Neo-Marxist Theories of the State and the Case of the New Deal." *Politics and Society* 10 (1980): 155–201.

Skocpol, Theda and John Ikenberry. "The Political Formation of the American Welfare State in Historical and Comparative Perspective." *Comparative Social Research* 6 (1983): 87–148.

Skocpol, Theda and Kenneth Feingold. "State Capacity and Economic Intervention." *Political Science Quarterly* 97 (1982): 255–78.

Squires, Peverill. "Why the 1936 Literary Digest Failed." *Public Opinion Quarterly* 52 (1988): 125–33.

Stedman, Murray S., Jr. "American Political Parties as a Conservative Force." *Western Political Quarterly* (1957): 392–97.

Thomson, C. A. H. "His Excellency's Loyal Opposition." *Fortune* (February 1937): 67–71, 188–89.

———. "Research and the Republican Party." *Public Opinion Quarterly* 3 (1939): 307–13.

Tufte, Edward R. "The Relationship Between Seats and Votes in Two-Party Systems." *APSR* 67 (1973): 540–54.

Unseem, Michael. "Classwide Rationality in the Politics of Managers and Directors of Large Corporations in the United States and Britain." *Administrative Science Quarterly* 27 (1982): 199–226.

Weir, Margaret and Theda Skocpol. "State Structures and the Possibilities for 'Keynesian' Responses to the Great Depression in Sweden, Britain, and the United States." In Peter B. Evans, Dietrich Rueschmeyer, and Theda Skocpol, eds., *Bringing the State Back In* New York: Cambridge University Press, 1985.

Wilkenson, Thomas and Hornell Hart. "Prosperity and Political Victory." *Public Opinion Quarterly* 14 (1950): 331–35.

Wittman, Donald. "Parties as Utility Maximizers," *APSR* 67 (1973): 409–98.

Unpublished Doctoral Dissertations

Boskin, Joseph. "Politics of an Opposition Party: The Republican Party in the New Deal Period, 1936–1940." Ph.D. diss., University of Minnesota, 1959.

Evgen, Henry O. "The Republican Strategy in the Presidential Campaigns of 1936 and 1940." Ph.D. diss., Case Western Reserve University, 1950.

Morris, Harry W. "The Republicans in a Minority Role, 1933–1938." Ph.D. diss., University of Iowa, 1960.

Stein, Judith. "The Birth of Liberal Republicanism in New York State." Ph.D. diss., Yale University, 1968.

Index

Designer: Linda Secondari
Text: 11/13 Garamond
Compositor: Maple-Vail
Printer: Maple-Vail
Binder: Maple-Vail